'Drop

Drifting Off,

Being Excluded

Joseph L. DeVitis & Linda Irwin-DeVitis
GENERAL EDITORS

Vol. 22

PETER LANG
New York • Washington, D.C./Baltimore • Bern
Frankfurt am Main • Berlin • Brussels • Vienna • Oxford

John Smyth and Robert Hattam
with Jenny Cannon, Jan Edwards, Noel Wilson, and Shirley Wurst

'Dropping Out,'

Drifting Off,

Being Excluded

Becoming Somebody Without School

PETER LANG
New York • Washington, D.C./Baltimore • Bern
Frankfurt am Main • Berlin • Brussels • Vienna • Oxford

Library of Congress Cataloging-in-Publication Data

Smyth, John.
'Dropping out', drifting off, being excluded: becoming somebody
without school / John Smyth, Robert Hattam with Jenny Cannon,
Jan Edwards, Noel Wilson, and Shirley Wurst.
p. cm. — (Adolescent cultures, school, and society; v. 22)
Includes bibliographical references and index.
1. High school dropouts—Australia—Interviews. 2. Youth with social disabilities—
Education—Australia—Case studies. 3. Success—Australia—Case studies. I. Hattam,
Robert. II. Title. III. Adolescent cultures, school & society; v. 22.
LC146.5.S59   373.12'913'0994—dc21   2003002328
ISBN 0-8204-5507-5
ISSN 1091-1464

Bibliographic information published by **Die Deutsche Bibliothek.**
Die Deutsche Bibliothek lists this publication in the "Deutsche
Nationalbibliografie"; detailed bibliographic data is available
on the Internet at http://dnb.ddb.de/.

Cover design by Lisa Barfield

The paper in this book meets the guidelines for permanence and durability
of the Committee on Production Guidelines for Book Longevity
of the Council of Library Resources.

© 2004 Peter Lang Publishing, Inc., New York
275 Seventh Avenue, 28th Floor, New York, NY 10001
www.peterlangusa.com

Printed in the United States of America

CONTENTS

PART III
INDIVIDUAL, INSTITUTIONAL AND
CULTURAL IDENTITIES

PART IV
CONCLUSION

ILLUSTRATIONS

FIGURES

TABLES

ACKNOWLEDGMENTS

The Students Completing Schooling Project upon which this book is based was funded by the Australian Research Council (ARC) from 1997 to 1999 and involved a partnership between the Flinders Institute for the Study of Teaching (FIST) at Flinders University; the South Australian Department of Education, Training and Employment (DETE); and the Senior Secondary Assessment Board of South Australia (SSABSA).

The focus of the research reflected both an Australia-wide and an international concern at the time about the sharp decline in students completing high school. The main intent of the research was to provide a forum for the voices of students in order to inform the education community about the factors that facilitate student retention and success in the post-compulsory years of schooling. The research focused on the range and interplay of factors between students' lives, the structure of schools, and the constraints of a publicly valued credentialling system.

The project had a complex organizational structure, and we wish to acknowledge the following people.

The Research Team responsible for implementing the project included Professor John Smyth, Chief Investigator (Director, FIST); Robert Hattam (Research Co-ordinator, FIST); Jenny Cannon (SSABSA Research Officer); Jan Edwards (DETE Research Officer); Dr Noel Wilson (FIST Research Officer) and Dr Shirley Wurst (FIST Research Officer). Dr Geoff Shacklock was a member of the team in 1997 and the first half of 1998, and Dr Margaret Cominos was a member of the team in its early stages. The Management Group that provided oversight of the project included members of the research team; Stephanie Page (DETE); John Liddle (DETE); Judith Lydeamore (SSABSA); and Graham Benger (SSABSA). Ken Lountain (DETE) was a member during 1998.

An Expert Group offered ongoing advice and commentary to the management group, and included Susan Cameron, Dr Chris Dawson, Jim Dellit, Wendy Engliss, Nigel Howard, Dr Jan Keightley, Tanya Rogers, Janette Scott and Mark Williams.

This project was supported by a research grant from the Australian Research Council and funding from the South Australian Department of Education, Training and Employment and the Senior Secondary Assessment Board of South Australia. We acknowledge the crucial support of the Department of Education, Training and Employment and the Senior Secondary Assessment Board of South Australia in the ongoing management of the project. Flinders University also provided the space in the form of a sabbatical for one of us to bring this book to a conclusion.

We also express our appreciation to Ada Warren and Lynden Jillings for their transcription of the data, Susanne Koen for editing, Tim Saunders for graphic design, Judith Lydeamore and John Liddle for editing advice, and Solveiga Smyth for her incredible support through all the stages of the research and in the final formatting of the manuscript. Noel Wilson undertook the amazing job of converting a mountain of interview transcripts into some accessible portraits.

Portions of this book appeared in the original research report of this project, entitled *Listen to Me I'm Leaving: Early School Leaving in South Australian Secondary Schools* (2000) by J. Smyth, R. Hattam, J. Cannon, J. Edwards, N. Wilson and S. Wurst. Some sections of chapter 1 appeared in J. Smyth, and R. Hattam, "Voiced research as a sociology for understanding 'dropping out' of school", *British Journal of Sociology of Education* 22 (3), 2001, pp. 401–415, and some portions in J. Smyth, "Researching the cultural politics of teachers' learning" in J. Loughran (ed.), *Researching Teaching: Methodologies and Practices for Understanding Pedagogy*, London and New York, Falmer Press, 1999(a), pp. 67–82. Chapter 5 appeared as J. Smyth, "Making young lives with/against the school credential" *Journal of Education and Work* 16(2), 2003, pp. 128–146. A version of chapter 6 appeared as J. Smyth, J. and R. Hattam, "Early school leaving and the cultural geography of high schools", *British Educational Research Journal* 28 (3), 2002, pp. 375–397. We are grateful to *Education Links* for permission to use the quote from Rob White in Chapter 3, and to Belinda Probert for permission to quote from her paper "Fast Capitalism and New Kinds of

Jobs" (1998). Our appreciation to all rights holders for permission to re-produce material indicated above.

Finally, this book would not have been possible without the courageous participation of the 209 young people who shared their stories and who through ethics procedures gave permission for their words to be used. While we have tried to represent their views as accurately as possible, not everyone associated with the project may necessarily agree with the way we have done that. The interpretations and the responsibilities that flow from that are naturally ours.

John Smyth and Robert Hattam
23 July 2002

PART I

INTRODUCTION

CHAPTER 1

CAPTURING THE VOICES OF EARLY SCHOOL LEAVERS

The problem, after all is not with the voices that speak
but with the ears that do not hear
(Casey, 1995, p. 223).

I n this chapter we want to lay out something of the argument and the scaffolding that lies behind the study we report in the remainder of the book.

Getting Oriented

At the outset, we should say that this was an Australian study (which we called the Students Completing Schooling Project) conducted in the period 1997–1999, and thus it may introduce some idiosyncrasies that are uniquely local. On the other hand, our reading of the extensive international research literature suggests that the issues go much deeper than locality: they are global, pervasive and protracted in nature, they are poorly understood, and they are invariably mischievously constructed to serve certain interests while denying others.

The issue of young people who "drop out" and the circumstances of their failure to complete high school or secondary education has been the subject of conjecture and contestation for more than three decades. What is interesting above all about the overwhelming direction of the policy, public and educational debate that has swirled around young people in this category is what Fine (1990) has referred to as "making controversy". In other words, there has been an active construction of what is occurring and what needs to be done to fix it, but precious little that casts light on meaning or understanding. In Fine's (1990) words, most of the representations effectively demonize young people and their non-completion of schooling, and give "a shaved and quite partial image" (p. 55). The language that has tended to saturate public and policy discussion has been around the notion of "youth at risk".

It is important at this early stage of the book that we introduce the voices of the young informants, parts of whose lives constitute the basis of the study we are reporting upon. Unless we do this we run the risk of speaking over their experiences, or else dismembering them into small bits. Below is what we are calling a "portrait"—one of many we will provide throughout the book. We provide it without interpretation or commentary. We think it important that what young people said in the study be allowed to speak for itself; that is not to say that as researchers we have no voice, for we clearly do. As we explain later, there has been only minimal editing of these portraits.

Portrait #027[1]
Jack: Myths and Labels and a Little Bit of Luck

I was bored, basically, just the way that they were teaching and stuff like that. It just seemed like I was not learning anything, I wasn't trying. I don't know, basically I wasn't getting anywhere, and it didn't look like I was going to. I had a job, a part-time job at the time, and I thought I'd leave and go to that job at the supermarket, just basically to get out of school, because I wasn't going to leave school if I didn't have a job. It was just part-time, like just over nights and stuff, and then they put me onto full-time just helping around the shop, And they put me into fruit and veg.

Then I got a phone call one morning from a guy from TAFE [Technical and Further Education] and he said—because I went to one of those TAFE open days and I was the only one that wanted to get into this course, that day—so he wrote my name down and he rings me up and he said, "I found your name in my diary, do you want a position? Someone has just dropped out". And I said, "Oh right, when do I start?" and he goes, "Tomorrow", and I went, "Alright then". So I left and went to that and then I was just finding that really hard, like just all the paper work and stuff, I just found it difficult.

It was in furnishing and cabinet making and that's what I wanted to get into. I'd been working at the supermarket for six months when TAFE rang up. Then I was in the course for a while, a few months, and I started two weeks late, so I was behind in the work and I'm not all that bright, so I was starting to fall behind even more. Once I start to fall behind I'm that kind of person that thinks, "Well, why bother at all. And I thought, "Oh I'll try and finish it anyway". Because TAFE are always getting phone calls from companies saying we need someone.

So this company rang up. They found this guy that was in my class, and he decided that he didn't want the job, and they said "We need someone quick". This was up at [xxxxx] and this was why this kid didn't want it, because he didn't want to go up there. So they walked into the class and they said, "Alright, who's got a car?" And I went, "Well I do", and he goes, "Well here, talk to this guy", and handed me a phone and I get on the phone and he goes, "How are you doing?" I said, "Yeah, my name's Jack", "Yeah", he goes, "You got a car?". I went "Yep". He goes, "Can you come in tomorrow?" I went, "Yep". So I went in there, I had a week probation, and then he said, "Alright, you've got a traineeship". Yeah, so that's what the position was, it was a traineeship, and then about two weeks later he said, "No, stuff it, we'll put you on apprenticeship". You've just got to, like, be in the right place at the right time. Yeah, and I don't reckon that school's the right place at the moment.

I was halfway through year 11, I'd just finished the second term, first semester and I failed Business Studies and then that pretty much says that I have to go back and do year 13 and I'm thinking, I don't even reckon I can make it to the end of year 11, so that's pretty much why I left.

Yeah, and I had a reputation and I couldn't shake that. Like in year 8 and through there, basically I was just in a rebellious stage, I guess, and just running amuck and then up through, like got out of that and went into a different group of friends in about year 9, and then I tried to change, started trying and it just didn't work. So I thought, well, I have to go to school, I might as well just bludge [shirking responsibility or hard work] my way through it, so started not really trying and then when it counted I tried, and that's how I was making it through.

Yeah, but I wasn't exactly the worst, either, though. I wasn't like one of these kids that goes to school and does drugs all day, and graffiti and stuff like that. I just didn't do my work, made jokes in class and stuff.

Yeah, because basically some of the teachers were alright, some of them weren't, and the ones that weren't [were] the ones that gave me a hard time, I just thought I'm not going to take this and gave them an even worse time back and so. Yeah. And then teachers talk, of course. I mean one time I had this fight with the Maths teacher, and in the next lesson, or a couple of lessons later, I walked into Woodwork and I got on well with the Woodwork teacher and he said, "Come on Jack, what's the problem, you're not getting on well in Maths?" I said, "How do you know that?" and he said, "Oh, us teachers talk". I mean, this is gossip.

I don't know, it's basically "them and us" like there's teachers and there's students and a lot of the friction is the discipline that they try to give us. Like our school didn't have a school uniform and they brought in a school uniform. Well, that was that. And they just took it way out of proportion because everyone's had it so easy. It's like, why are you doing this now? There was no problem before apart from that fact we had those security guards because of the stabbings and stuff.

Yeah, but like, it's just little things that teachers do all the time, it just gets on the nerves of the students. Like, I mean, you're allowed to wear plain blue tracksuit pants but [if] they've got a little Nike or something you get detention, like for lunchtime. On the other hand, we had maroon jumpers [sweaters] with the school name written around the collar, and if you wore a plain maroon jumper, you'd get detention. I just can't see the difference and I couldn't see the difference then and I just didn't feel it was necessary to be sitting in the detention room doing nothing when there was no problem with it, so I started to argue the point and getting myself into more trouble.

They might have had good reasons, but they didn't discuss them with the students first. It was basically, "We've got a school uniform, and you have to wear it". And they said, "Alright, what uniform do you want? We'll make it so that you like it". So this is where we got tricked. They said, "Do you like this one, this one, or this one?" And we had to pick one. And so we said, "That's the best". So we picked that one. "Alright". And we had to wear it all the time and we're saying, "This is a really stupid school uniform", and they said, "Well, you picked it". We say, "Well, you didn't give us much to choose from". "Well you chose it. We asked you what you wanted and you chose it".

Ok, at [the] supermarket you wear a uniform. That went down alright because it was that far out that you knew that you couldn't wear the slightest alternative, I mean you go there and you have to be in it basically. It's for the customers, it's making money for these people, it's a part of your job and you're getting paid to do it. Yeah, you get paid to do it. You go in there and you can see why you're wearing it in there. You're wearing it to look presentable, to be neat, to sell the product. I mean, if you walked in, in daggy clothes and dreadlocks and stuff like that, and saying, "Hey lady, need some help?" they'd fire you straight away.

Yeah, they'd either fire you or they'd make it hard for you. It's kind of the same in school; they can't fire you so they just make it hard for you. I mean you go to school to learn, you don't go there to be told how to dress.

Basically my [xxx] teacher was the one that I got my bad reputation from because I used to kick up, and like they always take the compliments but whenever it comes to a disagreement they always say, "Well don't talk to us, talk to the principal". You walk into the principal's office and he's thinking, "Another student, let's just agree". And then he'll say, "Well, right, I'll think about it".

When I was at school I began to like a few of the teachers, like I had going up through and like just talked to them and stuff and I was known, as

"That's Jack". All the teachers knew my name. "That's Jack", but it's "Just watch out for him. He's not a real trouble maker but just keep an eye on him". Yeah. I don't know, it's like I was known as the kid that if you try hard enough you can make him work, but you've really got to try. But I don't know, I just didn't like the way that they were running things, and just didn't try.

They have different rules for different students, different rules from different teachers. You get a strict teacher, you tend to get into a lot of trouble; you get an easier teacher, you get away with murder. If you're one of these goody goodies getting straight A's and stuff you can pretty much wear what you want, but if you're one of these people that tries to stand out a bit and you wear the slightest thing wrong, that's it, "Go to the detention", "Go and get expelled" and stuff. I mean I think they've taken it too far to a point where you're not allowed to learn any more, you're there to be disciplined, you're there for the teachers to make themselves look good. They all keep their red slips just waiting to pin someone, yeah. Everyone just gets sick of taking all the shit from the teachers and they just feel like rebelling, and that's what they do.

I mean, I've been talking to my friends that have left school as well, and it's basically they just want to go back to school so they can get expelled, just go back for a week so they can just stick it up all the teachers that have always been saying, "Go away". Discipline gets to you really. Like I can understand it for those people that have really stuffed [messed] up, really making it hard for other people. But they start to get carried away with just little things like swearing in the school yard and stuff, that's a way of life now. I mean, as you grow up through different generations, it's different. Stuff like different clothes, different language, different everything and they're trying to stop it, they're trying to make it their generation, their way back how it was, and it's advancing. I mean you go into school and you say "shit" and the teachers just crack up, "Detention!". You go out into the workplace, you don't say that and they pay you out [hassle].

Basically you go to school, you go into the classroom, you sit down, given your work, you sit there, you do it or you don't do it. Then you go home and come back the next day, you sit down, the same chair, the same classroom and you do that every day and like, then you just start to think, because my parents make me go to school every day, "What would happen if I didn't turn up today?" So I wouldn't turn up today and then I'd think, "Well, it's not going to make any difference if I turn up the next day".

Yeah. I had to ride my bike each day and, because both my parents work, I didn't have a car at that stage and it doesn't matter whether it was pissing down in the middle of Winter or stinking hot in the middle of the Summer, I had to ride to school, or walk to school, and I was getting really sick of that. And finally you get there and you think, "Why did I bother?"

So I went behind mum and dad's back and went to get the papers to leave school and then of course the school rang up and said, "Jack's just applied to leave school". And they said, "Oh well, if you really want to leave that much, then you can leave", and then I ended up getting full-time work straight away. I was surprised they rang my mum and dad because whenever you stuff up in school they're always saying, "It's your decision to be here, you don't have to be here. You've turned 15, if you don't want to be here you can get out". And then I said, "Alright, I want to leave then", and they said, "Well, you can't". So all through school they've been saying, "Leave, you're allowed to leave", and then when it comes to it, they say, "Oh no, don't leave".

TAFE, you know, it's more the practical side, more what it's really going to be like. It's not like at school, you don't have a teacher looking over you the whole time going, "Don't do that, don't do that. Don't talk to him. You're wearing the wrong stuff". I mean, when you're at TAFE you go, you walk in, you sit down and hear what he has to say, he talks to you for a bit and then says, "Right, this is what we've got to do". You either do it or you don't do it, but there's none of this uniform, or it's like go out and have a smoke. But at school you've got teachers patrolling you. You're outside of the school bounds and so you take one step to the left and wham. It's just irrelevant.

And at TAFE no-one knew me, made assumptions about me. I went in there and if I tried I was just like the next kid, and you can't afford to be a smart ass; if you do something wrong they'll kick you out. They just want to find people jobs and if you're not willing to try then they'll find a job for someone else, so basically if you don't want to be in there and you don't try, then you're not going to be in there. At school the most that they try to do, I think, to try and find you a job is sending you out on work experience, but at TAFE you've always got the people coming in saying, "Alright, we've got a position here, who wants it, who wants to go for it?"

Yeah, school doesn't matter, everyone's done school. We were saying to this guy because he's never had a job in his life, "Why don't you go out and get a job?" And he says, "I don't need to, I'm doing year 12", and we said "Well, you're going to need experience. I mean you go to an employer and they're going to say, what experience have you got?" And you say, "I've got year 12". And he's going to have all these other people in front of him and he's going to say, "Well, so has this guy and this guy and this guy". You need something under your belt other than school and you've got to get that stuff under your belt early and not necessarily stay to year 12.

If you ask most of the kids—heaps of people—"Why are you at school?" "Because I have to be". If you say to a lot of people in TAFE, "Why are you in TAFE?" "Because I want to be". And that's the difference.

So I can't see a point in going back to school. I couldn't really see a point in what it would do for me. I don't think it would benefit me at all, even if I went there and passed all the subjects, got straight A's, I don't think it would benefit me if I went after another job. I think it would benefit me more if I went around to other companies and said, can I do work experience for a week, and have them write a letter of recommendation that I can work out in the work force, that I can do this, that I can do that. I mean jobs lead onto other jobs and all you need to do is to get out there and get that first job and then it can always lead onto other jobs.

Or you can be lucky and just work it like me.

Michelle Fine has been prominent among a small but influential group of international scholars and researchers (see for example Kelly & Gaskell, 1996) who have pursued their research in the direction of exposing the "litany of threats now saturating the popular, policy, and academic literatures" (Fine, 1990, p. 55). As she argues, much of this ritualistic chanting has been constructed around shaping, shifting and traumatizing the public imagination around issues such as the purported decline of international competitiveness, the shrinking taxpayer base and the rising crime and social restlessness, that supposedly will flow directly from the premature exit of young people from school. As she put it:

> Perhaps no field surpasses public education as the space into which public anxieties, terrors, and "pathologies" are so routinely showered, only to be transformed into public policies of what must be done to save *us* from *them*. (Fine, 1990, p. 55, emphases in original)

Central to the line being pursued by commentators like Fine is the argument that while the "dropout problem is a real issue" (p. 65), categorizing and stigmatizing young people, their lifestyles and their families as "the problem" deflects attention away from the wider contributing factors and makes them invisible. What is created is a kind of "ideological diversion" (p. 65) that distracts our attention:

> [t]he notion of "at risk" . . . offers a deceptive image of an isolatable and identifiable group of students who, by virtue of some personal characteristic, are not likely to graduate [from school]. (p. 64)

What gets banished, of course, from the kind of viewpoints Fine is critiquing is the de-industrialization and collapse of huge swathes of the manufacturing sector of western economies and the accompanying impoverishment of inner-city communities. Instead:

> our attention floats to the individual child, his/her family, and the small-scale interventions which would "fix" him/her as though their lives were fully separable from ours. (p. 64)

Building on this kind of thinking, in this book we want to explore and map what social geographer David Sibley (1995) calls "geographies of exclusion"—his reference to "the human landscape as [being able to] be read as a landscape of exclusion" (p. ix). Like Sibley, we want to "foreground the more opaque instances of exclusion, opaque, that is, from a mainstream or majority perspective" (p. ix). As Sibley puts it, "These exclusionary practices are important because they are less noticed and so the ways in which control is exercised in society are concealed (p. ix). But most importantly, from our point of view, here:

> explanations of exclusion require an account of barriers, prohibitions and constraints on activities from the point of view of the excluded. (p. x)

When we think and talk about who gets to be included in social spaces, and schools are social spaces, there are well defined "implicit rules for inclusion and exclusion" (Sibley, 1995, p. xi), that determine who is welcome and who gets to be ejected or exiled, metaphorically as well as actually speaking. The institution of schooling is such that expectations abound as to what constitutes comportment, and there are clear and well articulated views about what is "deviant", "out of place" or likely to threaten the "image" of places called school. It is when the boundaries are contested, when the barriers are experienced and confronted that we begin to get some clues about how power relations and social control are exercised.

We, therefore, see the issues raised in this book as fitting within the genre of what Roman (1996) refers to as "the missing presence of youth themselves" (p. 1) as speakers with political legitimacy around issues affecting the conditions of their existence, schooling being among the most prominent of these. But as Roman points out, there is a need to do more than simply access the voices of young people:

> [m]erely including youth at the table during state policy debates will not necessarily resolve the crisis of representation raised by the issue of their politically disenfranchised, trivialized, or silenced voices. (p. 1)

What is crucially important, in addition, here, is the calling into question of the official policy constructions by "thinking against the grain" (Roman, 1996, p. 2), which is to say:

> developing the epistemic, methodological, and political stances to alter, as well as to challenge, official policy discourses that naturalize the spectacle of youth-at-risk. (p. 2)

The kind of analysis we are interested in is:

> sympathetic to the structurally complex reasons for students leaving or being pushed out of school [that] point to the lack of meaningful relations between teachers and students, students' reactions to restricted economic opportunities, and mismatches between home values and school values. . . . (Roman, 1996, p. 2)

Tackling the issue in this way moves us beyond the "burgeoning discourse of 'monological deficit' assumptions" (Roman, 1996, p. 3). Such an approach enables a proper critique of the issues, while at the same time avoiding the slide from "institution to individual" (Fine, 1996, p. xv), in which young people engage in "self-blame" and "embarrassed regrets" (p. xv).

Reflecting upon her own earlier research that "perhaps too glibly [portrayed] dropouts as critics", Fine (1996, p. xii) argued the need for a research approach that tangled directly with political decoys that "deflect . . . our attention away from structural conditions that purge students from schools . . ." (p. xiii). What we need, Fine (1996) argues, are research approaches that courageously confront public policies that "pummel the souls of those gutsy enough to question" (p. xv). As Fine put it, students who refuse to be institutionalized and who resist the "social magic" that comes with having an institutional identity

> may leave . . . or they may drown . . . Either way, schools are structured so that critics pay a price (academic, economic, or mental health) and their analyses melt into self-blame over time. To study dropouts per se, we may lose sight of the critique. (1996, p. xiv)

Apple (1986) put this in terms of the need to alter the "terrain of debate" (p. 174) in ways that expose the "poverty of at-risk analyses" (Margonis, 1992, p. 355), even where those deficit analyses have shifted from blaming victims to blaming institutions and "identifying failure before it occurs and shaping students likely to fail into productive and dependable citizens" (p. 344). Such "false humanitarianism", as Freire (1970) labels it, further positions these young people as passive subjects or "consumer recipients and not as active co-participants involved in shaping their life conditions" (Fraser, 1989, p. 155).

What we seek to provide here is a contemporary reading of early school leaving that has been developed through dovetailing our understanding of what young people have told us, with existing theoretical insights from the educational literature. By "early school leaving" we mean leaving school before successfully completing high school.

But from the outset, we need to acknowledge that the account presented in this book is not an exhaustive analysis of either the literature or the "data" collected in the study. The relevant literature, in so far as we drew on it, includes the contemporary sociology of education, the social psychology of identity formation, the political economy of education, the nature of the school–labor market interface, the sociology of youth, and theories of school culture and credentialling. Also, the "data" drawn upon in the study was immense and involved 10 megabytes of interview material (Cannon, 1998). In aiming to make such a complex project readable, we have used broad brush strokes to map what we believe are the most significant issues.

In the research reported upon here we have interrogated this question: what are the interferences to completing post-compulsory years of schooling (years 11 and 12), culminating in the award of a credential? Our aim is to develop a set of arguments in response to this question.

In trying to make sense of early school leaving, the research team interviewed over 200 young people who had either recently left school or were seriously contemplating leaving school. There were a number of themes that characterized the process of navigating a transition into adult life. These included:

- the decision-making processes of young people around school leaving;
- their experiences/perceptions of school, work, the leaving process, hanging in at school, and their experiences of returning to school;
- young people's "vernacular theories" (McLaughlin, 1996) of the social world, especially how they imagined the arrangements of schooling worked for them or not;
- their subjective states during the last days of their schooling; and
- the complex lives of some individual students, which act as a frame for understanding the nature of the school system and the society they live in (Anderson & Herr, 1994; Herr & Anderson, 1997).

Interrupting Habitual Readings

Our intent in coming at this issue afresh is to try and develop a "new" reading of what's happening—a reading that demands careful contemplation of what schools are "up to". Having said that, we also know that our account will come "as the always-already-read" (Jameson, 1981, p. 9). We read the word and the world "through a set of assumptions, socially shared and often unconscious, that frame knowledge and our relationship to it" (Mac-Pherson & Fine, 1995, p. 185).

We do not believe that many existing interpretations of the process of leaving school do justice to the lives of early school leavers. Our reading habits invariably "position" these young people into categories and world views that don't seem to improve their chances of success at school. Certainly, falling school retention rates[2] mean that the policy aim of universal retention is a fading dream. Rather than continuing to fit these young people's complex lives neatly into categories or theories that don't seem to be working, we believe that it is essential to reconsider the issue of early school leaving. This doesn't mean abandoning accumulated wisdom, but it does require being prepared to examine "how students are made 'voiceless' in particular settings by not being allowed to speak, or how students silence themselves out of either fear or ignorance" (Giroux, 1991, pp. xv–xxvii). A reconsideration of this issue requires an awareness of the differentials of power that are evident in most relationships—what gets said and what gets listened to are always understood to be marked by un-equal power relations. Being sensitive to power involves a responsiveness to passivity, silence, rebelliousness and alienation.

The silenced voices of students in schools also need to be understood in relation to a socio-cultural milieu in which youth policy is based on youth as "trouble" (Cormack, 1996) and media representations of youth that promulgate moral panics about "dropouts", "juvenile delinquency" "gang violence" (to name only a few) that render young people as the subjects of pathology, deviance or blame (Roman, 1996). "Youth, its cultures and sub-cultures, have always been seen as a social problem in the minds of the general public and policy makers" (Brake, 1980, p. 167). This process of stereotyping, we believe, banishes many early school leavers to the mar-gins of society, a place in which "they cohere momentarily around defi-ciencies", because they are "represented as unworthy, and immoral, or pit-iable, victimised, and damaged" (Fine, 1994, p. 74).

The witnesses in the Students Completing School Project were early school leavers who, we believe, are reliable witnesses in that they know more about why they left school early than anyone else. But such a view is contrary to the conventional wisdom. Schools are power structures in which the clear unfettered voice of students is rarely heard. The school is invariably premised on inequitable power relations, controlled through sanctions and reinforced by moral imperatives about what should be done.

This is equally true whether the issue is curriculum or behavior, what is to be learnt or what is to be worn. In such a climate teachers' voices describe and produce truth, while student perceptions are easily disregarded on the grounds of immaturity, prejudice, pathology or mischievous intent. And, of course, fear and punishment and moral chastisement produce their own inevitable distortions, which may subsequently be used to prove the claims of unreliability. In this study we have attempted to provide a space for young people that is free of fear.

The strength and power of these voices are undeniable. We invite the reader to hear these voices with the openness and clarity of their production. That is, to hear them without judgement, without imposing some preordained truth upon them. We know that for some this will be a difficult task.

We also need to come clean and admit that this account is our interpretation. It is but one interpretation, and not one necessarily agreed upon by the rest of the research team. Having said that, we hope that we have written this account in a way that opens up serious contemplation of the issue of early school leaving, and that our account will enable readers to examine their own theories about it. Perhaps our most difficult struggle in writing this account has been to represent the issue of early school leaving in a way that opens up debate rather than leading to closure. We want to call attention to the realization that there are no innocent researchers (Fine, 1994) and there no are innocent readers. We are all politically, socially, culturally and socio-economically situated and hence need to come clean on whose interests we serve when we aim to make sense of early school leaving. We have all "got agendas" we want to achieve. There is no clean, pristine and value-free place from which to examine early school leaving.

In going beyond our habitual readings we need, therefore, to pay attention to the categories we use; to examine the words, the names, the metaphors; and to interrupt the stereotyping that "positions" those who leave school early. Young people who leave school early are often referred to as "dropouts", both in the literature (Natriello, 1986), and in public discourse. In referring to the educational literature:

> the experience of "dropouts" has often been distorted and misrepresented . . . the very term *dropout* implies that students exercise a clear choice to leave school without graduating, and yet a fair number of students are pushed out or simply fade out. (Kelly, 1993, p. 9)

In Fine's (1991) words we have been "framing dropouts", where the term framing refers to a "frame-up" or a conspiracy to incriminate. Fine calls attention to the way "dropouts" are too often stereotypically represented, as a frame-up, as "depressed, helpless, and even without options . . . as losers" (pp. 4–5). For Fine, the frame-up obscures the "structures, ideologies, and practices that exile them systematically" (p. 5):

> [T]he question was no longer why a student would drop out. It was more compelling to consider why so many would stay in a school committed to majority failure. (Fine, 1991, p. 7)

Certainly many young people interviewed in the current study reported having to deal with being treated as a "dropout". "You get the occasional joke" (#015) about being a dropout from friends—but more seriously, some young people also reported that leaving school early was perceived in a negative way:

> Well I've had a lot of people when I've worked, and when I've been working they've been saying to me what's a young kid like you doing working, you should be at school, and so, like, that's what's been getting these ideas in my head. (#032)

> [I]t is employers, because they look down on people who quit school, as slackers sort of thing. (#127)

Rather than refer to "dropouts" we prefer to use the term "early school leavers" (Dwyer, 1996; National Youth Affairs Research Scheme, 1997). There is an implicit value judgement here. Our use of the term "early school leavers" affirms a commitment to the view that all young people should be encouraged to stay at school to successfully complete the postcompulsory years, and we have written this account from such a position.

We don't believe that any long-term sustainable improvements in school retention rates will be possible unless the complex interacting factors that interfere with successfully completing school are adequately understood and addressed. Interrupting the stereotyping of early school leavers requires more than just being careful about the labels or the names used to describe these young people. Stereotyping early school leavers might also be understood to involve the process(es) of interpretation that homogenizes, naturalizes and rationalizes them away.

When we *homogenize* those who leave school early, we consider them as a collective. We lose sight of the differences between them. A significant issue we had to grapple with in developing our account of early school leaving was guarding against presenting a single simplified account. There isn't one early school leaving story. We need to guard against understanding early school leaving in terms of theories that want to simplify the issue, such as the following: they leave school to go to training—not all early leavers do; or they leave school because they cannot cope—not all early leavers cannot cope. Of course there are other simplifications on offer as well. The interviews in this study strongly suggest more complex dimensions. Instead of simplifications we need a theory capable of handling complexity.

When we *naturalize*, we accept early school leaving as "just the way things are". This view appears to be widespread. It seems as though many believe that what is happening in schools is somehow an inevitable playing out of nature. We do not believe this to be a useful view. Rather, we believe that what goes on in the human world (of schools) is a product of human action, and hence the contemporary social world (that is, early school leaving) is viewed as but one possibility. We believe early school leaving is socially constructed. It depends upon certain conditions, and is a product of the institutions, systems and culture(s) we create and sustain.

When we *rationalize* away early school leaving we rely on "moral boundaries of deservedness that thread research and policy" (Fine, 1994, p. 74). That is, we "believe that we can distinguish (and serve) those who are deserving and neglect honorably those who are undeserving" (Fine, 1994, p. 74). The logic goes something like this: "we're doing our best under the circumstances—and those who leave early haven't tried hard enough". This moral boundary is implicit in the central challenge of the credential the young people in this study were struggling to acquire. In the words of the policy review document, it is necessary

> to ensure that mainstream post-compulsory students undertake a coherent range and depth of study which will equip them for adult life, work and further study and which is within reach of all such students, *given their serious application to the tasks*. (Gilding, 1989, p. 30, emphasis added)

Of course the caveat of a commitment to a course of study "within reach of all"—"given their serious application to the tasks"—opens up a space that makes it difficult to examine the arrangements that are in place for post-compulsory schooling. It lets the system off the hook, so to speak, and places the blame squarely on the student. If readers of this study acquiesce to this caveat from the outset, then they will find it difficult to hear the voices of early school leavers. For instance, how can such a view make sense of student alienation in the post-compulsory years? With such a caveat, it does not seem possible to consider how schooling might be made to work for an increasingly diverse group of young people wanting "to take part as adults both in the economy and in society generally" (Gilding, 1988, p. 3). Given that schooling still seems to fail those from lower socio-economic backgrounds, and that staying on to complete schooling is still very much skewed in favor of children from wealthy families, invoking such a caveat also laminates over any socio-economic or cultural dimensions to the problem.

Naming the Problem—Perspective Is Everything

Being concerned with early school leaving also means paying special attention to how we name "the problem". For *educational policy makers*, "the problem" is named in terms of "falling retention rates". But, naming the problem as "falling retention rates" hides the complexity of contemporary post-compulsory teaching and learning in schools. For those working in schools *(teachers and principals)*, the problem is often understood in terms of catering for an increasingly diverse student clientele. It is not about retention rates; the issue is that schools are being asked to offer a meaningful transition into adult life for the diverse population of students intent on "staying on" beyond the age of compulsion. This struggle for relevance is even more acute in schools that draw their students from communities most affected by contemporary micro-economic reforms of the workforce (Wyn & Lamb, 1996). *Schools* are interested in why students are "dropping out" of school; they are also asking why students are "staying on" (Paterson & Raffe, 1995). For schools, the retention "problem" means being concerned with the many disaffected pupils whose presence puts an added strain on life in classrooms. For *students*, the problem is one of navigating a transition to economic independence in a world characterized by:

> a new social condition of suspended animation between school and work. Many of the old transitions into work, into cultures and organizations of work, into being consumers, into independent accommodation—have been frozen or broken. (Willis, 1986, pp. 162–163)

Staying on at school and leaving early are both being read by young people in the light of dramatic changes to the labor market. The call for the "clever country" (an aspirational term used by politicians in Australia), for an education and training-led recovery, is unconvincing because the labor market for young people has all but collapsed (Spierings, 1995), except for part-time, unskilled work. Young people staying on at school can have profound implications for families who have to decide if they can provide the material, social and cultural resources that will enable their young to continue to successfully inhabit school culture. The question is whether schooling is relevant (Batten & Russell, 1995) to the possible future trajectories of these young people, given the resources available to them in light of their desired futures.

For *parents*, the retention "problem" is often experienced as angst. They wonder what will happen to their children when they leave school without credentials, and move into a precarious job market characterized by a creeping credentialism (Commonwealth Schools Commission, 1987).

They worry about how they will cope with the stress of having a child completing the post-compulsory schooling credential—which involves measuring up in a competition that has always favored those groups in society who already have access to material, cultural and social capital (Bourdieu, 1986).

The problem being investigated here, therefore, looks different depending upon the vantage point from which it is viewed.

If, as researchers and readers, we are to work against "protecting privilege, securing distance, and laminating the contradictions" (Fine, 1994, p. 72), it is important to erode the stereotypes. For our part, in this book we have attempted to construct a text that amplifies the plural voices of early school leavers. We want the reader to hear the "uppity voices" (Fine, 1994, p. 75) of early school leavers as "constructors and agents of knowledge" (Fine, 1994, p. 75). We believe that the voices of early school leavers need to be considered as "subjugated knowledges" (Foucault, 1980, p. 82). Putting it bluntly, the knowledge of young people is subjugated knowledge because there is often a failure to elicit it in the processes and practices of traditional mainstream high schools. In addition, when young people do "speak", their voices are very often not heard. As a culture we don't seem interested in "knowing" in a dialogic way: that is to say, knowing that affects how we might act in the future, what young people know about themselves, and how they make sense of their lives. What seems increasingly evident is that there is a need to struggle to open up a space of enunciation for early school leavers. It is not only that they are silenced—a view that was central to the design of this study—but that even when they do speak, they cannot be heard.

Developing a Research Orientation

A Sociological Perspective

Understanding post-compulsory schooling requires a "sociological per-spective" (Proudford & Baker, 1995)—one in which subjectivity and con-text are mutually constitutive and embedded in a dialectical relationship (Seddon, 1995). Through situating everyday life within a socio-economic and socio-cultural milieu, such a perspective avoids the pitfalls of viewing "human behavior as the product of [completely] autonomous individuals making decisions and acting on them" (Freeland, 1991, p. 191). Such a perspective also avoids profoundly misunderstanding the fact that "young people are born into an . . . already structured society, and [that] those structures constitute barriers to equitable access and participation well be-fore the child reaches school age" (Freeland, 1991, p. 196).

From a sociological perspective, schooling might be regarded as a so-cial and cultural location in which a number of logics or imperatives strug-gle for significance. Struggles for control of what goes on in schooling are played out daily in classrooms and staffrooms, but significant and defining boundaries are organized institutionally and as such are periodically set-tled. A settlement, as a framework, contains struggles within manageable limits. A settlement can be understood in this instance as an "unwritten social contract . . . [or] a bargain, a historic compromise . . . struck between the different conflicting social interests in society" (Hall, 1988, p. 36). Historically speaking, at least during the past ten years or so, the practice of teaching and learning in post-compulsory schooling has been broadly defined in terms of an "educational settlement" (Freeland, 1986; Reid, 1998). This settlement often goes by the title of a "general liberal" educa-tion, and in post-compulsory schooling in South Australia, this settlement has been codified as the SACE (the South Australian Certificate of Educa-tion)—the credential awarded to students who successfully complete year 12 of secondary education.

Such an educational settlement needs to be understood in the broader context of a post–World War II political and economic settlement often referred to as the welfare state, in which struggles by trade unionists, fem-inists, environmentalists and human rights activists, to name only a few, have affected institutional and lifeworld arrangements against the grain of the interests of those pursuing capital accumulation, private ownership and the maximizing of profit. Quite clearly, the educational settlement that has been an important feature of the welfare state is now being signif-icantly disrupted by the recent changes in the relationship between the federal government in Australia and the market. Such disruptions, along with the collapse of the youth labor market and a "creeping credentialism", put added pressure on young people as they navigate a transition into the work force.

The increasing precariousness of these "new times" (Hall & Jacques, 1990) also puts added pressure on the education and training sector. The transition from childhood into adult life, from dependence to economic and emotional independence, is managed in Australia within the institutional arrangements of school, Vocational Education and Training (VET) and universities. Significantly for this study, the pathways available to Australians "in order to establish an independent adult identity for themselves" (Dwyer 1995, p. 147) still reflect a society stratified according to "factors such as socioeconomic status, gender, race, ethnicity, region and homelessness" which "combine to determine just who will be most vulnerable in the transition to adulthood" (Freeland, 1991, p. 191).

The Research Methodology

To address the broad research question alluded to above, the study pursued four interactive and complementary methodological strands, reflecting something of the complexity of the topic and the need to investigate it in multiple ways. To summarize, these strands are:

- *quantitative:* examining the extent of the "problem";
- *qualitative:* listening to what young people understand is happening during early school leaving;
- *students-as-researchers:* enlisting young people to also listen to their peers' explanations/descriptions of early school leaving; and
- *longitudinal:* tracking a number of young people during the three years of the study.

In this book, however, we are only reporting on the second of these strands. Our intent is to try and capture the voices of young people so as to understand how they interpret and make meaning of their lives and, in particular, what part staying on at school and completing the credential, or leaving early, has played in that process.

It may be helpful, however, to give a brief statistical glimpse of the issue we were investigating.

The Extent of the "Problem"

We have placed the word "problem" in quotes to unsettle the common meaning of the term. Falling retention rates might be viewed as the research problem. Falling retention rates might also be viewed as a policy problem for governments. But leaving school early might not be viewed as a problem for those who are doing it. In fact, for many young people it seems that leaving school early is a sane option when considering what is happening in their lives, the way they are being treated at school, their aspirations for the future and their access to resources they can use in the process of making a life for themselves.

We needed to review the ways in which student participation in post-compulsory schooling was represented statistically so that we could make informed choices for the qualitative phase of the research—a phase which involved interviewing (ex)students to ascertain the reasons why they had either left school early or why they were "hanging in" at school. The intent in the interview phase was to access the understandings of a group of (ex)students that represented the significant categorizations of students who had left school early.

The research team conducted a search of the various statistical representations of early school leaving in the literature and in local research reports concentrating on retention and completion rates (Hattam, Edwards & Cominos, 1997). A more detailed account of this information, including a brief discussion of its accuracy and our reasons for using the terms "apparent retention rates" and "apparent completion rates", is contained in Appendix A of Smyth, Hattam et al. (2000). Below is a table representing a summary of apparent retention rates up to the time of the commencement of the study.

While the retention figures do not provide an entirely accurate picture, it does appear as though retention to year 12 is on the decline, at least in the part of Australia where this study was conducted, and at the time of the study. A part of the problem with the accuracy of apparent retention figures in the state of South Australia is the number of part-time students. South Australia does have a large number of part-time

TABLE 1.1 Apparent Retention Rates in South Australia 1986–1997

1986	1987	1988	1989	1990	1991	1992	1993	1994	1995	1996	1997
54.8%	60.2%	66.6%	66.7%	72.1%	83.5%	92.7%	86.3%	81.7%	71.4%	68.4%	66.9%

Source: Australian Bureau of Statistics, 2000, 4221.0.

TABLE 1.2 Retention, Completion and University Entrance for the Year 8 Cohort of 1992

Year 8 cohort	Total year 12 enrolled in SACE in 1996 as a percentage of year 8 cohort	Year 12 enrolled in SACE in 1996 and gained SACE in 2 years as a percentage of year 8 cohort	Year 12 enrolled in SACE in 1996 and did not gain SACE in 2 years as a percentage of year 8 cohort	1996 SACE achievers who enrolled at a South Australian university as a percentage of year 8 cohort
16 943	12 583	7 436	5 147	4 683
100%	74.3%	43.9%	30.4%	28%

Source: Australian Bureau of Statistics 2000, and Senior Secondary Assessment Board of South Australia, unpublished data.

students studying post-compulsory courses, and these do not feature in the statistics.

We have used the term "apparent retention rate" to describe the proportion of year 8 students who were in year 12 five years later, and "apparent completion rate" to represent the percentage of students commencing the post-compulsory years of study in 1995, and who were enrolled in 1995 and 1996. This choice seems appropriate given that we have attempted to track a cohort of students who could have completed the credential in 1996. Table 1.2 represents the retention, completion and university entrance rates for this cohort.

The data broadly indicates that the reforms in post-compulsory schooling that were developed in the late 1980s and early 1990s in South Australia seem to have been unconvincing for a large proportion of young people. That is, young people have not been convinced that post-compulsory schooling should be a part of their transition to adult life, and the proportion that feel this way is growing.

Composition of the Interview Cohort

Disaggregation of retention and completion data reveals significant class, gender, race and geographical dimensions with regard to rates of early school leaving. It was important in this study that we be attentive to this diversity. We also included students with disabilities, even though we were unable to find accurate statistical data on this group. In themselves such data can tell us very little about why the category differences exist. But they do suggest lines of questioning that may help inform our understanding of why such differences occur. Bearing these distinctions in mind, we believed it was important to select young people to be interviewed from across these categories. We also included a group of young people who were still enrolled at school but were at risk of leaving school early.

In all, 209 young people were interviewed, with the spread being as follows:

- 147 were "leavers", and 62 were "stayers";
- 102 were females, 107 were males;
- 18 of the young people were interviewed twice;
- 147 were from the metropolitan area, and 62 from the country;
- 9 male and 10 female Aboriginal students were included;
- 33 had a disability;
- half of the young people were school card holders,[3] and
- 174 were from government schools, 25 from Catholic schools and 10 from independent schools

Locating over 200 young people who had already left school or were at risk of leaving school early was difficult. In the first instance we asked a range of schools in various locations in South Australia to help. We asked for the details of recent school leavers including some males and females and some "school card" and some "non-school card" holder students. When this strategy was exhausted we used a range of other strategies, including asking other youth organizations for help.

Generalizability

We believe that the kind of qualitative information we have gathered in this study has considerable power in terms of its generalizability. By this we do not mean that we have produced knowledge that is propositional, predictive or law-like in nature. Rather the information we have obtained through the interviews is highly generalizable because it is "epistemologically in harmony with the reader's experience and thus to that person a natural basis for generalization" (Stake, 1978, p. 5). Generalizability, thus defined, derives from within a person as a product of their experience and "the tacit knowledge of how things are, why they are, and how these things are likely to be later on or in other places with which this person is familiar" (p. 6). The essence of generalizability of this kind lies in "generalization to a similar case rather than generalization to a population of cases" (p. 7). And similar cases are recognized in terms of a similar complexity or pattern, rather than as having a similar (arbitrary) classification as a group. Demands for representativeness thus become subsidiary in importance to the need "for assurance that the target case has been properly described" (p. 7).

This construction of generalizability is very different from generalizability as described statistically, where generalizations may be made only to random groups within simple classifications.

Thus, there was no particular reason to select students for interview as if they were randomly selected from the total population. We know that the percentage numbers of students leaving school early are different for students according to gender, class, Aboriginality and rurality. We wanted to have a reasonable number from each of these particular target populations simply because we do not know whether the reasons for leaving are qualitatively different between such classifications. Within these categories of students, selection on the basis of variety, richness, complexity, awareness and willingness to talk honestly are likely to be better precursors of generalizability than is a mindless selection of random numbers and names.

Student Voice as a Research Methodology

The research literature on "voice" and "silence" is extensive. A paper was drafted (Shacklock & Smyth, 1997) which reviewed how these concepts are being used in social research with a special focus on their use in educational research involving "youth". What follows is a summary of an expanded version of that paper (Smyth, 1999b).

The term "voiced research" is a relatively new way of characterizing the inclusion of perspectives previously excluded, muted or silenced by dominant structures and discourses. Voiced research starts out from the position that interesting things can be said by and garnered from groups who do not necessarily occupy the high moral, theoretical or epistemological ground—they actually may be quite lowly and situated at some distance from the centers of power. Shacklock & Smyth (1997, p. 4) claim that "in the telling of stories of life, previously unheard, or silenced, voices open up the possibility for new, even radically different, narrations of life experience". Fine and Rosenberg (1983) push this notion a little further still when they argue that:

Critical perspectives on social institutions are often best obtained from exiles, that is, persons who leave those institutions. This is perhaps why exiles' views are frequently disparaged as deviant and in some cases conspicuously silenced. (p. 257)

Voiced research is, therefore, political in that it has an explicit agenda of reinserting, in multiple ways, opportunities for expression that have been expunged because dominant social visions hold sway. There is always continual struggle over whose views get to be represented, and smaller voices, those which are less audible, get "drowned out by others louder, more dominant, and putatively more epistemically legitimate" (Shacklock & Smyth, 1997, p. 4). In post-compulsory schooling, who gets to speak for and on behalf of students and who gets listened to is an artefact of power and who gets to exercise it. In this study, then, it is the "subjugated knowledges" of early school leavers that, while considered unworthy by those making policy, ironically hold the promise of providing the most powerful explanations.

What, then, characterizes a voiced research approach?

Because of its epistemological commitment to a more democratized research agenda, voiced research has to be construed in such a way that it provides a genuine space within which young people can reveal what is real for them. This means that research questions can only really emerge out of "purposeful conversations" (Burgess, 1988) rather than interviews (whether structured or unstructured). The operation of the power dimension in an interview where the researcher has the question and he/she is trying to extract data from the interviewee has all of the wrong characteristics for a more participatory approach. The notion that what is worthwhile investigating may reside with the research subject, and may only be revealed when a situation of trust and rapport is established, can rest uneasily with some researchers. Not having tightly pre-formulated questions but being sufficiently confident in the capacity of (ex)students as research subjects to come up with research questions that are sufficiently "respectable", is a very different game even for many qualitative researchers. At issue is who has the power to determine what is a worthwhile or robust research question, and young people as subjects are in a vulnerable position in this regard. When taken seriously, this approach represents a significant reversal of the way power generally tends to operate in research projects; the researchers "know", and young people are expected to willingly comply in supplying information. Voiced research of the kind we were pursuing here struggles with these dynamics of power.

Starting from situations of immediacy for the research subjects can generate more than a few tensions for the resource-strapped researcher. Having discussions stall, reverse, go down cul-de-sacs and head off on incomprehensible tangents is a constant and real test of the authenticity of the researcher and her/his democratic commitment to this apparently less structured style of research. Exploring and explicating complexity does not rest at all easily with the requirement of policy makers for rendering simplicity, reduction and utility in research—all aspects that run counter to voiced research with its tendency towards cacophony, multiplicity and idiosyncrasy.

Out of this work the following interview strategy shown in figure 1.1 was developed (Shacklock, 1997). The research process for the first phase—the *reconnaissance phase*—adopted the broad concept of the interviews as "purposeful conversations". We sought to make the interviews as unstructured and non-confrontational as possible through a relaxed conversational style of interaction. The research team recognized that they had a "purpose"—finding out why/how young people make decisions about leaving or staying at school, but also that an open and non-invasive process was more likely to produce richly storied accounts of leaving and staying. The often-used opening request, "Tell us about when you left school and what was happening at that time", usually worked well at providing a set of issues for follow-up questions and conversation. Importantly, what followed was grounded in the young person's experience of school and not in any assumed expertise or overbearing "need to know" on the part of the researchers.

In the initial phase of making sense of the interview data, a process we called thematizing, the research team coded the transcripts using coding that was suggested by the transcripts. No attempt was made to try to fit the interview transcripts into any pre-existing categories. As the thematizing process unfolded, it became possible to group these codes under a set of significant themes which included attendance, class, curriculum, disability, easing out, failure/success, family, femininity, harassment, labor market, masculinity, peers, popular culture, post-school, pregnancy, pressure, race, relationships, rurality, SACE, school culture, schooling relevance, suspension/exclusion/expulsion, self concept, sexuality, substance use, teachers, transience and values conflict. During the thematizing process, the research team coded each of the transcripts with up to five of these themes as a method of categorizing the dominant stories. In other words the transcripts were categorized according to which of these themes appeared to be most significant.

Each transcript was also coded using Dwyer's (1996, p. 12) archetypes for leavers "positive", "opportune", "would-be", "circumstantial", "discouraged" and "alienated". We were keen to check out how useful these

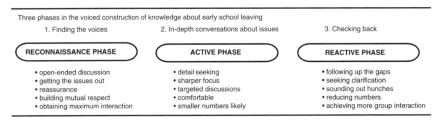

FIGURE 1.1 The Interview Strategy

categories might be for pushing our analysis. In the end, it was impossible to assign Dwyer's categories to many of the informants. For example, many of them could be described as "positive leavers" in terms of where they were going to, but they were also "alienated leavers" in terms of their experience at school. We therefore abandoned these categories.

For the second phase of the interview strategy—the *active phase*—the research team decided to re-interview a small number of the interview co-hort, around 20. This second round aimed to achieve the following:

- to use a much more structured interview process;
- to track some students longitudinally. What were they up to a year on from the first interview?
- to follow up on significant themes; and
- to go after silences—such as sexuality/homophobia (Haywood & Mac an Ghaill, 1995; Kenway, 1995; Mills, 1996), domestic violence (Weis, Marusza & Fine, 1998), physical space (Malone & Hasluck, 1998), ethnicity and suicide.

For the third phase—the *reactive phase*—the research team convened small groups of young informants to react to some of the theorizing. We met with some of those interviewed in phase two, and also met with some undergraduate students studying education. An intensive workshop process with members of the education community was also a significant aspect of this phase.

The broader purpose of the interviews was to engage in some theory building.

Dialectical Theory-Building

In practicing "dialectical theory-building" (Lather, 1986; Smyth, 1998a), the intent was to find a more informative way of accounting for early school leaving—one that moves considerably beyond the largely "victim blaming" explanations we have at the moment. We draw our inspiration about the importance of dialogue between theory and practice from Ira Shor's *Critical Teaching and Everyday Life* (1980) and *When Students Have Power* (1996), where he engages in a wider search for the cultural interferences to critical thought. In our case, the search is for more complex explanations, beyond individual student deficits for the noncompletion of schooling. What Shor does in an exemplary manner is to show how the impediments to everyday life are embedded in larger social forces that surround us, rather than being located in the immediacy and shortcomings of personal idiosyncrasies. Understanding the world in this way means moving beyond concrete and psychological interferences (Shor, 1980), and looking instead at the systematic, structural, institutional and ideological levels, for forms of awareness that provide explanations.

"Dialectical theory-building" is a heuristic device (Smyth, 1998a) through which data constructed in context are used to clarify and reconstruct existing theory. At the same time, the efficacy of existing theories is challenged as they are subjected to the interrogation of generative themes unearthed from the everyday experiences of those whose lives are being investigated. What is being attempted is the continual modification of existing theoretical constructs to reveal "counter interpretations" (Lather, 1986, p. 267) through a more intimate understanding of the views of participants. At the same time, sedimented layers of meaning and understanding are being uncovered about the complexities of the lives contained in the interview conversations. In the case of young people not completing schooling, this means theoretical vantage points are used to sculpt interpretations out of complex verbal accounts given by young people at the time of making their decisions.

Coming a little closer to what we want to be dialectical about, we want to provide a more fleshed-out explanatory account of early school leaving that is informed by the voices of students, but in a way that is framed by the larger orienting categories/theories of policy contestation; multiple youth identities; transitions from school; curriculum, assessment and credentialling; and the cultural geography of the school.

We have attempted to represent, or to concept map a constellation of orienting theories as seen below and presented in later chapters of the book.

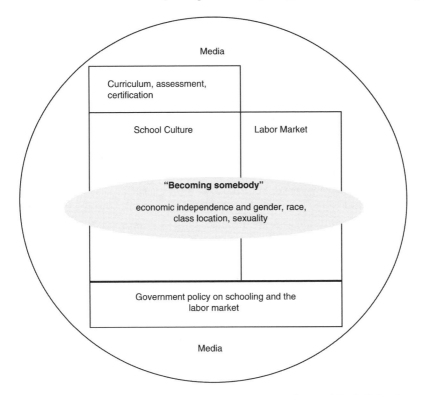

FIGURE 1.2 Constellation of Orienting Concepts to Understand Early School Leaving

Representing Lives in Portraits

In deciding how best to represent the material we had collected, the research team believed it important to affirm the need to honor the complexity of what had been heard about young people's lives. Often in research reports the voice of the informants is spliced in at appropriate spots to make a point or stimulate a discussion. While this strategy was used in most of this account, we also wanted an alternative way of representing student voice that would undermine what usually amounts to separating out details of people's lives. It was clear that to understand early school leaving it was essential to be able to keep in mind the complexity of young lives. Early school leaving is not reducible to this or that factor. Early school leaving is a process that occurs in the context of all the things that are happening in a young person's life. Thus, the particular form of representation used here drew broadly from the approach of the Australian

Human Rights report on Aboriginal young people who were taken away from their parents, the "Stolen Generation's Report", *Bringing Them Home* (Human Rights and Equal Opportunity Commission, 1997).

To achieve this we reorganized the student responses, explanations and conversation into a short (2–5 page) coherent statement saying "this is me and this is what I've been doing", that captured the mood, style and essence of the student discourse. There were of necessity some omissions of detail (some of the transcripts ran to more than 100 pages over two interviews), but we found that with careful selection and crafting, most of the story could be told in the student's unedited language.

As indicated earlier, we sought to minimize the overt interference of the researcher in the story as presented. We wanted something as close to the voice of the young person as possible. Given that the researcher's voice gets plenty of space in our account, we saw little need to intrude in the construction of these portraits. In many cases the resulting portraits were returned for comment to many of the young people who attended the "reactive" group workshop, with generally positive reactions.

Here is another such portrait.

Portrait #138
Baz: Got Ya!

I was repeating year 10 about a year ago and I left school because of a number of things building up pressure and I couldn't handle it after a while. I'd be getting followed around the yard at recess and lunch by these two teachers. Just watching me all the time. I used to run away from them but it was hard, so after a while I got mad at them and ended up smashing a door. In a temper, I just got that irate, I just slammed it and it smashed.

I used to be a bad kid, I admit to that. Just muck around, not do the work and that. I used to wag school [absent], swear at teachers, tell them to get fucked and just walk out of the room. I was going through a stage, you know. Just didn't think school was worthwhile. Last year I was trying to do the work and I did want to pass. Before that I didn't. So I was getting good grades, and that just makes you feel better. Like I used to get E's and I was bringing it up to C's. And I wanted to get a good job, like mechanic or computer technician, and it's good money too. You know, the maths teacher realized and he said to me that I was doing good now. But he was the only one that said it. And these two other teachers were always hassling me.

Like when we first moved up here to the country I was pretty bad, but then I realized I had to change and like these teachers wouldn't let me. At the high school in Exmouth I got suspended. It was for fighting other kids. I was getting picked on. There was this big gang of them. I think it was because I liked this girl and I was going out with her and her boyfriend was one of the gang.

Yeah, my parents split up when I was about seven. They were fighting all the time, and I was in the middle of it for months. It was pretty bad. I remember I got clobbered around the head because I was standing in the way, saying don't fight.

I was living with my mum, and I did good at primary school for a while, but after year 7 I decided to live with my dad, cause my mum was always going out and getting drunk at the pub and stuff like that. So I moved to another school in Exmouth and then my dad moved so I went to this school down south and it took me a while to make friends. Then when I did, I got into the wrong group, and I got suspended and had to move back to Exmouth with my mum and another school. Then she got a new boyfriend and we moved up to the country. I was at five schools in my first three years at high school.

Anyhow, these two teachers would hide behind walls, and sneak around corners just to watch me. I tried just walking away, like the principal said, but they just kept on following me, watching every move I made. And Bob and me, we'd be hiding, just watching them, because I knew they were doing it. One time all these girls had their arms around me and he came out of his office shouting at me, because he was on the top floor, and told me to go into his room and he wrote down on the incident report I was choking them. The girls done a statement and they said I wasn't choking them. He said sorry that time. But I still got suspended for handling girls, or something. Maybe I was. But it was mutual, you know.

I don't know why he kept on. He used to be helpful. Maybe he changed when I liked his daughter and I said to her that I wanted to go out with her and that. And at one stage he told his daughter to keep away from me and if she went near me she'd get grounded. Just because I'm talking to her and I'm friends with her.

My mum talked to the principal a couple of times, but nothing changed. Then there was this last time I got suspended. It was raining, and Mr F kicked me out of the SACE (South Australian Certificate of Education) room. Then I went into the courtyard. I walked out the door and went in the courtyard and stood under the shelter there. Then I got kicked out of there by Mr F again, so I sat in front of the detention room because there was shelter there, just a bit on the side of it. I got kicked away from there. Still didn't complain about it, I just moved. Then I went in the activity hall. Mr J got involved then and when I was told to leave there I just slammed the door so hard. It smashed the glass. Then I just walked out and stood in the rain, just sat there in the middle of the rain.

The Principal, before she suspended me, she said she wasn't going to tell AUSTUDY (Australian Study Allowance) because she was going to give me correspondence, so I could do it at home, because I asked her could I. Then some other teacher went ahead and told AUSTUDY and [I had to pay back] like $310 . . . . My mum rang AUSTUDY and they said a teacher from the school rang up. That's when I went off school really. I mean, that money is what I live on. And I was thinking it's not worth it because I know as soon as I go back they're just going to start picking on me and after a while I'm not going to handle it and I'm going to lose the plot again, and I'll just get suspended.

So I worked on a farm for a while picking grapes. Applied for a job with the supermarket. Got an interview, but they told me to wait till I get my licence. Then I got into a TAFE course at the start of the year. A pre-voc multi-trade course. Did welding, occupational health and safety, drawing. Didn't really know what I wanted to do. I liked working on computers, and I was getting good grades on that. I finished the course, but didn't get to pay my fees because it was $700. So I didn't get the certificate. Then I moved back to Borderville to live with my aunt, and decided to be a computer technician. So that's looking OK.

Life is good. I still play soccer. Scored a goal last week. Social life is good. Plenty of friends. Girls, yeah. And getting into this TAFE course is making me feel good. My dad will be pleased. He used to tell me that if I didn't pull my socks up, I'd be a no-hoper. Pity about school. I would have gone all the way to year 12. I would have been in year 12 by now.

Organization of the Book

The remainder of the book is organized around chapters that follow the broad metaphor of mapping the context and arenas of influence around the decisions young people made to exit schooling and the barriers or constraints put on their completion of schooling.

In part II, we provide some of the theoretical and thematic categories pursued in the second section of the book.

The issue of early school leaving is situated in chapter 2 within the wider setting of globalization, the state and schools. We make the argument that while young people are making choices, these choices are being framed for them by wider sets of forces. In navigating a transition for themselves, young people are constrained agency. We show the ruptured and disrupted nature of these pathways and how aspects of the global interact with the local at the level of the state: for example, "going for a job", "getting training", "on the path to university". Furthermore, schools also begin to loom large here in the ways they structure relationships hierarchically, through, for example, an emphasis on teacher-centered pedagogy, subject specialization and the reinforcement of conservatism through entrenched tradition.

Chapter 3 starts with a theoretical entree into Snow and Anderson's

(1987) notion of "doing identity work", and sets up Ira Shor's (1980, p. 48) notion of "interferences" as a way of reading the interview material from young people, as they encounter obstacles in their project of "becoming somebody" (Wexler, 1992). Here, we begin to unravel some of the issues around young people's identity formation, including the impact of media culture; the generation gap and the breaking down of authoritarian relationships between adults and young people; the growing forms of alienation among young people (suicide and substance abuse); and the central role friendships play. Finally, we briefly map the school-to-work interface as young people navigate a path to economic independence.

In part III we continue with the notion of "doing identity", this time through a series of closely inter-linked categories.

Chapter 4 explores the constellation of class/gender/race as sites for disciplining identities, and we see that these elements constitute the presence or absence of forms of capital to which young people have access in varying degrees. The chapter concludes by drawing these themes together within the category of "interactive trouble" (Freebody, Ludwig & Gunn, 1994) as young people struggle with the influence of the matrix of class/gender/race in power relations.

In chapter 5, we explore the apparent breakdown of the "linear" or "propulsion" pathway to university, seen by many of the young informants as being the dominant influence. We report on how the young informants in this study made complex decisions, particularly around the credentialling process. There is support here for Wyn and Dwyer's (2000) thesis that some young people are not propelled through schooling by the lure of a credential; quite to the contrary, they reveal a high level of agency in constructing alternative biographies for themselves that undermine the policy trajectory. Far from being victims who "drop out", these young people presented in individualistic ways what amounted to accommodation and resistance to the impediment of a policy credential for university entrance, which they labelled as irrelevant, despite its declared intention to be inclusive of all.

The voices of young people on what school meant to them provided the fabric of chapter 6 as they described with incredible insight, precision and clarity the cultural geography of the high school. Some startling insights were provided here into school cultures that worked and those that inhibited the broader life project of the young people.

PART II

CONSTELLATION OF ORIENTING CONCEPTS

CHAPTER 2

CONTEXTUALIZING EARLY SCHOOL LEAVING: GLOBALIZATION, THE STATE AND SCHOOLS

Navigating a Transition

The metaphor of "navigating a transition" is a useful way of talking about what young people are doing in and around post-compulsory schooling. The notion of navigation assigns young people a sense of agency: they have a measure of self-determination, albeit constrained through parental authority and their location in a terrain marked by social class, gender, sexuality and race. As such, "young people are a highly differentiated group" (White & Wyn, 1998, p. 324) based on their location in the circuits of power that operate in society. The interview material in this study supports the contention that young people are engaging in "consciously chosen action" (White & Wyn, 1998, p. 315); they are invoking their own volition, will or choice, although often in a context not of their own choosing; and they are attempting to make the best choices they can in their context. The following comments from young people in the study give a sense of the agency with which young people are working:

You've just got to go for it. (#006)

It's my life now and I've got to run it. (#059)

I've had to be strong because I've had a lot to deal with all at the one time. (#103)

If you don't want to do it, you're not going to do it really! (#122)

As Dwyer and Wyn (1998) argue, transitions to adulthood should not be considered as a "linear progression from the world of school into the world of work" (p. 286)—as a predictable, straightforward and natural process that is driven by psychological maturation. Instead, young people are having to make sense of, and navigate, a transition in a complex and changing world, a world that is characterized by disjunctures between formal education and the labor market; these amount to an unpredictability of vocational integration in a radically restructuring labor market that offers little more than impermanence and insecurity. Instead of linear transitions from school to work, "[t]hey are establishing different patterns of response which involve complicated mixes of study, work and family life" (p. 294).

Mapping Context—Globalization

We believe it is important to ground the voices from the interviews in the material conditions and the context in which young people navigate their post-school destinies. But what does it mean to "contextualize" youth lives in these times?

In the recent past, it would have been possible to make sense of or to construe life in schools in a "context" of state bureaucracies (Seddon, 1995). It is significant to note that policies about post-compulsory schooling, curriculum, assessment and credentialling, in the state of South Australia where the study was conducted, are a state government responsibility. These policies, which in South Australia define the arrangements for the South Australian Certificate of Education (SACE), affect what teachers do, and what students experience in schools. We elaborate in more detail in chapter 5. But we believe that the process of globalization also needs to be considered if we are to adequately contextualize and understand contemporary life in schools. It is this wider context that we will sketch out later in this chapter. But for the moment, we need to provide a little background.

During the late 1980s and early 1990s, the arena for educational policy development in Australia experienced a gradual move to an increasing involvement of the federal government (Knight, Lingard & Bartlett, 1994; Knight & Warry, 1996; Lingard, Porter, Bartlett & Knight, 1995). This expansion of the sphere of influence of the national government has continued. By the end of the 1990s, life in schools was increasingly influenced by technologies of power that operated globally (Smyth, 1998b; Taylor, Rizvi, Lingard & Henry, 1997). Educational policy then, as now, was framed within a neo-liberal discourse (Pusey, 1991; Kelsey, 1995; Giddens, 1994), that operated as a dominating rationality, or a "regime of truth" (Foucault, 1980, p. 131):

> [S]uch a policy is based on an increasingly close relationship between government and the capitalist economy, a radical decline in the institutions and power of political democracy, and attempts at curtailing "liberties" that have been gained in the past. (Apple, 1993, p. 21)

> For the neo-liberals, capitalistic enterprise is no longer regarded as the source of the problems of modern civilization. Quite the opposite: it is the core of all that is good about it. (Giddens, 1994, pp. 33–34)

The complex process called globalization is not only affecting the nature of educational policy, but it is also affecting everyday life, civil society and the economy. We need an account, therefore, that is capable of understanding complexity and that connects globalization to young people's lives and to what happens in classrooms:

> This complexity is apparent in the "world" in which young people live, including: the effects of globalization on some aspects of youth culture; the restructuring of national and regional economies; the increased significance of educational credentials and the casualization of the youth labor market. Complexity is also apparent in the way in which young people approach these issues. (Dwyer & Wyn, 1998, p. 296)

The process of globalization is significant in this study because these changes are profoundly affecting the terrain upon which young people are having to navigate their futures. Deciding whether to stay at school or not is now very much affected by the way nation states manage globalization. In tapping into an emerging global economy, Australia finds itself in a difficult transition phase involving a profound structural adjustment. The welfare state is being wound down with a concomitant drive towards privatization; international competitiveness has become a mantra; transnational corporations increasingly affect what is happening locally; and the official policy discourse is one of headlong pursuit of the transition to a "knowledge economy" (Kemp, 1999, p. 1). But the structural adjustment process affects communities in different ways. Many in the Australian community are being disenfranchised from the economy, and hence from financial independence; in South Australia in particular, this includes many rural communities and significant portions of metropolitan Adelaide (the capital city). We agree with Bauman (1998) that globalization should be understood as the "new world disorder", and might be better termed as "glocalization" (Robertson, 1995). For Bauman, glocalization infers globalization for some and localization for others:

> Glocalization is first and foremost a redistribution of privileges and deprivations, of wealth and poverty, of resources and impotence, of power and powerlessness, of freedom and constraint. It is, one may say, a process of world-wide re-stratification, in the course of which a new world-wide socio-cultural hierarchy is put together . . . What is free choice for some is cruel fate for some others. (Bauman, 1998, p. 43)

While it is not possible here to unpack all the complexity of the emerging global (dis)order and its impact on how young people navigate their futures, we want to argue here for an expansive view of globalization which seeks to make sense of how political-economic, socio-cultural and technological changes at the global level reach into everyday life. We can only provide a thumb-nail sketch of this complexity and hope that it will alert the reader to the impact of globalization on the world of school, including what is happening in universities, the vocational, educational and training (VET) sector and the world of work.

We begin with a sketch of how we understand "globalization" and its impact on the world of work, and then outline briefly some defining features of the contemporary secondary school and some trends that seem to be emerging as a consequence of globalization.

The Process of Economic Globalization

Worldwide forces are dramatically changing the way we live our lives:

> Vastly improved forms of information technology, instantaneous communication, and a capacity of international capital to move around the world at short notice to take advantage of local circumstances (most notably, cheap labor), has meant that corporations as well as governments are faced with unprecedented levels of volatility, uncertainty and unpredictability demanding quite different kinds of responses—both in terms of work organization as well as workplace skills. (Smyth, Dow, Hattam, Reid & Shacklock, 2000, p. 3)

Smyth (1998b) also argues that decisions about the nature of everyday life are increasingly being removed from the control of national (and democratically elected) governments, and are now made by transnational economic forces that operate largely outside the scope of any single government. Castells (1989) argued that there are really three identifiable aspects to this wider economic restructuring:

1. a fundamental re-alignment of the relationship between capital and labor, such that capital obtains a significantly higher share in the benefits of the fruits of production;
2. a new role for the state in the public sector, which is not so much about reducing the role of government intervention in the economy, but a changing of its style; and
3. a new international division of labor in which low cost labor is profoundly shaping what is happening in the "developed" world.

For Smyth (1998b), there are a number of outcomes occurring with regard to the first of these contemporary trends. These outcomes might best be summarized in terms of higher productivity through technological innovation; lower wages, reduced social benefits, and less protective working conditions; decentralization of production to regions of the world with more relaxed labor and environmental restrictions; greater reliance on the informal economy, that is, unregulated labor; and a weakening of trade unions, which is the single most important factor in increasing the level of profits (Castells, 1989, pp. 23–25).

As to the second of these trends, Smyth (1998b), drawing upon Castells (1989, p. 25), argues that we are not witnessing the withdrawal of the state from the economic scene; rather we are witnessing the emergence of a new form of intervention, whereby new means and new areas are penetrated by the state, while others are deregulated and transferred to the market. For Castells, this emerging redefinition of the role of the state embraces the deregulation of many activities, including the relaxation of environmental controls in the workplace; the shrinkage and privatization of productive activities in the public sector; regressive tax reform favoring corporations and high income groups; state support for high technology research and development and leading industrial sectors; priority and status for defense and defense-related industries; the shrinkage of the welfare state; and fiscal austerity, with the goal of a balanced budget.

Regarding the third trend, Smyth (1998b) sees the opening up of new markets through global expansion (or "internationalization") becoming possible as a consequence of several noticeable developments: industry taking advantage of the most favorable conditions anywhere in the world; capital taking advantage of "around-the-clock capital investment" opportunities; corporations homogenizing markets and making up market losses in one area through increases in another (pp. 26–28).

In trying to make sense of the impact of economic globalization on the Australian economy, Probert (1998) provides a neat summary of the features of the new work order:

- The *decline of many traditionally important industries* and occupations that went with them—in particular, many manufacturing businesses, with the most recent and spectacular losses being in places with few alternative employment industries (steel making in Newcastle, New South Wales, and paper making in Burnie, Tasmania). Job losses in these industries have been mainly blue collar men's jobs.

- The rapid growth of *new service sector industries*—such as financial services, tourism, hospitality and health, and the accompanying expansion of white collar, clerical and personal service work, much of which has been taken up by women.

- The *changing composition of the labor force* reflecting declining employment rates for men, particularly for older men, and the increasing employment rate for women; but also the collapse of full-time employment among young people. Thirty years ago most women working full-time were teenagers; today most women who work full-time are much older, and many have dependent children.

- Sustained and unacceptably *high levels of unemployment and underemployment*, concentrated particularly at the low skill/less educated end of the labor market.

- A very rapid increase in what have been called "irregular" *or "contingent" kind of jobs*—jobs that are temporary, or part-time, and in particular, jobs that are casual. Around 26 per cent of all employees are now employed casually, the vast majority also on a part-time basis.

- New *patterns of work organization* have appeared which are based on quite different principles to those of the post-war boom. These forms of work organization are found in a wide range of industries and include team-based work, fewer levels of management and supervision, multitasking if not multi-skilling, and the need for communication skills.

- Significant changes in the *industrial relations framework* which has historically played a major role in regulating job content, working conditions and pay for most Australian workers. We now have an emphasis on enterprise level bargaining, and even individual bargaining through Australian Workplace Agreements, with far fewer jobs subject to [regulated conditions]. (p. 2, original emphasis)

What is particularly disturbing, in relation to early school leaving, is the absence of any serious analysis of the effect of this new work order in the secondary school curriculum. It seems that young people need to work it out by themselves. Having said that, we need to point out that some of the informants in this study had very insightful analyses of the contemporary labor market. This next portrait is an example.

Portrait #028
Joel: Seeing the Changes

Leaving school? Well the original plan was for me to finish school. Yep, finishing my SACE. But I had trouble with my parents, from about year 6 on all through my high school. I ended up fighting and ended up leaving home.

Year 11, week five of first term, I left then, 'cos I had to get a job because I couldn't handle it. Too much stress. I didn't go to school for a few weeks around that time, and ended up giving up. I want to be a chef. That's what I'm doing now, so I didn't need a full education anyway. The stress levels? Well, we were in what they would say was the badder group, you know, the bad people.

My parents they say, "Oh, you think the world is different now. But when you're older you'll see it's actually the same". I don't agree with that. Forty years ago all the economy was different, living was different, surviving, getting a job. So now we're still getting the same knowledge that they got 40 years ago. The way I see it, looking back, is how long have they had the same teaching methods, the same textbooks, stuff like that? A long while! A long, long, long while.

I mean, I left school and started my life, and I've looked at it. The generations are getting younger. For example, I was speaking to a few of my 20 year old friends, and they say, we started on marijuana when we were 17, right. Then I look at the generation before us, and they started like a few years below that; I started a few years below that, down to 11 year olds; 10 year olds are starting it now. And it's just getting younger and younger. And that scene, like if they're doing what we're doing now, but younger and younger, then it'll stuff them up more now, but they're getting all the experiences younger so they're going to mature faster in that sense.

Following from that is, if they're going to get more experience at a younger age it means they're going to get fed up at a younger age and they're going to be still kept in the system. So schools need to change. They're going to need different methods. They can't, like, use what they've been using for 40 years any more. Everything's set for you still. You have to do this, you have to go by these rules, you know. Such as homework, which is what most people don't like. It's where the stress factor comes in, because that's your break time. Your break time is study time still. And you want it to end. You've had enough. In year 10, I did homework twice in the entire year. I didn't like it. I said I'd rather fail than be doing homework.

That's why you get all these students getting all stressed out, because they do want to succeed. They do want to do really well. Because you still need your SACE to get a good job, whether you think it's relevant or not, you need that. And that's when their theory starts. Wooh, to survive you have to follow this; you have to go by this to get to there, whether it's irrelevant or not, you know. You're stuck with it until you're 15. And if you leave when you're 15—unless you're doing like my trade or you go straight to TAFE—you're pretty much screwed. Like some people at fifteen don't have the maturity to leave. They just leave because their friends left or for some reason they just, "Oh I've had enough of this", and they just, you know, get drunk and then get stoned. Yeah, and then get into heavy drugs and then just fade away. Yeah, to just forget about it kind of thing. Then they either get on top of it all, or it becomes their lifestyle, that's what they're used to, and they just continue with it.

What was relevant to adults 20 years ago is only partially relevant to us. It's like, we want to develop from that. We don't want to keep going back to the same. They need to say to the students, "What do you think you need?" For instance, they got a student lounge together by the time I was in year 11, and everyone said, "Yeah, we should be able to smoke in there". And they said, "No, it's against the law". You know, and then people look at other schools like Jefferson High, where adult re-entry students can come back and they can sit in a chair and have a cigarette. And it's just such a pitiful reason that they can't have a cigarette, and they're stressing out because they can't have one, and the teacher won't let them go and have one; so they bludge [shirking responsibility or hard work] and then they get suspended, you know. Yeah, because they make it bad. We make allowances to go do it, whether it stuffs us up or not, you know. Totally different worlds. They don't want to do it. That's why you get "trouble makers" and that. The school didn't spend time finding out what he actually wanted to do. Instead they tried to get him to do what they wanted him to do. And that ain't going to work.

My parents are the same. They think that I'm the bad one because I've been with the wrong people and I might smoke a little bit of marijuana. So I'm bad, you know. No matter what the relevants [sic] are, they think I'm bad. Even my good points are irrelevant because I do this. It's really my mother. She full-on disagrees with what I'm like and how I live and who my friends are. And, you know, I'm not allowed to have any friends around my house because they're bad. They don't want to hear what I do out of home when I go out because, you know, it's irrelevant to them.

Yes, the trouble started when I started changing. Having my own thoughts. Yeah, and they just didn't agree with me, so they decided instead of listening to me and what I had to offer, they thought, mm, we'll fight him and get him. Their hard line made me go my own way more, fight them more, you know. Try to get my point across. They listened, but they didn't hear. They didn't want to know. They said, "Oh we'll change, help you out the way you want" and that, but they never did.

And they never let me do anything, they never let me go out, explore to see what actually went on. They thought, "Right, you're not mature enough yet so you can't do it". But the way you get maturity is to go out, find out what's wrong and what's not. They say, "Don't do that, otherwise that will be bad for you". But you don't actually know that because you haven't done it.

I've moved back home now because I couldn't survive. I was getting less money than my rent so in the end I ended up spending three grand and moving back in the period of a month. They're going better, but I figured out a self-plan for myself. As soon as I walk in home through that door I change, I go to what they want. I gave up to them, they can think what they want. Some of my friends come around, and it's like, you're weird man, why are you acting like that? You're nothing like what you normally are, when you're at home. Because I can't, you know. I've got to act the way they want, otherwise trouble starts. Sometimes I get pissed off, and just give it away for a week or so and then it goes back to normal.

My dad, though, listens to me now, and I have some reasonable conversations with him, and he tells me, through experience, you know, how that would work, and why that wouldn't work, and stuff like that.

They wanted me to finish school. That was their full intention. Like, I've got dyslexia and they changed my school when I was in like Primary school to this school where they've got a special teacher. The only one in South Australia who could help me to spell. I can't spell for shit, you know. But everything else is fine.

Half the stuff at school I saw was irrelevant. I tried harder in Maths and English because I thought that was relevant, and I like PE because I used to be a real fit person, and I used to be a State champion, long distance. I was in like 2000 metre Olympic training squad. Stuff like that.

It was worth the effort in some ways but not in others. I was thinking what I want to do. I was sitting there in class, and going, well, this is useless. I don't want to be learning this, but I have to. I'm going to the toilet now. I'll see you at the end of lesson. Even just walking around the school, you know, it's making me feel better than actually in the class with what they wanted to teach me. I still play sport and that. I don't like sitting on my arse and not doing anything.

I didn't like English but I found it enjoyable, because I really excelled in year 10. I had a really good teacher. He'd make jokes and pay out [tease] the students, and we used to pay him back, have a good time and that. It made me want to learn, you know. And if you wrote a story he wouldn't mark it on the grammar or the spelling, it would be like on the actual idea and how you put it together and, you know, the start, the middle and the finish—how it all corresponded. When he left we all did a card for him and bought him a book. And on this card, I made a spelling mistake. He said,"Don't change it, it's good to remember you by."

Some of my friends, they really care, you know. But hell, the way I see it, things in this world are going downhill so quickly, they are just descending mighty quickly. Very depressing. But some of us think, why is this happening, you know. Why are these people doing this still? Like with the money. I don't think this world should be used by money. Look what money has done to us. It's got poverty and it's got riches, you know. So instead of using money to make us better or to make us work hard they should change it so that the world is working as one to better ourselves, not in competition, but better. So the whole State works as a community, working as one, to better themselves. Then there would be no poverty, there would be no wars, you know. It would be getting better and then like the pollution problem would solve itself, because of the techno. Everyone is bettering themselves . . . , because technology would be getting better . . . everyone is bettering themselves. You save money. Money wouldn't matter, man.

I'm almost 18. I find it very hard to explain myself and put what I'm actually thinking in words. But I'm seeing all these different things, and it's a lot different to what is actually happening, and I'm getting all these different words and things in my head how society has to change. Some of it might be fantasy. But I'm getting to a point where I'm going to see, like bona fide things. When I'm older I most probably will have more idea how to go about it. I feel really strongly about doing something about it when I'm older. And I think, I can change this, and I'm thinking to myself, you know, maybe in a few years I should get into politics or something, and actually do something about it.

The totally different world Joel is talking about above is not just different because of the changes in the economy—there is also a socio-cultural and technological dimension.

Socio-cultural and Technological Globalization

Transnational corporate capitalism has developed the "informational society" (Luke, 1991) or "society of the spectacle" (Debond, 1970; Agger, 1992) as a society of electronically mediated consumption communities:

> To fuel the growth of transnationalised capitalism, more and more of the everyday lifeworld must be colonised by the corporate coding system reducing autonomous non-commodified behavior to scripted/packaged choices projected across hyperreality. (Luke, 1991, pp. 18–19)

Those with the capital have access to television, global communications and the information superhighway (Kellner, 1995). We often take for granted our own privileged positions. This privilege is de-mystified when we remember that most of the world's population has yet to make a telephone call! The convergence of technological and socio-cultural globalization involves "monstrous media conglomerates—ABC/Disney, Time Warner/Turner, SONY/ Colombia, Paramount/Viacom/Blockbuster, CBC/Westinghouse" (Kellner, 1995, p. 47)—that aim to commodify information and entertainment as rapidly as possible to maximize capital accumulation. This confluence of wealth and media ownership is also well known in Australia: see, for example, Rupert Murdoch.

Living within these transnational consumption communities includes two conflicting vectors, one from above and one from below—a colonizing as well as a post-colonial dimension (During, 1992). In the 1990s, Australians experienced increasing amounts of popular culture that was colonized/Americanized/homogenized. Deregulation has meant that every city has the same shops, the same films, the same music, the same fashion, the same news and the same food. If culture is understood as also providing the tools for meaning-making, or for making sense of our experience, then our consciousness is colonized by "corporate capital's codes, scripts and packages" (Luke, 1991, p. 19). We are seduced into behaving as collaborators/consumers/clients in the good life that is known as "possessive individualism" (p. 13).

In its post-colonial dimension, the convergence of technology and culture has meant the emergence of spaces for freedom of speech that are out of reach of the censors, be they military regimes or the thought police of democratic countries. As an example, there are web-sites that offer a space to carry critical comment that is censored in the mainstream press of countries such as Serbia, China and Malaysia that are struggling against undemocratic regimes. As well, globalization offers the possibility of living hybrid lives (Luke & Luke, 1999), in a kind of "third space". In such a third space, cultural difference is not obliterated, made deviant, or considered pejorative—but rather held in tension, as a quality to be sought after.

What is most significant about globalization is the impossibility of considering the local without the global. The global constitutes the local, and vice versa. Our everyday lives are now profoundly affected by changes to the economy, technology and culture, changes that have a global reach. For young people this means navigating a transition in a world in which the local and global are increasingly intertwined; a world in which the pathways to financial independence, such as going for a job, getting training or entering university, have been disrupted or intruded upon by global effects. To bring the discussion back to the local, we will now consider these disrupted pathways and the effect of the global on the local:

> Globalization is fragmenting the Australian labor market, creating "work rich" and "work poor" districts in our cities and regions. Regions in South Australia are part of the periphery in the Australian labor market. This periphery has a greater share of the national unemployment, poverty and inequality and a declining share of the population and employment. (Spoehr, 1999, p. 92)

We move now to explore what these wider forces mean in the context of young people engaged in early school leaving.

"Going for a Job"

Young people who leave school before finishing their post-compulsory schooling credential, often do so with a view of "going for a job". But in South Australia they have to contend with the state's sharply declining economic fortunes, and if they live in those regions Spoehr describes as the "periphery", then their prospects look even bleaker.

Spoehr's (1999) analysis of South Australia's economic position reveals the following:

- the economy is skewed towards highly protected manufacturing industry, but has done better than expected due to strong growth in chemicals and the transport industry;
- "[a]t the beginning of 1998 there were around 58 unemployed people for every job advertised in South Australia" (p. 94);

- the unemployment rate is consistently worse than in all other mainland Australian states;
- there is a sustained decline in full-time employment: the "number of full-time jobs declined by 1.5% or around 7000 in South Australia over the three years to 1998" (pp. 95–97);
- South Australia has the highest proportion of under-employed people in Australia, with nearly 8 percent of the labor force preferring to work longer hours than they are currently working;
- South Australia has the highest level of long-term unemployed (those people unemployed for more than 12 months) in Australia;
- youth unemployment rates were the highest in the country over the 12 months to September 1998; and
- youth unemployment rates vary considerably, "with rates well above the State's average in southern and northern Adelaide" (p. 101), and also among "young women in the rural areas of southern and eastern South Australia" (p. 101).

These conditions have changed little since 1999.

At this point it is appropriate to engage again with one of the young people interviewed. Many of them did leave school to go for a job, or, as in the case of Roy, to start their own business.

Portrait #088
Roy: Thanks a Million!

I left school about six months ago after first term, year 11 at xxx. I was doing Physics, Chemistry and two Maths. In year 10 at xxx they sort of thought that's what I should do.

Why'd I leave? I sort of see school as you do all this stuff, get a bit of paper and you end up working for someone else. It's not really me. Why'd I leave? Basically because I was too busy running the business.

You see, I had this PC since the start of '96 and then I just went out to this computer place in Pine Road and met this guy and went back there on the weekends and then helped him and he taught me about hardware and stuff. He didn't pay me but he gave me parts and stuff as well. I soon learnt how to fix every problem that we had, and from that I sort of fixed a few computers and started building them and selling them and it sort of went from there. I learnt a lot from him and then started my own completely new business.

By the end of the year, that's last year, business was getting up a lot. I started failing a lot in tests. Chris and I we had plans for new software, so we started to get into that. School wasn't teaching me any more about computer hardware and the electronics of it. And I didn't learn much about software in computer class. Ideally I just wanted to set up and run my own business.

The other thing was where I was living in xxx, because my dad remarried, and his wife just wouldn't let me use the phone, wouldn't let me get another phone line put in, wouldn't let me have customers come around, wouldn't let me store my gear anywhere, so it was just crazy. So I moved back to my mum's house at White Lakes.

My dad, he didn't support my business in any way either. When I decided to leave school he jumped up and down. You know, I got distinctions in the Australian school science competition and in Maths. Funny though because my dad he was sort of an inventor. Came up with a lot of ideas. He's got his own company.

At the moment I'm only targeting businesses. Before I was running a computer business for home users. But I just found setting up a home computer for someone that has little or no skills whatsoever is really hard and annoying because you've got to teach them everything and the other thing is they all want it done for nothing. Whereas a business like yesterday, they just wanted two machines networked so they could run this software package, so they had one big expense. No worries, I got the bits, went there and put it together.

Anyhow, I wanted to manage a business, instead of doing all the work. So now I know quite a bit about programming and design. But Don knows all we need to know about programming, like he's done three years at uni [university], so now I just tell him what to do and he does it. I'm really in the management side. He can see the product, but I can see its potential, and this product is looking at making millions. So I'm already set up in information technology with both software and hardware and I've got another couple of businesses happening with different services and stuff. The main company is called Royce Business Solutions. Spelt with a C. Yeah, Rolls Royce, touch of class. Lots of people are interested in investing to get hold of the software we've designed.

I was always more interested in managing. I can remember in year 6, my brother gave me a job saying I'll pay you 5c for every flyer you stick in a mail box. So I went to school, found three mates, paid them 2.5c for every flyer, sat back, did nothing but get paid 2.5c for every flyer they stuck in a mailbox. And I'd just think up things, you know, like I got involved in video surveillance. I got a 10x zoom lens for this camera and then I built a circuit so then I could get a computer joy- stick, plug it into it, then use a joystick controlled zoom and focus it. Just come up with little ideas and stuff.

Looking back at school, I got along with most of the teachers pretty well. Except for a few who really bossed me around and sort of told me what to do and that. And the school counsellor was pretty supportive about the business with people to see and information and stuff.

Yeah, I was sort of interested in the science courses like Chemistry where you get to play around with stuff. And programming computers was interesting in a way. The actual work was pretty boring but they were getting there. And I did Japanese in year 8. That was a bit of a bludge, but it might actually come in handy now. But overall school wasn't getting me where I wanted to go. And the teachers weren't really happy about the mobile phone, you know ringing in class. By the way, if you're after one, I'm an authorised dealer.

But really, basically the teacher is giving you the work to do and you've got to do it, which seems exactly the same as you would be if you were working for someone. And universities? I find them a good place to find employees, you know.

Roy's story was unusual in that he managed to find a niche in an emerging part of the labor market connected to the globalization of information technology. There are some positive stories of young people getting jobs relatively easily. The following portrait though is more representative of the lives of young people living on the periphery of the new work order.

Portrait #024
Mark: A Good Life

I was in year 11, I left round about last December for a couple of reasons. First of all, I had two cars to run. I was on AUSTUDY and 'cos my mum's on a sole pension, I have to pay her money to support me, food and board. And from that I've got $5 a week to live on, for myself. I had to put petrol and insure the car. I had two cars. I recently had one towed away 'cos that got defective. It was unregistered. And my engine blew on me, so that's why I've spent thousands of dollars on it, and it would have taken me years to fix on $5 a week.

Cars are a sort of hobby. 'Cos I mean, I smoke and the only thing I do is drink. Don't do anything else. I mean, don't have any other interests. I start work at 5 in the morning and finish at 4 o'clock; and I eat, sleep and back to work again, sort of thing. I work as a factory hand, at just, like, a chicken place.

It's not a bad job. I mean, it's got various things. I do deliveries now. They take responsibility in me. When I started, I was just like washing a few things and cleaning and now I've gradually moved up. But in the way of my future, I don't see, oh, I'm not getting very far in that. Yeah, and I've made a couple of new friends. I go out with them. And of course, fix my car, like, by myself. I've learnt a lot about cars, but nothing that, you know, certificate kind of way. It's all up here—but not on paper.

I've got other interests. I mean, at age of seven I fixed the vacuum cleaner. Didn't know what I was doing, but you know, just taught myself, but now I've picked it up. And I did work experience at Force Electronics. I went there and I repaired all these VCR's and I knew what I was doing. But I didn't have a certificate. And that's one of the reasons I left school, because I wanted to do some electronic engineering, and I've got a German background. But because of the SACE I couldn't do German and Electronics and I did Maths, Physics and all that, Chemistry. All the top, you know, top subjects. And for what I wanted to do, Electronics, if I wanted to go to uni, it would have helped me a lot.

I'm not sure if I've passed year 11, 'cos on my Chemistry exam the car runs out of petrol and it's 5, 6 kms away from the school, and I couldn't get there on time and they're not going to let you in after a certain period. So I just thought, oh, well, exam's done! I mean, that was my last exam I think from memory, so I thought, oh, well.

At school my grades were pretty good, like A's, B's a couple of C's and because I'm like growing up every one was saying, oh, you don't go out and enjoy your life? I'd no money to do that; and I was stuck there and I thought, want to do this, but I have to finish school and I've got my car. What am I going to do? And I thought the easiest way was just leave school, and get a job.

I was recommended by a counsellor at my school to leave school. And a couple of friends also. 'Cos I told them my interests and they go, oh a TAFE course would be better for you. And I go, oh I have to finish school. And they go, oh no, you can get in through year 11. Oh right, cool! Anyway, I told the counsellor my interests, and I said I want to be an engineer of some sort, and he goes, oh there are a couple of TAFE courses you can do. So he recommended me to a pre-vocational course.

So that's the next thing I did after school. Yeah, only did it for two days. It was metal work, machining. That was up at Oceanside. I had to get up at 6, 6: 30, catch a train to the city, wait and catch the Oceanside train and then I was already late, so I had to run then. I was already 10 minutes late. As well as that because of my exams, I was four weeks behind everyone else. The counsellor gave me all these sheets. I read them and I thought, oh that's alright—got electronics in it. Cool! So went for the course, rock up [presented at], metal work, and he explained to me all the different types of things in it. I said, oh well, can't hurt to try them out, 'cos I'd already quit school.

When I went for my course selections for SACE they have certain standards. And like I passed most of my requirements but the grades didn't match with it; and with the German and Electronics in year 10, I did Pure Maths ABC, Physics, Chem, and when it came to the crunch, I couldn't do German and Electronics because, I don't know. You're meant to get 22 units, I think.

If I could go back in time, I'd change my subjects around; redo things. Money side wouldn't have been a problem. But I guess I would have missed out on a social life, and I would have had no car. But I don't know, I'm a teenager, I'm meant to enjoy life. And at the end of the year my social life took over my school. 'Cos I got good grades all at the start of the year and I lost interest basically. I mean I'm good on Physics or the science side, but not the language. I've got no idea. And that's something I wanted to learn, and I was doing it since primary school, but I couldn't. I found it hard.

I think the pressure's really on everybody at the moment. That's certainly how I think it is. I mean, just another blue-collar worker. I mean, if you want to be respected in this world, you have to have a good job, good money, a family so to speak. And just have a perfect life. And not everyone has a perfect life. I guess I'm one of them. Maybe 'cos I haven't got like, a full family. I went through a divorce, seen violence at home, and that's sort of matured me. I just stand up, just stand up to my dad at a very small age. And I've grown up a lot quicker in a small part of time. And I think I've grown up too quick. And that's something that I didn't realize.

There's good bits at school. You've got your friends. I mean, school's like a job. If you work for it you get your grades; if you work your hours you get your money. But if you bludge, you don't get money; if you bludge you don't get any grades. That's something that I didn't realize when I was young. And I guess experience plays a part; 'cos I didn't know what the real world was like.

When you first start at high school you think, oh well, high school's a big deal. You know, you've got a long time ahead of you. I mean, time flies when you're having fun. And then it comes to year 11 and you think, right, choose. What you want to be? And it's like—never really thought of it. And then you look back at your subjects you chose like, previously, previous years, and you think, why did I choose that? And I've stuffed up here! And so you're stuck to that, and you've, like, you've closed your options off. Like, the door gets narrower.

I did music. In years 8 and 9. I played the organ; and that wasn't part of the curriculum, so I had to take up the clarinet. And I didn't like that at all so I quit. Blowing into a piece of wood didn't really give me much satisfaction. The organ was what my grandfather did. And I sort of look like him, and act like him. And I don't know, I had a natural talent as well for it—but I never had the opportunity to do it.

What I want out of life is to know that, like, if I complete something, I know that I've done it and I know that I can be proud of it. I can say, hey, look what I've done, I can do this! And I don't know, I guess be proud of it. And if I do something I don't really like, I do it—I mean, I got to be proud of it—but I don't know, it's not the same.

Because I want to do my own thing. Other people have their own interests and all those interests are mixed together and it's all going to rub together. Some people want to be a mechanic and some people want to be a doctor. Some people, I don't know. I don't know. I reckon if maybe school found your interests just a bit earlier, it would help a lot of people find, well, natural talent, I guess.

Mark's portrait reveals some of the "choices" young people are making—should I go to university, should I get a job, should I try and get some training, or should I stay at school?

"Getting Training"

Training is another possible choice for young people as they navigate their futures. This sector too underwent significant reforms during the 1990s, including the vocational education and training (VET) sector being opened up to private providers; the national recognition of the skills and qualifications of all new apprentices and trainees; and an increasing number of young people taking up the option of studying VET in schools. Robinson and Ball (1998, pp. 67–68) have provided a summary of young people's participation in vocational education and training:

- young people are combining full or part-time training with part-time work;
- the percentage of 15–19 year olds in VET has fallen over the 1990s from around 30 percent to around 20 percent; and
- there is a shift away from the vehicle and building occupational groups, and an expansion in the "clerks" and "salespersons and personal service workers" occupational groups.

Just as globalization is having an impact on the labor market, it is also having an impact on the VET sector.

"Going to University"

What is happening in and around post-compulsory schooling is affected by the arrangements for entrance into universities:

> The pattern of higher education participation in Australia has changed substantially over the latter half of the twentieth century, moving from an elite status in the fifties, with less than four percent of the 17 to 22 year age group participating, to a mass system with 30 percent of that age group participating by 1995. (Ramsay, Trantor, Charlton & Sumner, 1998, p. 15)

Of special importance to this study of early school leaving, however, is the priority given to students of low socio-economic status in higher education policy. Some of the national trends reported by Ramsay, Trantor, Charlton and Sumner (1998, pp. 22–23) are presented here:

- "progress in access and participation for students from low socio-economic backgrounds has been particularly slow";

- mature entry programs are "not providing an effective entry mode for older students from low socioeconomic backgrounds"; and

- there is a complexity of issues facing low socio-economic status students including the "compounding impact of multiple disadvantage"; "the range of subjects available and/or chosen at senior secondary school can also restrict access to university . . . with inadequate counselling and inappropriate subject choices often limiting their ability to meet university requirements".

In summary, then, participation in higher education has dramatically increased in recent decades, but those from low socio-economic status (SES) backgrounds are still greatly under-represented:

> Trends in low SES access to higher education indicate that students in this group are significantly under-represented at all levels of university education, with increasing disparity at higher degree levels . . . A range of special access programs for low SES operates across Australian universities but it appears that careful review and more extensive measures may be required to combat multiple disadvantage, cultural expectations of university and many other compounding social and cultural factors. In addition, recent changes to funding of higher education and the general policy directions of the current Federal Government are counteracting any impact these programs may have. (Ramsay, Trantor, Charlton & Sumner, 1998, p. 27)

So not only is there a global deregulation of the economy and an international division of labor, but the higher education and training sectors are also being deregulated. Pathways to financial independence that once operated much like public highways are increasingly having "tolls" placed on them. In navigating a future, young people are now consumers of pathways, and are having to "choose" between staying on in schools that increasingly cater for university entrance, and which tend to favor the already wealthy; going for a job in a collapsed youth labor market, in which access depends on knowing someone; getting training in a sector that is increasingly asserting the user-pays principle; or going to universities that are charging more in terms of fees but doing less in terms of access for those traditionally under-represented.

At this point we need to re-focus the discussion. So far, we have briefly sketched a context for considering early school leaving with a special focus on the impact of globalization on "going for a job", "getting training", and "going to university". But the part of the "context" we have not yet discussed, which may be the most important in terms of this research, is the actual leaving process. Most young people "negotiate" this while still at school, no matter how tenuous that might be for some of them. The question becomes: what does the contemporary secondary school look like, and what trends do we notice in terms of globalization?

The Nature of the Contemporary Secondary School

> Why is it, in spite of the fact that teaching by pouring in, learning by passive absorption, are universally condemned, that they are still entrenched in practice? (Dewey, 1966, p. 38)

The members of the research team, at one time or another, had all been practicing secondary school teachers. This first-hand knowledge of the complexity of life in schools provided an important interpretive frame, not only for the conduct of the interviews, but also for making sense of the interview material. The need to acknowledge the complexity of secondary schools became increasingly important in the drafting of this account.

We are especially keen in the representation of this account of early school leaving, not to place the "blame" entirely on "the school". We do not believe that blaming schools is either productive or an accurate reading of what is happening. To blame schools would be inaccurate and somewhat unhelpful. However, this is not to suggest that we won't have some strong things to say about a number of counter-productive practices that we believe are being sustained in schools.

One way to view the complexity of life in schools is to analyze schools historically and sociologically. If we view schools historically, then we notice a process of school reform that has been underway for some time (Goodman, 1995). We also notice what is often taken for granted, seen as natural—"that is the way schools are". But, on the other hand, reality suggests that schools are very contingent, and influenced by discourses that operate in circuits of power. As an example, in recent times, schooling was very much structured by the prominence of IQ testing and practices like corporal punishment. These two practices were accepted, in their day, as "natural" parts of school life. Many significant school reforms do not arise from:

> a generative discussion about the kind of society we wish to create collectively. . . [but] . . . place teachers and their students in the passive role of merely getting prepared for a destiny that someone else has determined for them. (Goodman, 1995, p. 7)

Schools are being reformed through discourses that promote such ideas as "international competitiveness" (Smyth, 1998b), "outcomes" (Smyth & Dow, 1998), "choice" (Ball, Bowe & Gewirtz, 1996) or "mimicking the latest advancements in business organizational development" (Goodman, 1995, p. 12).

A sociological perspective on the other hand, situates everyday life within a socio-economic and socio-cultural milieu. Such a perspective considers the inter-relationships between history, the economy, the political process, culture and everyday life. Such a view argues that life in schools is controlled through structural, ideological and disciplinary modes (Smyth, Dow, Hattam, Reid & Shacklock, 2000). Control (or power) limits "the range of practices and relationships possible in classrooms" (Gore, 1995, p. 166). Power/control works in many ways and usually simultaneously, as

- power from above—the use of regulations, sanctions, surveillance, rewards, and punishments;
- discursive coercion—distorting human communication and thereby the use of human reasoning in power relationships; and
- control/power that is productive at the level of discourse and hence constructs/authorizes what is defined as "good" teaching and learning.

In the next section we outline in very broad terms a constellation of features that not only represent important boundaries but also constitute constraints to be struggled against. According to Elmore (1987), we need to look at the "continuity of practice" of secondary schools in order to understand them. In recent case studies of some Australian secondary schools (McInerney, Hattam, Smyth & Lawson, 1999; Smyth, McInerney, Hattam & Lawson, 1999), the following constellation of features was found to define life in secondary schools: (a) hierarchical structuring; (b) subject specialization; and (c) teacher-centered pedagogy. These are not necessarily characteristics that pervade all secondary schools; rather, they are parts of an educational legacy that still exerts a significant influence on the way we think and enact schooling, especially in high schools.

But, before we outline these features it is important to note that the "core business" of secondary schools, regardless of whether it is intentional, is demonstrably one of youth identity formation (Griffin, 1993; Fraser, Davis & Singh, 1997; Grundy, 1994; Tait, 1993). What transpires officially, as well as unofficially, in schools reflects this preoccupation with the transition from childhood dependency to adulthood autonomy and independence. Secondary schools might be best understood as places in which young people are attempting to navigate their futures, while in a continual state of metamorphosis. Of course, this process of navigating a transition sets up a tension for those charged with providing education in secondary schools. The tension is between two competing imperatives: that of staying in control versus that of facilitating the transition to autonomy and independence. This tension has intensified in contemporary secondary schools. The traditional—"children are seen and not heard"—autocratic approach is no longer acceptable; it simply does not work very well any longer, because of a growing "acceptance of a democratic approach to human relationships" (Balson, 1995, p. 3). Such changes in society have come quickly and now teachers and students "face the dilemma of not knowing what to do" (Balson, 1995, p. 3). Balson might be overstating the case a little, but there is a heightened level of confusion about the practice of democratic relationships in schools. This confusion is exacerbated because, in many schools, students often do not "bring discourse habits which allow a democratic group process to take place" (Shor, 1990, p. 345). Many teachers still "behave traditionally in the classroom, in that they act as delivery systems for . . . an undemocratic culture" (Shor, 1990, p. 347). Many secondary schools often contain as many as a thousand students, and:

> [t]hey often do not have ways of getting to know their students or to incorporate or appropriate their lives into what goes on in the school. This sometimes makes them appear as harsh, inhumane and uncaring places. (Smyth, McInerney, Hattam & Lawson, 1999, p. 10)

Hierarchical Structuring

It seems to matter little what the policy rhetoric states or what a school might say about the democratic nature of its decision-making structure: schools are still largely organized around a hierarchy in which power is unequally dispersed. This hierarchy is sustained institutionally. Smyth,

McInerney, Hattam and Lawson (1999, p. 9) argue that at the apex are the educational policy makers, head administrators, principals, deputies, co-ordinators, subject experts and specialists of various types; in the middle are teachers who, in most cases, discharge the technical functions of teaching within an overall framework largely set by others; and at the bottom are students who, in most cases, have only minimal or token say over how their school lives are structured. It is widely acknowledged that this disparity in power is the "cause" of much alienation in secondary schools for many students (Cumming, 1996; White, 1996; Wyn & White, 1997). Tensions abound in circumstances like these where such discrepancies are not only obvious but legitimated and taken for granted.

Another form of hierarchy also structures the life of secondary schools. It operates through the curriculum—understood as what is taught, how it is taught and how it is assessed. In Australia, the curriculum is still significantly skewed in the direction of selection for entry to university. The question of who will attend university has a profound influence on the nature and shape of the post-compulsory curriculum in Australia, and consequently on the teaching and learning practices that dominate post-compulsory classrooms:

> The existence of a credential that opens the gate to university and lucratively paid employment, or to other career paths likely to be economically worthwhile, makes secondary schools very significant sorting devices (Pring, 1989). Secondary schools and the way they constitute what is important about schooling play a pivotal role in who gets to have a share in society's rewards, and these opportunities reflect existing advantage or disadvantage. (Smyth, McInerney, Hattam & Lawson, 1999, p. 9)

The selection pressure on schools manifests itself in a range of ways.

Behind the rhetorical claims of "choice" and "diversity" in the post-compulsory curriculum lies a hierarchical curriculum structure. Connell (1998) provocatively refers to this as the "Competitive Academic Curriculum (CAC)". This is a curriculum marked by:

- an abstract division of knowledge into "subjects";
- a hierarchy of subjects (with Mathematics at the top);
- a hierarchical ordering of knowledge within each subject (a fine-grained distinction between elementary and advanced material);
- a teacher-centered classroom-based pedagogy;
- an individual learning process; and
- a formal competitive assessment (the "exam"). (p. 84)

Teese's (1998) historical analysis of the post-compulsory curriculum in Australia reveals that "social inequalities have been maintained primarily through the operation of academic hierarchies" (p. 401). Teese has exposed the nature of the "hierarchy of subjects" that Connell refers to above. He argues that the development of the contemporary "curriculum hierarchy" that privileges Mathematics and the physical sciences has come about as a consequence of the way that universities in Australia (but we suspect also elsewhere) have asserted their control over the secondary school curriculum. The imposition of quotas and the move to standardize results across subjects has enabled universities to rank students using a single score:

> The subjects with the highest correlations were also those whose examiners aimed at test homogeneity, pre-testing and validation of items, and pre-coded multiple choice formats to maximize reliability of assessments. The long-term effect of these developments was to channel the most able students into mathematics, physics and chemistry, and to a lesser extent into certain modern languages. (Teese, 1998, p. 409)

Teese also argues that such a "curriculum hierarchy" sustains a stratification of educational opportunity that is marked by both gender and social class. University selection processes that are based on competitive achievement, parading as a meritocracy, actually sustain social inequalities. Secondary schools, because they exist in a credentialled society and because they act as gatekeepers are, therefore, active makers of students' life chances, whether they choose to openly acknowledge it or not. This process is "reinforced [at least in Australia] by private schools" (p. 414): "[p]rivate schools extend the power of universities over the curriculum by enabling middle and upper-status parents' power through the curriculum" (p. 403).

Teacher-Centered Pedagogy

A selection process for university that is based on the competitive academic curriculum puts pressure on teachers to churn through large quantities of pre-determined content using didactic or transmission approaches to teaching and learning. Didactic teaching has the following features: the learner is treated as a passive vessel; there is a high reliance on acquisition and rote learning of canonical and axiomatic knowledge; there is a prevalence of testing for the "right" answer; learning is decontextualized and knowledge fragmented; and sub-routines or sub-skills are separated from understanding the larger context into which they fit and which gives them meaning (Lohrey, 1995). Like Dewey (1966), we believe these are conditions that inhibit learning.

Subject Specialization

Selection pressures that are oriented towards a sorting and sifting function in the post-compulsory curriculum also mean that the curriculum is based on what universities regard as prestige or elite forms of knowledge. Put another way, secondary schools are probably best known for their compartmentalization of knowledge (Cusick, 1973): a reference to the fact that teachers spend much of their time working with students within particular subject matter specializations, passing on those specialities to students.

The imperative for subject specialization and teacher-centered approaches means individual teachers take classes for short periods of time (lessons) in a highly structured timetable. A significant influence in sustaining traditional ways of offering curriculum in secondary schools is the faculty structure. Such a view of knowledge serves to further undermine an inter-disciplinary curriculum, and the architecture of traditional high schools also reduces the likelihood of student-centered and team teaching approaches. Most traditional high schools do not have many large teaching and learning spaces.

Life in Secondary Schools

In summary, then, life in secondary schools has been structured through historical processes that have seen selection processes distort the post-compulsory curriculum and that have resulted in the reproduction of social inequalities. The imperative of selection for university entrance now means that secondary schools sustain the following constellation (Smyth, McInerney, Hattam & Lawson, 1999), and hence inter-related, set of features:

• the day is organized by a timetable with discrete units of time allocated to specific kinds of subject matter;
• for each unit of time, a single teacher works with a group of students in a single classroom;
• schools are architecturally designed to support efficient surveillance of separate classroom spaces;

- within a given classroom, the teacher initiates instruction and teacher talk dominates teacher-student interaction;
- knowledge is defined as mastery of discrete pieces of information received from external sources;
- the teacher-student relationship is institutionalized and marked by an imperative to transmit content and use competitive forms of assessment; and
- curriculum development is managed in faculty structures.

There is also a powerful culture of complacency that operates around secondary schools. The perplexing question remains: "If traditional schooling has been good enough in the past, why change it?" This is especially evident in schools that see their purpose almost solely in terms of getting their students into university. Such a view is held by the community at large and by many members of the teaching community. To step outside of this and develop what may appear to be a "radical" alternative— that is, a school that looks markedly different from others—involves pushing away from heavily defended territory. That is not to say that there are not some "radical" alternative schools, but that the large majority of secondary schools, often referred to as mainstream, seem complacent. This culture of contentment is presently being disturbed, though, by those who are advocating notions of middle schooling and VET in secondary schools.

This next portrait captures some of the reasons why some teachers in some schools are trying to implement middle schooling and a VET curriculum.

Portrait #087
Jodi: They Don't Listen

To be honest, I think the education system sucks. They spend so much time trying to teach kids what they think they'll need to get a job or go to uni or something, whereas they should be teaching them more about life. You know, things that you really do need to know to be able to be successful as a person. Like Mathematics or English or science get them to university or a career, but they don't have a clue who they are. And health lessons and stuff, they talk about health and your body, but they skip out all the important stuff, like about how to deal with different things that happen in your life.

The schools have got this big authority power-play thing and instead of trying to work out what this kid is thinking or why they're doing what they're doing, they don't do that, they just think this is the rules, you do this so, or you get into trouble. I've got a lot of friends that have left school and we've been kicked out or whatever—they just get told one thing and they do the exact opposite and it's because people don't learn to deal with situations like that.

I noticed a big difference when I left high school and went to TAFE. At TAFE you feel more comfortable with the way they treat you and give you the benefit of the doubt in the first place, and treat you like equals. That gives people more drive to want to be there and want to learn things as well. At school you're treated like a kid and half the teachers yelling this and yelling that, and you just put your back up and think I'm not going to take this, I don't need this. So you get all huffy and react the wrong way and get into trouble and go through the [punitive] system again.

Problems started to kick in at year 9. I know everyone says have respect for elders, and I know I'm a lot younger and less experienced, but I look at them exactly on the same height as me and you know if they're going to treat me like shit I'm not going to stand there and take it. I'm going to tell them, you know, you can't do this.

Yeah, basically just being treated like a non-human being, like if you're five minutes late to school, which can happen for thousands of reasons, then you've got a detention and then you have to stand there and pick up other people's rubbish. Teachers suss out people who are just a little bit more, you know. I got suspended once or twice for smoking cigarettes, or even for having cigarettes in your bag it's automatic suspension. Lots of my friends have been suspended or kicked out of school for the same reason. It's got nothing to do with education. And I can remember getting suspended for getting sent to time-out room twice in a month and the reasons for getting sent there were talking in class and writing a letter instead of doing my work. You know, little things like that could be dealt with in other ways.

Every person is different and everyone has to be dealt with differently and that's why they supposedly have counsellors at school. So if a kid's really stuffing up and doing some terrible things you need to get them and sit them down and say, you know, what's going on? What's your reasons for doing it? What do you want to do? Like where do you want to go in life? Because no one wants to be in trouble all the time. No one wants it. But you get a name for yourself and then it's like some teachers just wait to pick up the tiniest thing and jump in.

So I was doing well in English, Drama and Art. I find I can learn anything if I put my mind to it. But in subjects that didn't matter to me, or I just didn't like the teacher, I would just sit there and write. Like I love English and I used to write heaps of poetry and stories in, like, Maths. So some subjects I was failing, that was my choice, but I was quite capable of passing year 12 if I wanted to. They just put me in the vegie [lowest stream] Maths or something because I didn't like Maths. I went from year 10 at Hillside to Anatomy and Physiology at university level at TAFE and passed all of it.

Like schools don't focus on your mental capability, they just focus on your behavior. Maybe I wasn't an easy student. I didn't do horrible things. But they knew I'd be smoking and they wouldn't be able to catch me. And I'm a very opinionated person. They'd say you're being cheeky. And I'd say look, I'm not, I'm just saying this is what I think. And they'd say, no, you can't, you don't say that, you shut up. And I'd try, I'd try so hard and I'd say, look I'm not trying to be cheeky and they'd think it was just me being cheekier. I think they automatically don't listen and think that what you have to say is irrelevant because you're a student, you're a child. They don't listen.

I went back there. My best friend goes to Hillside and she's doing year 11, and she stayed at my house one night and I went in at the lunch break to take her lunch because she hadn't taken anything. And the deputy comes up to me and says, you have to leave, I'm going to call the police. I said excuse me, if it was her sister bringing her lunch would you be calling the police too? I just thought that was a really rude thing. I said I went there for three years, you can't . . . I just thought, hi Jodi, how are you going, you know. What are you doing now? Is everything going well? Would have been so much better. It's just, I'm going to call the police.

I wasn't an overtly disruptive person unless someone really annoyed me. I got suspended twice, once for smoking and once for being in time out, and they wanted to send me to some learning center, and I said no way. So they said we can't kick you out, but we think it would be the best idea to move on. Well I was just turned 15, and there was no way I was going to leave and just sit around. So this other deputy, not the one that asked me to leave, he went to TAFE and got all the information for me and helped me get into the course.

So I went to TAFE and did a pre-vocational hairdressing and beauty therapy course and that went for 12 months and I finished that successfully. Now I'm looking for an apprenticeship. That's not so easy. I've applied for a few but nothing has really come up yet. It's a four year contract, so they're really picky, but I can't go any further unless I get a job in a salon. And so far there's never been less than 50 people applying for any job.

I'm only 16, and if I get a job by the end of this year I've got three and a half years until I'll be qualified at hairdressing and that's what I want to do, because I want to go travelling overseas and that's a really good job to have because you can work anywhere. After that it depends. I might be happy. If I'm not I don't see any reason why I won't go back to school. I'll only be 21.

I'm a really creative person. I actually enjoy doing hair. I practice a lot like I've cut all of my friends' hair. If I had my own business I'd be rich. And I enjoy the communication. I'm really into people's self esteem. There's so many people who just feel really shitty about themselves, and I know hair's not really the answer to that but people, it does boost them, and gives them more confidence. I like making people feel like that.

The interest in middle schooling, in particular, has gained momentum recently for a variety of reasons, including concern about the disruptive transition that often occurs between years 7 and 8[1]; concern that for many young people schooling involves "alienation in the middle years; and interest in reinvigorating the curriculum in response to the changing nature of adolescence (McInerney, Hattam, Smyth & Lawson, 1999). Jodi's story, told above, powerfully resonates with these sorts of concerns. VET in schools has also gained momentum in recent years because of renewed concern about the linkage between school and work, and the need to offer relevant and credentialled alternatives to the competitive academic curriculum.

These two recent reform initiatives give us added insights into the powerful structural forces that sustain the continuity of practice we mentioned earlier.

Simply put, the insertion of the middle schooling approach, especially into high schools, might be understood to be about developing pedagogy (Cumming, 1996) that:

- emphasizes the student-teacher relationship;
- engages students in negotiating the curriculum (Boomer, Lester, Onore & Cook, 1992);
- involves constructing a curriculum that is sensitive to the social and cultural milieu impacting on the construction of student identity (Smyth, Shacklock & Hattam, 1999);
- encourages collaboration between teachers and students in the learning experience; and
- favors a success-oriented assessment that is designed to give feedback on what has been achieved.

Both middle schooling and VET require significant reforms in secondary schools. Both require a major shake-up in the traditional way that secondary schools are structured. The traditional timetable, the faculty structure, competitive assessment, teacher-centered pedagogy and subject disciplines all coalesce to impede these two developments. Without careful planning around such issues, secondary schools run the risk of further perpetuating existing class inequalities in society.

What Does All of This Mean?

At the beginning of this chapter we argued that we could only provide a sketch with which to foreground the context for considering early school leaving. It is clear that young people are navigating a transition into a globalizing world, in which:

- the labor market is rapidly becoming more part-time and temporary;
- manufacturing is collapsing and information and service industries are growing;
- analysis of the new work order is almost absent in schools;
- the pathways to financial independence, such as going for a job, getting training or entering university, are most often difficult, confusing and troublesome, especially for those from families that have been either traditionally or recently disenfranchised from the economy; and
- the secondary school seems to be on the verge of making some significant reforms in structures and practices that have historically favored those going to university.

In the next chapter we continue to map out a context for considering early school leaving, but we also move to consider how the process of youth identity formation operates in the project of "becoming somebody", and the importance of biography in decisions being made to stay on or leave school.

CHAPTER 3

BECOMING SOMEBODY WITH
OR WITHOUT SCHOOL

I'm not going to be a down-and-out. I'm going to be someone (#100).

Well I really want to become something (#043).

These two quotes from young people in this study nicely capture what is meant by Suarez-Orozco's (1987) and Wexler's (1992) term "becoming somebody"—a useful way of thinking and talking about the process of identity formation of young people. We need to have a vocabulary to talk about this process of young people's deliberations on their lives. The term "becoming somebody" is particularly evocative. At one level, it might be understood as "the daily project of establishing a social identity" or the "construction of the self" (Tait, 1993, p. 40). It names the idea of young people making a life for themselves. At another level, "becoming somebody" might be thought of in terms of a "desire for recognition, and protection over time and in space and always under circumstances not of their own choosing" (West, 1992, p. 20). The notion of becoming somebody might be summed up in these two quotes from quite different sources, one American and the other Australian:

> They were not struggling to become nobody, some high postmodernist definition of a decentered self. They wanted to be somebody, a real presentable self, one anchored in the verifying eyes of the friends whom they came to school to meet. (Wexler, 1992, p. 7)

> At the start of year 11 I knew I wasn't going to do year 12, so I thought well I may as well find . . . I mean I'm not going to leave school and do nothing. (#030)

The project of becoming somebody has two interwoven strands: how young people navigate an entry into the labor market, and their simultaneous efforts to develop a socio-cultural identity. It is difficult to understand the complex process of youth identity formation without understanding the interplay between young people's desire for economic independence and their struggles to establish, confirm and in many cases endure a socio-cultural identity.

Youth Identity Formation

In this chapter we describe how the biographies of young people are being constructed and contested (Yates & Leder, 1996, p. 40). We do this from the position of an emerging understanding of early school leaving that is interested in the "less visible—that is to say, the behind the scenes, negotiations of power" (Anderson & Herr, 1994, p. 59). Herr and Anderson (1997) describe young people's process of identity formation as occurring "within and against the context of schooling" (p. 45).

Not only is youth identity formation largely absent from policy discussions, but, until recently, the sociology of education largely avoided such questions (Wexler, 1992). By pursuing this line we want to make a contribution to an emerging critical social psychology of the school that attends to the "individual-society relation" (p. 6). As such, we are interested in "how society is in the individual" (p. 6). Often this individual-society relation is discussed in terms of a tension between social structure and youth agency, or alternatively between "consciously chosen action and external restraint" (White & Wyn, 1998, p. 315). The tension between agency and restraint can be understood in this study as focusing on the way young people negotiate their own meanings, lives and futures, in the context of specific socio-cultural, political and economic circumstances (White & Wyn, 1998). Such circumstances involve selection, inclusion and exclusion and other forms of boundary maintenance work inside of regimes constructed by wealthy, white, male heterosexuals.

White and Wyn's (1998) "contextual understanding of youth experience" offers a powerful model for working this individual-society relation, one that views young people as a "highly differentiated group" (p. 315) and that resists simplified portrayals of complex lives. Such an understanding is sensitive to the "social practices through which young people construct identities, negotiate their space and place and are in turn defined in an ongoing struggle which has many dimensions" (White & Wyn, 1998, p. 324). Our focus here is on the nature of young people's negotiations with schooling, and especially the ways in which such negotiations are socially and politically situated. A contextual understanding of youth that works the individual-society relation understands identity as a "kind of interface or conceptual bridge linking the two" (Snow & Anderson, 1987, p. 1338). That is, identity is understood to be a complex process in which young people are working on generating and maintaining a sense of meaning and self-worth at an interface between their inner life and the social context in which they live. Such a contextual understanding of youth lives might be understood in terms of the following set of questions:

- How do young people navigate a transition from school into adult life?
- In what ways do young people make sense of the role of schooling in their future?
- How do young people work the economic, cultural, social and symbolic capital they have at their disposal in navigating a future?
- In what ways does schooling ameliorate, or not, the inequalities of capital to which young people have access?
- How are youth identities constructed by the school/school credential?
- Which identities flourish and which ones wilt?
- Which youth identities get to be commonplace in and around post-compulsory schooling?
- Is post-compulsory schooling providing a culturally powerful "rite of passage" for inducting youth into these "new times"? (Hall & Jacques, 1990)

Questions like these provide a framework for the investigation into young people's lives in and around schooling. But before we proceed further with our analysis, we present the following portrait as indicative of the kind of issues we have just raised.

Portrait #211
Kelly: I've Been Pretty Mixed Up

In year 7 I went to this alternative school. It's for people who can't go to normal schools. I didn't do any work. I was usually sent home or just left. I done a bit last year and I went for about four weeks this year. But there was nothing there, they didn't make you, well they tried, they'd ask you to work and like you know if you wouldn't work they'd say well go and have a smoke or go home. The work was year 5 and 6 stuff anyway. It was bullshit you know. I wanted to do high school work. Year 8 and 9.

The first time I got suspended in year 4 it was for just refusing to do my work 'cos the teacher was being a bitch so I just walked out and they sent me home for the day and I wouldn't leave so then they suspended me. Then two Vietnamese girls gave me shit, so I tipped cold water over them when they were in the toilet. A bucket of cold water. And I got suspended for that. It was freezing cold water and we'd just come out of the pool and they'd just finished getting dressed in their dry clothes. I don't suppose it was fair 'cos you know two wrongs don't make a right. I understand that but I didn't then, you know.

Maybe if I was a teacher, I would have looked at counselling for a person that young and find why they're misbehaving. I'd be trying to get to the reason of it. I realize now that was what I needed because my uncle had died. Like I was really close to him and he'd died about half a year before and I just didn't get over it.

So then I was getting suspended every time I'd go back. I'd get suspended straight away for mucking up, you know. Stuff like abusing teachers when they told me to do something and I didn't want to do it. Sending me out of the class for no reason. I'd whisper to someone or talk to someone and someone would pass me a letter and I'd read it or put it in my book and she'd come up and rip it up. She even ripped up my painting one day and I just up and went off, I'd had enough.

Or reasons like taking too long in the toilet doing my makeup you know and hitting the principal. I remember I wrapped the portable netball ring around his head. Yeah, and I threw a chair at him and I rushed him with a chair and put him up on the wall and the chair, the metal parts were skinny, and I jammed the chair and him into the wall and the chair stuck in the wall. I guess I had mixed up emotions and I didn't know how to express myself other than being violent.

Then in year 7 they kicked me out. They sent me home with a letter and told my parents to come in for a meeting and my dad went in and they told him well we don't want your daughter back here, she's causing too much trouble. I mean I would have done that too if someone had broke into my school and stole the cash box. Even though it was sort of done with some of the other people. But it was just a one off thing. We only wanted the money so we could go to the pool.

They didn't do nothing really. They tried to get the AEW [Aboriginal Education Worker] to sit down and talk to me and do things with me during the day but I'd just tell her to get fucked as well. Get away from me, I don't need your help. She thought that just because she was the same color as me that I was going to be nice to her. I was at first, but she wasn't there to help me. More to pinpoint me at everything I'd done and listen to everything the teacher said. I'd just push everyone away you know, and I'd just worry about my friends. And when I went to this other school I thought oh, you know, this is wicked. Everyone here does crime. This is cool. Then later that year I just got sick of it and there was nothing there for me and I realized, you know. I woke up to myself a bit and I thought, you know, that I'd love to go to high school.

So two months into last year I went to high school in year 8. My dad kept telling me don't muck up, just sit down and do your work otherwise you're burning all your bridges behind you. But I just couldn't, you know. The work in schools is shit, like it's not useful, it doesn't get you anywhere. That's what I think anyway. They should have given me more English and Maths, and I want to be a hairdresser, a beautician and a dancer, and school didn't offer any of that for me. So I didn't bother. I wanted to but I was getting locked up you know, just fucked up. I was going downhill. I was supposed to start a hospitality course, bar and waitressing, this year, but I broke my bail. My bail conditions were to show up at the course and do what they tell me to do, bang bang bang. That's it and that's all there is to it. I tell them I want to be a hairdresser and beautician and they make me do a hospitality course. Do they listen? Maybe, but they don't take it in. I suppose that's what I do as well sometimes.

You know, I've been pretty mixed up. I never had my mum there, you know. She was always, my mum was a heroin addict, OK. She'd go out for a few weeks and then she'd finally decide to come home and she'd stay one night and then she'd leave again and then my uncle died and she got a new boyfriend and she told us she was getting married and WHAT! I was only eight. It came to me as the biggest shock in the world. I thought you know that was one of the bridges I burnt as well. I thought my mum's leaving me for a man. Why's she doing this? I thought it was my fault and so I blamed myself, and I don't know I just hated myself and hated everyone else because I blamed myself and my mum and my family for everything that had happened.

Yeah, looking back I was pretty mixed up and out of control. But I also reckon the teachers, you know, they set me up.

7 Months Later: Love Me Tender

I did four months time. I got out of here in April. I met this guy and I was sort of going out with him, and he's a junkie, and he said, oh, do you want a hit? And I said, what is it? This is like the day I got out and he says, it's heroin, and I said oh yeah, alright. He gave me half a cap, and I was just off my head. Then every time we'd get money, me and my best friend Melanie, we'd go down to Hillsbury and score. First we'd just do it on the weekends, and then it started happening every second day, and then I started thinking that I needed it and then I started using it every day. I'd go through three caps of heroin a day, three to six caps a day. That's at $50 a cap. I got some money from my mum for clothes. But I had to steal a lot.

With the needle, you know, I'm off my head already before it's even gone in. Your blood starts going like boiling and you just feel so good just looking, watching yourself jack back a needle, and you forget all your problems, you're just having a good time. You're somebody who'd got not a worry in the world. Sometimes it was like no, I've got to stop this. And I couldn't, I didn't have the willpower. And I was losing it, I was honestly losing it and I got raped. Then I started using even more.

By now Melanie, she's screwing the dealer for heroin. She's a little junkie. She's going nowhere. And my boyfriend, Jim, he was out by this, he took me up to his place. It wasn't so bad that first day, and then my head just started throbbing and then I couldn't walk and then the only time I would get up was to go to the toilet and spew. For six days I was just sweats, hot and cold. Just aching. You know, when your hands get cold and they throb and ache. That's what it feels like from head to toe. My body felt like it was inside out with petrol tipped on it. And I was stressed out a lot. My hair, I'd brush my hair and it would come out. And then it was like hello, this is reality, this is the life you have to live. You can't be smacked off your head for the rest of your life, because one day you're going to have a hit and it's going to be the last hit. Like my uncle, who had to have a hit behind my aunty's back just before Mothers' Day when he knew the risks. So he left my cousin, who was only 11. And now he's getting sent to Glenside. He's on medication. He sleeps at his dad's grave.

So I'm back in here. When I was addicted I done an armed robbery. Sometimes I try to think and I get confused in my thoughts. I hear voices in my head, and it scares the shit out of me not knowing why. I haven't told anyone here because nobody in here understands. My mum understands and she's very supportive. I mean she's pretty well respected because she's a very smart lady, but she's got enough stress. Yeah, I tried to kill myself in here about two weeks ago because everything was getting that bad, because of all the head fuck and shit, you know. Excuse my language. I reckon I really do need to see a counsellor, because I cry myself to sleep every night.

I've never got back to school, but I want to go through to year 12. I was off the heroin and if I could have got two months at school I could have said to the judge, look, I've been going to school, give me bail. I'll prove myself. So they don't believe you when you tell them that you're trying to get your act together, the judge and that. They just think they're right all the time. They don't understand, they don't know me, and they don't want to. They don't care. Criminals go into court every day. They give them this, give them that, let them out, put them in.

I could be lying dead in a gutter, now, if I hadn't got back with Jim. Raped and murdered, you know. He rings me every night, he's supported me through a lot. It was him believing in me that helped me believe in myself. I love being honest with him, you know. Like we'd lay in bed and talk about everything. We broke for a while. Then getting back was like, wow.

He said to me, I believe in you, I love you, Kelly. And that made me cry, because I'm very emotional and stuff. When I first started going out with him he was only thirteen, and people said, Oh, yous aren't in love, yous aren't going to last.

You know, I met him when he was here. We'd only seen each other a couple of times on the outside, and had never really spoken. He got one of the girls to ask me out, and one night, it was summer and I accidentally left my hair tie down at the pool, and Sue, she's a really nice staff worker, took me down to get it. The boys were out in the courtyard playing basketball and I put my hands up through the bars and he put his hands up and held my hands and I don't know, just like the sun was, it was sunset and just the whole way it happened, yeah. We looked at each other, like looked into each other's eyes and I don't know I just. I was only 12 and I was so young and I just had, I don't know, my heart was going brrr and I had this amazing feeling go through my body and just from that day we were going to be together for a long time and I hope that we're going to be together forever.

Interferences

In focusing on the interaction of family, culture and school we want to map the "interferences" (Shor, 1980, p. 46) to completing schooling. By interferences, we mean those obstacles that undermine the completion of schooling. These interferences constitute a network of mutually supportive social processes that operate "'simultaneously in daily life at both the ideological and institutional levels" (Shor, 1980, p. 49). Many of the young people we listened to spoke of interferences to school completion as "social and pervasive, not as personal problems" (Shor, 1980, p. 48). When we listened to our interview material, with a view to understanding the interferences to completing school, the following themes resonated loudly:

- the ongoing problem of a "generation gap" as well as a power gap between teachers and students;
- how friendships and antagonisms get played out and often hinder school completion;
- how schools assist or hinder the process of becoming economically independent;
- how family location positions young people in a class-organized experience, which often means that the demands of private life undermine completing school;

- how various forms of masculinity and femininity may interfere with completing school; and

- how Aboriginal students are still having to deal with potent forms of racism that undermine completing school.

We will discuss the first three of these in this chapter, and the last three in chapter 4.

Green and Bigum (1993) use the term "aliens in the classroom" to illustrate the generation gap between teachers and students. The term "aliens" conjures up the notion of an increased separation between teachers and students. "Aliens" in this sense is a category that disrupts our "common sense", and provides a space within which to contemplate the possibility of a changing relationship between adults and children, especially between teachers and students. The term "aliens" also comes with a science-fiction dimension—that young people are increasingly "cyborgs" (Harraway, 1991), connected into emerging forms of information technology in ways that many adults/teachers do not fully understand. Certainly, many students have levels of information technology literacy that surpasses those of most teachers. Young people have a more intimate connection to information technology–rich forms of popular culture than many of their teachers. Many young people use such media-saturated culture as resources for identity formation. Thinking about having aliens in the classroom might also be a useful way of understanding a range of changes affecting young people, including the impact of media culture on youth identity formation, a profound democratizing of relationships that is manifesting itself in the culture, suicidal ideation, the use of illegal substances, and the struggle to become economically independent in an institution (the school) that demands compliance and dependence.

The Impact of Media Culture

Placing the process of becoming somebody in the middle of the frame in our analysis of early school leaving reveals the growing impact of media culture on identity formation in contemporary societies. Giroux (1994) put this well:

> For years, I believed that pedagogy was a discipline developed around the narrow imperatives of public schooling. And yet, my identity has been largely fashioned outside of school. Films, books, journals, videos, and

music in different and significant ways did more to shape my politics and life than did formal education, which always seemed to be about somebody else's dreams. (p. x)

What seems to be happening is an increasing level of contestation between the school and media culture for significance as a site of social, cultural and identity formation. We take media culture to mean:

[c]ultural objects like music, dance, fashion, television, movies, magazines, advertising, art and vernacular [which] are part of a technological and aesthetic "sensorium" (Aronowitz, 1992) in which individual and collective identities are defined, created, displaced and denied. These cultural objects exist as products of capital and are consumed aesthetically and politically as commodities that have economic, as well as cultural value in subject formation. (Smyth, Shacklock & Hattam, 1999, p. 74)

Having said that, we believe that schooling still plays a significant role in the identity formation of young people. Schooling is still a gate keeper for (re)producing economic futures and providing "representational resources" (New London Group, 1996, p. 64) to help young people make sense of their lives. The term "representational resources" refers to knowledge, skills and understandings that enable us to read the word, language and the world: visual signs. But for some students, school cannot compete with what media culture has to offer. Sometimes this means that homework cannot compete with TV:

There is something a lot more interesting than doing school work like um there's a really interesting like TV program that you want to watch. I usually sometimes do that. When it's too good I thought bugger it, I won't do my homework tonight, you know. Or you feel too tired or you want to do something else . . . you just don't feel like doing it and if I've I had a really bad day I just can't focus. So um yeah. (#198)

For some students, school as a way of life just cannot compete with the alternative:

I didn't want to do that any more. I want to make music. I want to be a producer and make records and be a DJ . . . because it's my life. (#001)

Many students take on the codes, clothes, language and lifestyle of various youth sub-cultures, such as "surfies", "skateboarders", and "townies" or in one case,

I had turned myself into a homy . . . a person that wears brand name clothes and stuff. (#100)

Often when taking on such identities, students experience "trouble" at school:

> I had a nose ring and I kept on wearing it and then Miss Smith . . . she was my English teacher . . . saw me wearing it and she said that's it, you're suspended. (#013)

In each of the above examples, the interaction with media culture led these young people to reconsider the efficacy of sustaining an academic identity that was seen to undermine or suppress their personal identity. For some of these young people, this was a significant part of the conditions that led them to leave school early. One of the ways schools regulate student identities, against the impact of media culture, is through the discipline of the school uniform, and hence the uniform becomes a site of contestation (Meadmore & Symes, 1996) for many young people. For many young people, the school's attitude to school uniform was another example of being treated "like kids". Many young people hated school uniform and were prepared to endure detentions for infractions. Some found ways to undermine the rules. For some students, the rules around school uniform were seen to be about conformity—a conformity that many were not prepared to endure because their appearance was so central to the performance of their identity.

Children Are Now Seen and Want to Be Heard

Many of us adults grew up at a time when "children were seen and not heard": a time in which the parent or the teacher still had some support for authoritarian or autocratic relationships with students. Balson talks of the autocratic parent as someone who thinks like this: "decide what you want your child to do, and use the threat of punishment or the promise of reward to induce compliance . . . Co-operation [means] simply doing as you were told" (Balson, 1995, p. 2). The authoritarian teacher is "an authority who transfers fixed knowledge to students. Knowledge is already formed and must be verbally delivered to the students. Students in the traditional mode are expected to absorb preset formulations spoken by the teacher" (Shor & Freire, 1987, p. 101). These autocratic approaches are no longer seen as being acceptable—they don't work any longer because of a general "acceptance of a democratic approach to human relationships" (Balson, 1995, p. 3). Such changes in society have occurred quickly, and teachers and students "face the dilemma of not knowing what to do" (Balson, 1995, p. 3).

Teachers are, therefore, struggling to come to terms with the changing nature of their students. Over the last couple of decades, "youth" have become less afraid of authority. Obtaining respect is more complex (the notion of "respect your elders" is not so simple); they expect more democratic ways of relating. They do not like authoritarian ways of relating and are prepared to speak back when they come across them. Some students have their own well-developed sense of justice that is not welcome in schools. But how to get a say on what is fair and what is not is difficult. The following comments by informants in the study sum up what this dilemma feels like to many students:

> That the school system sucks and the teachers feel . . . seem to think that because they are the teachers, that they have the right to tell the students what to do, and they don't really give the students any feeling or say in what, whether they think that's right or that's wrong. (#021)

> I used to have so many sickies, hated it. I just got treated like dirt at school basically. Hated school all my life. (#114)

In the everyday life of classrooms, students engage in contesting the teacher's intentions on a moment by moment basis. As Shor (1990) put it:

> Students bring their community idioms to the classroom, the dialects they have learned at home, but they may not bring discourse habits which allow a democratic group process to take place. (p. 345)

There is a struggle going on here against the remains of an undemocratic culture. Many teachers still "behave traditionally in the classroom, in that they act as delivery systems for . . . an undemocratic culture" (Shor, 1990, p. 347). Given the differentials of power that operate in schools, especially for young people who do not fit neatly into what the school demands of the ideal student, this dilemma, this tension between wanting to be heard but not having a democratic space provided, is most often borne by the student. The struggle around providing students with a voice in classroom life can be considered as a significant thread in many educational reforms during the past twenty years.

At the heart of such reforms is the view that the most productive contemporary classroom groups occur where:

> [M]utuality and autonomy are integrated. People accept differences. Conflict exists over substantive rather than emotional issues. Consensus is reached as a result of rational discussion rather than fear of rejection. (Social Development Group, 1979, p. 11)

In essence, this means that a classroom strategy involving the following is required:

- considering the power and affection relationships operating in the group;
- making provisions for student choice and feedback and especially negative feedback about what is happening in class; and
- focussing on the skill development of small group processes in the classroom.

Without such strategies, many young people find it impossible to find a space in which to voice their concerns about classroom life. A failure to find expression, to be heard and responded to, often leads to either outright sabotage or silence. The interview material from this study found a multitude of examples of young people experiencing what other educational research refers to as alienation at school. The phenomenon of "alienation"—understood as acting in an unacceptable way, such as running amuck or practicing a disaffected, disengaged passivity—is in fact a "rational" response by many young people to the particular social conditions found in classrooms. With no resolution to this feeling of alienation, early school leaving is seen as a "rational" strategy. Alienation as powerlessness might, therefore, be thought of in the following terms:

> as a product of the dual, simultaneous processes of marginalization and powerlessness. Marginalization basically refers to disconnection from mainstream social institutions. There are now several hundred thousand young people in Australia who, for all intents and purposes, have been cut off from the sphere of production (i.e. paid work in the formal economic spheres), who are being locked out of ordinary consumer activity (but who are nevertheless over-policed when they occupy the commercial spaces of the shopping center or mall), and who are precluded by economic circumstance from taking part in community life, including establishing a "home" of their own. This marginalization is often accompanied by a strong experience of powerlessness. Powerlessness has both psychological and institu-

tional dimensions. In the first instance, it affects how young people think about themselves, their abilities, confidence and creative powers to intervene and "make" or shape the world around them. In the latter case, many find that when they do wish to assert themselves they do not, in reality, have much leverage to do so. Conversely, they are often subject to coercion from others, including the unwanted (and often unwarranted) interference in their lives by state officials and government bureaucracies. (White, 1996, p. 25)

Alienation in schools has recently been given prominence among educators with an interest in the notion of middle schooling (Eyers, Cormack & Barratt, 1992; Cumming, 1996). Alienation has been described variously, in terms of "students whose behaviour was rarely problematic, but who appeared switched off, tuned out or simply not achieving" (Cumming, 1996, p. 1). This is also an appropriate descriptor for what is happening in the post-compulsory years. In this study we encountered many instances of a culture of silence at school:

Yeah and it makes you feel very alone and because there's a lot of fear. Going to school you get so much, you have so much fear in you, you don't know where you're going to end up at the end of the day. (#103)

I don't know, I always felt I was kind of trapped at school, you know, trapped in this one little stream where I had to go along and do it and I couldn't get out and live my life, but um. . . . (#127)

So I basically went into the corner and did my own thing and like . . . Whereas I sort of went in my hole and then when, sort of, I, yeah, I knew I wasn't getting anywhere or anything, I just thought, stuff school and just started doing nothing as well. (#114)

Another expression of alienation, and perhaps the one that first comes to mind when discussing this issue involves disruptive and anti-social behavior which includes: verbal disruption, physical disruption, unwelcome teasing, offensive and obscene behavior, physical aggression, displays of inadequacy, and verbal and physical resistance (Burke & Jarman, 1994). Many of the young people interviewed talked about "running amuck":

I was just—it was so sad, this poor teacher: we put him through hell. He was just boring, you know. You just get really violent, and the reason why we did that was because we were just so bored with what we were doing at school. And like, we've got, we did it basically for a reaction. We still do now. Like, from the teacher. Just to get their attention 'cos they were just too busy. (#064)

Yes. Just 'cos I don't want to do it or don't know how to do it. I just get bored and then I start mucking around and getting into trouble. (#128)

You just couldn't concentrate properly and all they did was muck around, so you just had to muck around with them. (#090)

I used to wag [to deliberately say away from school] every Wednesday and Friday because I didn't want to go to P.E. (#037)

I didn't understand the work so I mucked around. Since I've been back at school I've tried a bit harder. I just want to finish the year out. (#128)

because I'm not like religious and stuff and they're like all into like religious stuff like that. So I just sit there and run amuck, you know . . . I didn't like that school because I wasn't prepared to go to a Christian school. (#153)

Such alienation produces a stalemate in countless classrooms. Uncooperative students and unyielding authorities often fight each other to a standoff, what might be termed a student "performance strike":

I never got a single good mark, not ever. I did all my work and then I started getting bad marks. I just decided not to do any work, at all. (#037)

Many students refuse to perform under the current conditions of school and society. Many students know how to sabotage the curriculum but they appear powerless to change education in favor of constructive freedom. Their skills are ingeniously negative. They do not know how to make organized demands for change. Instead, they get better and better at aggression and sabotage, or they fall into deeper silences, or worse. Particularly disturbing manifestations of alienation are expressed through resorting to suicide and substance abuse.

Thinking about Suicide

Some of the young people interviewed reported thinking about attempting to commit suicide, while others had actually attempted to end their lives:

they picked on me a little bit and I got a bit uncomfortable with it, and I tried to commit suicide when I was about 11. (#100)

Yeah, I ran away because I had a lot of problems and I just thought the best way to get rid of her is to just run away. Then after that I was alone so then suicide feelings were coming on and . . . and then one time I actually did try and commit suicide and I ended up in a boarding ward [at the] Women's and Children's Hospital. (#103)

From what I gather, yeah, because I know I was one they were talking about because I tried suicide so then the teachers just don't look at you in the exact same way they used to. They see you with a problem and they don't really want to work with you. (#106)

I thought about suicide a couple of times, 'cos my life has been ratshit during school. (#114)

It kind of took over. Until you figure things out it's like school doesn't matter, you know. Here I am wanting to, a couple of stages there I wanted to kill myself. Does school really matter? (#121)

One stage I actually almost tried committing suicide by running in front of a car and then I had a close friend of mine run out in front of one when he was off his head on speed. He just drank a lot as well and he was saying that, that nobody cared about him and shit and it really freaked me out 'cos he was running in front of trains, and trucks, and buses and it just freaked me. (#198)

In some of these instances, some young people drew direct links between their experiences at school and thoughts of suicide. Some who had attempted suicide also believed teachers' attitudes towards them had changed when they returned (see #106 above). Post-compulsory schooling makes big demands of young people. Although there are a number of factors associated with suicide among young people, those most "emotionally vulnerable" (Furlong, 1991) found the demands of post-compulsory schooling too much.

Another expression of young peoples' alienation was their experimentation with various forms of illegal substances.

The Use and Abuse of Illegal Substances

About a quarter of the young people interviewed had significant stories around the use of "illegal substances". We use the term "illegal substances" to refer to cigarettes, alcohol, marijuana and others, such as heroin. The use of cigarettes is rife in the student population and is one of the many misdemeanors that "trouble making" students get suspended for. Quite often students who are "hanging in" at school find themselves involved in a cascading process culminating in early school leaving. Many schools make the most of the available disciplinary practices to get rid of "trouble makers". Being caught smoking at school was one of those. Once students were caught, they found themselves suspended, and experienced varying degrees of difficulty in catching up with school work upon return—something that bought its own retribution.

Many also reported binge drinking on weekends:

{Interviewer}: What I've heard from a lot of young people is that they do binge drinking. I guess that's where you go on a weekend and you drink really a huge amount of alcohol.

> You get paro! [Yeah, paro, thank you]. And you don't drink during the week—but the next weekend you go out and do it again. (#022)

Others talked about getting "stoned" at school and a few explained their experiments with heroin. Again, it is difficult to make claims about the linkages between alienation at school and substance abuse. It does not seem to matter whether they were alienated when they begin to "experiment" with illegal substances; they became so once they got caught! Smoking cigarettes, consuming alcohol and "getting stoned" might be more indicative of vulnerability than of trouble to be eradicated. What is clear is that schools seem unable to grasp the concept of addiction.

Not unconnected to this was the way in which young people related to each other as "friends".

Friendships

Not surprisingly, friendship and intimacy were considered significant reasons for staying at school, and hence constituted a significant site for doing identity work. That is, becoming somebody was being negotiated through relationships with peers. In many cases, friendship was *the* reason for going to school:

> Oh, loved it. Probably because I enjoyed going to school because all the people that were there I knew, my peers . . . you know, I'd say that would have to be the biggest concern at school, if you, your peers are having a good time. . . Peer thing is big, it's bigger than people think. Big. (#001)

> I'm only looking . . . . I only look forward to seeing my mates really. 'Cos I reckon, like, I reckon that's the whole point why everyone comes to school,

'cos that's where, like, they're whole beings; 'cos they meet all their friends and that's how everything happens. (#022)

I think like, with the kids our age, it's all about friends. (#070)

Yeah, I thought of school back then as more as, just let's just go see my friends, like a place where I could hook up with everyone. (#151)

Friendship, therefore, needs to be considered as a central category of analysis in making sense of early school leaving and should not be considered as trivial or incidental "noise" (McLeod, 1998). Importantly, from the interviews, friendship troubles emerge as defining moments for many young people in their ongoing deliberations about whether schooling fits into their plans:

if you don't enjoy the people you hang around with, you can't, you don't want to learn so you just leave, you know. If you don't, you know, if you're going to school and getting hassled out and you've got no-one to talk to or . . . then you won't have a good time so you won't stay there. (#001)

It's very important because you need someone there to help you out every now and again and if you've got no-one to talk to in class you just feel all alone and feel like there's no-one else there for you. You just sit there and do nothing. (#106)

Yeah. See when I left school as well, a lot of my, like all my friends had left as well, they'd either been kicked out or they'd left to go to other schools or they'd all got jobs and stuff, and so I didn't want to stay. Everyone else was doing their own thing so I left as well. (#151)

Not only is staying at school contingent on how friendships work out, for some young people, but their lack of friendships is part of the overall condition that leads to early school leaving:

Well, I just didn't, I didn't like school. I was one of the people that you know, I'd only have one or two friends. I didn't make friends very easy and so I said to my mum and dad, I said, I don't want to go school any more, and so we sat down and had a talk and. . . . (#008)

I didn't have time to come, I found when I came home I didn't want to do the work, I wanted to go and see my friends and because they were not doing nothing and I'd go around there and stay there and because they'd all left, basically, I didn't see the point in staying and I couldn't do the work anyway. (#083)

Having said that, we need to note that some students who find themselves on the outside in terms of peer groups, also find strategies to nurture a sociable space that enables them to stay at school:

> Oh. I'm in a group that's kinda like the reject group but we're the in reject group . . . Basically, we're like, we've ranged from year 9 to year 12. And we're a group that formed, I guess like, I've a group in my year level but I don't like hanging out with them at lunch and stuff like that. But I associate with them in class, so it's not like a loner in class. So we're all like, we all have a similar interest but we don't quite fit in like, with the groups that happen within, like, the year 11s, so. . . . (#120)

A focus on friendships at school shifts the gaze away from the teacher-student relationship and the (intended) curriculum as the important space for identity work, and it questions the binary oppositions of public/personal and reason/emotion. If friendships are seen as a significant site of identity formation in and around schools, then this often-ignored private sphere takes on fresh importance. No longer is emotion seen as some debilitating excess, instead, "feelings matter" (McLeod, 1998, p. 4):

> You know how it is in schools, if you do something wrong, they'll make a big thing out of it. [And everyone knows . . .] Yeah and everybody knows about it and they just humiliate you and there's none of that here. (#043)

> Everyone just wants to be popular, I suppose, not to worry about where the future is at that time. They just want to do things that they enjoy, that makes them feel good. (#059)

> Oh, seeing all my friends! Definitely! That's the only thing that really made me want to go to the school, you know. Socializing and being sort of like, someone that everyone sort of like, would stuff around with and stuff like that. Just made me feel good (#060).

> When I first started school, I said I was gonna finish year 12, but . . . it got a bit harder as I went on. I said, you know, I won't be able to cope with year 12 'cos one of my best friends did year 12 last year and he's pretty brainy and he had a bit of trouble with some subjects, so [Did he?] He made me think about it. (#135)

> I didn't like the attitude of the school, wasn't fitting in with the mentality . . . Crazy about boys, you might do drugs, you had nice clothes . . . the right

hair, that sort of stuff, and I wasn't any of those . . . that's the younger and I didn't fit into the younger teenage mentality and um I mean I did fight back in the end . . . not physical harassment . . . it took the form of payouts and social isolation . . . but it was still like I didn't have many friends there. (#121)

The last comment suggests that young people are actually making important assessments about their schools in terms of the nature and quality of the peer relationships that are being played out. The "attitude of the school" wasn't described here in terms of what the teachers were doing, or what was on offer in the curriculum—but rather in terms of the "teenage mentality", of the students. How young people negotiate this "attitude of the school" seems to deeply affect their ongoing engagement with school life. For some students, the "trouble" they found in relationships at school was enough to cause them to leave. For example, many girls experienced demeaning forms of sexual harassment:

I guess it sort of is more of an emphasis on the boys, I mean like with sexual harassment it's so, people don't actually think that they're sexually harassing you but when you get guys coming up to you calling you a slut or grabbing you or doing something, they just think they're mucking around. They're not. And that's like really serious behavior to me. Too many of the kids take it like because they don't know how else to handle it, they don't . . . you know it's . . . that's what I mean, people should be learning things about their rights as a person and about. . . . (#087)

Many boys too, have relationship "trouble":

Up in the country it was sort of, "how you going mate" and that sort of thing and you can fit in, but, I found that it's, well there's guy groups that it's cliquey, really cliquey, like you have to click in with the right people. (#003)

I had no problems in the classroom 'cos I could do the work and stuff like that. But it was a big problem in the school yard because I couldn't get on with other students really. And 'cos I was fighting all the time, and stuff like that, they told me I had to leave. (#060)

Like, you could be bright but you could also be popular—you just had to be careful about the way that you managed your friends, basically. (#020)

In high school . . . there's like constant pressure for fashion and you know, things like that. Like peer pressure, like you have to do this and you have to do that. (#042)

Many students reported getting into bad company:

I was in the popular group which got me into a lot of trouble as well. Into a lot of trouble smoking . . . Most of them got like suspended all the time, and detention. I was hanging out with the wrong people. (#012)

I felt sort of stuck. I mean, all my mates—they were still like, um, like, running amuck so to speak. And I wanted to move forward and then get a job. But then my friends held me back, so I was stuck in between. And now they've moved forward, and I'm behind them now. (#024)

For students who got in with "bad company", some schools did not have very sophisticated ways of making sense of what happens in friendship groups:

I used to hang around with, not hang around with, but like most of the people in my year level, like all of the trouble makers, like they were considered as like one big group and they used to like do it on purpose and stuff. Most of them got suspended and expelled and just a lot of them left and stuff and I remember [the deputy] saying to me that morning that "You're going to end up like all of your friends. We're going to get rid of you all", and I said, "So you are getting rid of everyone are you?" and he said, "Yeah, and you're going to be the next one". So it seemed like, I think they purposefully plan to get rid of all the trouble makers before year 12. (#037)

For some young people, intimate relationships with another person could mean changing priorities:

Well I guess, I think the first one out of all my friends to leave school and then my best friend, she got pregnant, and so she moved out with her boyfriend because they couldn't live at her mum's any more, 'cos her mum didn't like her boyfriend, so that's why they moved out. And my other friend Liz wants to move out just so she can party all the time [all laughing here]. That's one of the reasons why I'll move out as well. (#013)

Yeah, I was meant to go back to fourth term but I didn't. I chose to leave because I didn't want to be thrown out. Because at that time I was more worried about my boyfriend, and I got into drugs and I just didn't want to get suspended or expelled or anything so I left. (#174)

Racism also gets played out through friendships in schools:

Yep, it was my cousin and that was it. Other than that it was just girls, like I had another, a lot of other friends, but like if they was with their group of friends and then them other girls didn't want me to be there, like they'd like turn her against me and like oh, . . . because some of their friends didn't like me, like I get really depressed because you know, I couldn't help who I was and what I am . . . I just go back to my cousin, hang around with her all day.

Yeah. It didn't really worry me because as long as I knew who I was I didn't really mind. But other than that, them boys, oh I could just knock them, because they're so!—you know like if I was, I suppose—well like we used to have little boyfriends and that at school and I was going with one white fella and like them boys my color, they didn't like it. "You can't go with him because he's white", and "So what" you know, because, you know, and they used to give him a hard time so just give up, just didn't worry about it. (#173)

Of course, class relations are also played out in school friendships:

It's, I've found like over the years at school it was harder having not quite enough money, yeah sort of like you get jealous of other kids that have all these good things that you don't and it's harder for a kid to be pushed outside because it's not their fault but they get pushed away because they don't have what the other kids do. (#179)

For many young people, being at school involves doing "emotional labour" (Blackmore, 1996), "managing their own and other people's emotions"—"desire, fear, despair, caring, disillusionment, pain, anger, stress, anxiety and loneliness"—usually through developing "defence mechanisms to face the anxiety that threatened to overwhelm them" (p. 346). And some are already emotionally vulnerable because of things that are happening in their lives outside of school. Having to deal with strong emotional reactions to what's going on at school—emotions such as anger, fear, frustration, guilt and even contradictory combinations of these—only exacerbates such emotional vulnerability. Having to do emotional labor in the school, experienced as a disciplinary system that gives almost unlimited authority to teachers, who can treat students as total subordinates, leads many young people to reject school as an option.

What we also found significant around friendships was the tension between getting on with school work and sustaining friendships. Young people are going to school to be with their friends, but attending school is dependent on taking up, at least to some degree, an academic identity. That is, young people are doing significant identity work between adopting the identity of the successful student and sustaining/nurturing an identity through intimate relationships:

Like, because I can work at home, 'cos I'm by myself. 'Cos when I'm with my friends and that I still work but most of them like chatting and stuff. (#005)

But for some young people, who seemed especially resilient, this tension was in fact a part of the drama of school life, a part of which they were able to give some quite insightful descriptions:

Yeah, definitely . . . my culture does not fit into anyone's cultures because I'd rather be myself than anyone else, because I hate to be because like I could walk around school and everyone sort of like everyone else in their dress sense and their attitudes and that's wrong because the world is going boring as soon as everyone turns into everyone else. And the school is like that too. They have their own fixed set and if you're not intelligent, sort of thing, or if you don't suck up to the teachers, you're just not going to get anywhere. Whereas I don't suck up or try to be anyone else so I didn't get anywhere really. So I didn't really care as much if I quit school but I did in a sense as well because I was seeing my friends all the time and I lost that, lost a bit more . . . That sort of stuff I thrive on, watching people trying to be other people and trying to fit into everyone's shoes. It's really funny just to see how everyone just tries to be everyone else, whereas you're going to be your own person and everyone else reckons they're going to be their own person . . . [But they're not really] but really they're not because they're someone else. (#106)

So many people there they were just constantly after being popular and really, that sort of being popular is not really being popular, it's just being big and drawing attention to yourself, and also so many people there they try [to be] exactly the same as everyone else because they think, oh that person has friends, I want to be like them, and I never want to be like those people. I wanted to be myself and that's probably another reason why I didn't have huge groups of friends around me. (#127)

What we have highlighted in these last two sections is the importance of considering both the generation gap and friendships as very significant sites of identity formation for young people. It seems that unless schools can be especially sensitive to the impact of these aspects on young people, then increasing numbers will become "disaffected pupils" (Furlong, 1991), rejecting schooling and in the process being emotionally injured through the effects of marginalization and powerlessness.

The following portrait exemplifies this complex interplay between family, friendships, identity and having to do emotional work to stay at school.

Portrait #010
Sol: Secrets and Life

High school, you know, is all about social interaction. It's all about that. Going to school specifically to see their friends, but at the same time you're putting up with all these people who are really anti-social. Like City North High School is the sort of school where you're walking down the hallway and someone punches you in the back just for the hell of it. There's a lot of violence among the students and a lot of indifference amongst the staff. Just a lot of stuff happens, and no one notices or cares. High school politics is about who's in with who, who's against who. Like you can't be their friend because they're not my friend and you're my friend. It all just seems very silly to me. That's everywhere. At some schools the bickering turns to physical fighting. That's City North.

High school is designed to help the people that have got problems with their educational abilities, and to cater to the people who are your average everyday students; and if you don't fit into either of those groups, then it's not really built for you. It doesn't cater for people who learn quickly. They don't have special classes for people who are fast. They have as many problems dealing with the normal class. Like you don't get extended, you just repeat. Oh, you've finished? You're bored? Well, you can do the other half of the questions as well. You don't go deeper, you just get more. So I just really lost interest in it.

The whole assessment set up was the same. With a crappy little effort you get a 13 or 14. And then sometimes you'll try really hard and you'll get a 19 or something and it makes it seem like it's worth it. But then, everything you do from that point on you get lower marks because they're expecting so much. I found that with essays and stuff. I'd look at my essay next to someone else's essay and they've got higher marks than me, and if you take it to another teacher without the marks they say, oh yeah, yours is the better essay. It's got more points, you proved your opinion more strongly. But their essay still got better marks because they're not as good a student. I think they are trying to challenge you, but it doesn't. It's not fair, so why bother trying?

My school career since year 10 isn't very impressive to look at. I was at this country high school, and after year 10 I moved out of my mother's and moved in with my father, and went to City North High School till half way through year 12. Then I got kicked out of my dad's. So I got my own house, and tried to survive on $135 a fortnight. I was 17 then. So I left school. I didn't have enough time and effort to go to school and try and keep myself alive and try and juggle this ridiculously small budget. So I went back to my mum's in the country the following year and began year 12 there as an adult student. But again, I had to move out by myself and get into school by bus. It was quite a long trip and was horrific. There was paper and food and whatever else you could find being thrown around. And Cheryl and the baby moved in with me and I dropped out half way through the year.

This year I'm at an adult campus hoping to get into a psychology course at uni next year. It's a lot easier to get along with the people and the teachers actually listen to you when you say, oh well my car broke down or whatever. Or I'm really good at Maths, right? Our lessons are two hours with a break in the middle and pretty much every day I leave halfway through Maths. That's cool with the Maths teacher because I've already done the lesson's work. And I'm doing five PES (Publicly Examined Subject) subjects because I like tests. I'm just a test person. It means that half of my overall year takes 15 hours.

When I was younger, in a small country town—small country town values, if you don't fit into them, well then everyone looks on you hard. Generally it was OK, given the fact that a lot of people judged me on the fact that my mother is gay. It really doesn't have to do much with anyone. Like it has little to do with me, who I am. Well it doesn't and it does, both. I mean, what my mum does in her bedroom has got very little to do with who I am. It was an issue, and there was some name calling and stuff, but I also learnt to take advantage of it. Like as soon as you accuse anyone of picking on you exclusively because of that they stop picking on you, even though that's not what they're doing. I went spastic at one of the behavioral officers once. I can't remember what I was in trouble for. And I was saying like, oh you're just saying that because . . . , and it worked. I didn't get into trouble. I suppose kids always learn to take advantage of everything, no matter how much of a disadvantage it would seem to be. And there was one girl that I really liked that I had to break up with about 10 or 15 times, because she kept on going out with me, and every time her parents found out, you know, oh my god, his mother's gay, you can't go out with him. I guess when I was about 14 I resented that I was punished for her choices, but my anger wasn't so much directed at my mum as at the people who I thought were punishing me.

The reason I moved out to be with my dad was because my mum was having lots of fights with her girlfriend and at the time I felt that I was the cause, because it seemed to be the case, because they were fighting about all sorts of stupid things like who used the last bit of lighter fuel, or whatever. It's like, that's an important argument? That is worth punching each other out in the backyard, over. When I moved back, this is two years later, I found out it was all because my mum got raped and she got pregnant and that's what the whole contention was about. I really wish they had explained it to me at the time because I wouldn't have moved out if I'd known. Like I can understand how that dynamic triggered the arguments.

It's affected my relationship with Cheryl indirectly. The violence, that is. Like Cheryl gets violent sometimes and that makes me really uncomfortable. Like I've never known her to get violent with the baby, but she has been with me and that's a lot of the problem there. I sort of figure there's plenty of help for women who get beaten up by their husbands. There's no help for men that get beaten up by their partners. But that doesn't mean that the guy should sit there and stay there any more than the woman should in the same situation. We talked about it a long time before we broke up. She'd get a psychiatrist and go a couple of times and then, Oh I don't like this person, I don't want to go there. I love her, I don't want to lose her, but if I didn't leave her then I could see that I was going to stop loving her and I also want what's best for Jim. And that sort of thing in the house doesn't help kids.

Sometimes I feel like I'm doing the wrong thing. I feel that I should stay with her because she needs help but she's never going to get any help while I stay with her. And she needs that help more than she needs help in looking after Jim. I go over and help as much as I can, and I always look after him on Fridays, because I don't have school then. He's better for me than for Cheryl. She takes a lot of things personally like there's not even any real sentient thought behind it. Like he's fallen over and he's head butted her and she's like, Ow you hurt me. So she gets stressed at him. I tend to focus on the fact like he's a baby and he doesn't really understand what he's doing. But he's getting a bit more conscious now. I tend to treat everyone like that. Like if someone doesn't want something then you shouldn't try and force it on them. It's about understanding and not judging. Jim's got like a thirst for life. He enjoys it.

My dad, he's different. I've had a hankering to see him for a while now, but I'm a bit worried about it as well. My dad's not violent, he doesn't drink, he just has sex with children. When I was with my step mum in the city, he wasn't there. He was supposed to be but he wasn't because obviously she couldn't handle living with him under the same roof. Not that anyone bothered to tell me before I moved in. I suppose that's the biggest problem. I was living there for like a year and a half before anyone told me that that's why they weren't living together any more.

My mum and dad split up when I was about three. I used to see him every second weekend. I don't think he touched me. But he knew what he was like before he married my step mum. I know from other people he lived with before that. So like if he knows then why do you go and marry someone who's got five kids if you know you're going to do horrible things to them? He understands that it's horrible, he doesn't think that it's the right way to go or anything. He understands that it's not right, but that's what I don't understand, myself. Why do you voluntarily put yourself in a situation where you know you're going to fail, and with disastrous consequences. It's strange, I even had a pretty good idea that one of the kids had been abused, but I never made the connection with my dad.

I need to talk with him. It's strange like. There's a lot of my father in me and I sit here and I think about what I'm thinking and what I'm saying and how I'm feeling and I can see that, and it worries me. I want to talk to him and understand and like, I mean I don't think he's found an answer yet but maybe between us we can sort something out.

I settled on psychology because it's a way that I can understand myself better, and hopefully be able to use it to help other people both in understanding themselves and perhaps like do better with their lives or whatever. I think that's what I want from everything, more understanding. I've got this little question that I like to ask people. If you could trade, if you were given the choice, if you could go into this great big building where you can have absolutely, utterly correct information about absolutely anything that you choose to ask about. The only restriction is that you're not allowed to have contact with the outside world. What would you do? Would you be willing to be cut off from society, like not allowed to have contact, to talk to society about it, given that you could know all the secrets? That's my question.

I would. There might be stuff that's scary but that doesn't mean I don't want to know. That's me, I want to know. It's strange, I'm really curious and not at all curious at the same time. Like it's a respect thing, I suppose. I respect that if someone doesn't want to tell me something. Well that's cool, so I'm not curious in that respect, but I want to know and understand what's going on behind everything.

Becoming Economically Independent: Learning about Work without School

In this book early school leaving has been considered as a part of what Luttrell refers to as young people's "self-making process". According to Luttrell "students' attempts to assert a self (or at least an image of a self) and to have this self (image) recognized and valued by others is what life is all about in high school" (p. 94). In concert with others (Kincheloe, 1995; Farrell, 1996) we believe that this self-making process—becoming somebody—is what young people are up to as they navigate their lives from school towards economic independence. For most young people, the single most important imperative *is* navigating a path towards economic independence. Young people, all except the very wealthy, are engaging in navigating a place into the labor market as a matter of survival (Willis, 1977; Foley, 1990; Weis, 1990; Furlong & Cartmel, 1997; Fine & Weis, 1998). For most young people, there is no choice other than to find the means to pay their own way. Or as one young person put it: "When you go out into the real world and you work and you get by on your own and you do things on your own and if you work you're obviously supporting yourself" (#037). This process of becoming economically independent is not a matter of choice—a lifestyle choice—it's a necessity. The alternative, unemployment and poverty, is in clear view and concerns young people. "I don't want to fail, I don't want to be on the dole. I don't want to feel like I'm scum, you know" (#028). It is this imperative that drives many young people to leave school early. What is on offer at school is seen by many young people as not contributing to their project of making an independent life for themselves. As one young person put it, "school just wasn't going anywhere for me" (#002).

Whether for better or worse, many young people are unconvinced of the relevance of schooling to their self-making process. "Yeah, it was like a waste of time being at school because I learnt everything I needed to know, like by myself, without going to school" (#153). They are often less than convinced of the claims being made about schooling. They hear that schooling will provide them with the means to get a good job. All they have to do is work hard at school, put off the desire to make money now, and their future job prospects will be much better. All they have to do is be successful at school and the problems of navigating the interface between school and the labor market will take care of themselves. Many young people are unconvinced of the policy rhetoric. As one put it,

> if you want to do something like, 'cos I wanted to get a job and I wanted it now and I didn't want to wait until I finished school and do all [those] subjects I didn't want to do, continue going on an opposite direction to [what] I wanted to go and then just go back and waste all that time when I could have been working and doing what I wanted to do. (#006)

For this young person, staying at school was regarded as a waste of time. Becoming independent was about getting on with finding a job, and *that* could only be achieved by leaving school. What young people understand only too well is that the policy rhetoric doesn't match the reality.

The claim being made by some of these young people was that being at school did not provide the knowledge or opportunities needed to navigate the complex and changing interface between school and the labor market. One student put this in terms of the opportunities to find out who you are: "to find out what it is in life that I actually want to do . . . to find out who I am and then I'll know what I want to do about it [and] I definitely wasn't finding that at school" (#127). Another student was even more frank and more insightful: "I basically think the education system sucks . . . they spend so much time trying to teach things they think they're going to need, like in order to get a job, or go to uni or something, whereas they should be teaching them more about life and about . . . things that you actually really need to know to be able to be successful in life as a person" (#087).

In many instances it seemed that any efforts that were made by schools to assist young people in their attempts to navigate their way into the labor market were unsophisticated and often unhelpful. The school assumed that students actually understood the complexity of the changing labor market, and hence all students were making informed choices. Unfortunately what opportunities schools do have on offer are mostly pitched at providing work experience. Such programs fail to understand not only that many students already have part-time work, but also that the work experience is often not taken seriously by school and students. Work experience programs are generally not integral to the school's curriculum and are often seen by many teachers as interfering with the main game of school. The more important investigation into the complex nature of the labor market itself is mostly absent (Simon & Dippo, 1987; Simon, Dippo & Schenke, 1991). For example, most students in this study were unaware of contemporary industrial relations arrangements, and had little knowledge of how unions worked. School provided little or no place for students to actually discuss and examine their part-time work experiences which often involved exploitation of various kinds and even harassment. Most significantly, schools provided little opportunity for young people to actually broaden their aspirations for their future working lives, which for many of these young people were constrained by their own meagre social and cultural capital.

In this chapter we have explored the various facets of the ways in which young people see themselves as being involved in a project of becoming somebody. The extent to which schools were integral to that project or actively inhibited it was often a matter of heated contestation, but for others a matter of indifference. Having established that young people are active agents, in the next chapter we want to investigate a constellation of other factors that become crucial in this identity fomation.

PART III

INDIVIDUAL, INSTITUTIONAL AND CULTURAL IDENTITIES

CHAPTER 4

DOING IDENTITY WORK: CLASS, RACE AND GENDER

The term "identity" is now being used in a range of disciplines, including philosophy (Taylor, 1989), cultural studies (Hall, 1990; Kellner, 1995) and education (Giroux & McLaren, 1992; Giroux, 1993; McCarthy & Critchlow, 1993; Apple, 1996). The idea of identity formation is a relatively new and contested category in the educational literature (Hall, 1990; Walkerdine, 1990; West, 1992; Davies, 1993; Davies, 1994; McRobbie, 1994; Giroux, 1996; Skeggs, 1997; Wyn & White, 1997). Much of this contestation is around the "politics of identity" (Aronowitz & DiFazio, 1994) which focuses on the difficulties of making sense of the significance of class, gender, race and sexuality.

Not only is the category "identity" ambiguous, and at risk of becoming a "buzzword" with wildly different meanings, but it also competes with the notion of subjectivity. We use the term "identity" here because the term represents the "experience of being a person" (Davies, 1994, p. 3). "Identity", as an explanatory category can undermine the notion of an essential self—the one true, stable, unchanging self that can be discovered or that is considered as an "already accomplished fact" (Hall, 1990, p. 222). Rather, we see identity as "not something which already exists, transcending place, time, history and culture" (p. 225). Instead "identity" is best seen as socially constructed, as a "production", which is never complete and always in process. Viewed in this way, "identity" is more a matter of becoming, and when applied to young people it is about how they negotiate territories of class, gender, sexuality and race difference (MacPherson & Fine, 1995).

Class/Gender/Race in Constellation

The concepts of class, gender and race continue to offer considerable explanatory power in these new times. The interviews from this study affirm that class (or more precisely capitalism), gender (or more precisely patriarchy), and race (or more precisely racism), remain potent social forces in young people's lives. Capitalism has not withered away but has taken on "new" forms. Gender differences are still working to oppress women and girls, and racism is alive and well in schools, the culture and the labor market. Against the postmodern tendency to disintegrate such concepts because they hide more than they reveal, and the view that they are not nuanced enough to account for differences, we want to assert a need to hold on to a vocabulary that speaks about how networks of power construct youth identities (Walby, 1992).

In theorizing youth identity formation there is a need to struggle with two competing imperatives. The first is to understand, appreciate and interpret the uniqueness of individual lives. The second is to generalize and to discover similarities amid diversity. In effect, attention is paid to both sameness and difference.

We do not believe that the social fragmentation being asserted by postmodern social theory fatally undermines the categories of class, gender and race. Rather than abandoning these categories, we believe that an alternative to an either/or logic can be developed. That is, there is an alternative to a logic that reduces understanding to one primary determinant of identity formation, such as class or gender. There is growing argument around the need to take class seriously again—to "reinstate class" into social analysis. Skeggs (1997), for one, argues that:

> To abandon class as a theoretical tool does not mean that it does not exist any more; only that some theorists don't value it . . . Class inequality exists beyond its theoretical representation. (p. 6)

For others, like Aronowitz and DiFazio (1994), the category of class never lost its usefulness. Others, like Wexler (1992), argue that "class difference is the overriding organizing code of social life" (p. 8). From such a view-point, race and gender difference are negotiated *after* identities are structured in class terms. This does not resonate with our interview material. Having said that, the issue becomes one of how to theorize the intersections of class, gender and race as a set of dynamics that are significant in the formation of youth identity.

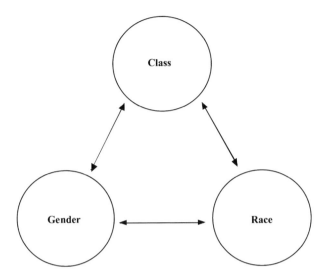

FIGURE 4.1: Constellation of Class, Gender and Race

Often this complex intersection is described in terms of a "commatisation" of disadvantage—class (comma) gender (comma) race (comma) (O'Brien, 1984). This amounts to a way of thinking about disadvantage as though it was somehow an additive. An alternative theorization involves pursuing a both/and logic in which the categories of class/gender/race are held in a constellation.

In constellation, we are constantly reminded of the mutual illumination of each category. In constellation it is not just a matter of adding issues from each of the categories, but rather of seeing how the problematic is reformulated as a consequence of accounting for the other dimensions; that is, a "new" set of questions or issues arise. Such a view resonates strongly with McCarthy's (1988) idea of non-synchrony. Rather than see the interactions of class, gender and race as a matter of adding oppressions, we need instead to be aware of "tensions, contradictions and discontinuity in the institutional life of the school setting" (p. 274). Rather than considering various forms of oppression—class, gender and race—as static and additive, we need to consider how such oppressions, understood as "efficacious structuring principles" (p. 275), get played out in qualitatively different ways in different people's lives. In constellation, we might move towards theorizing how "racial, class, and gender oppression are part of a single, specifiable, and historically created system" (Sacks, 1989). Weis points out:

that race, social class, and gender are structured into [schools, credentialling arrangements and the labor market] to begin with, and that students . . . are responding to concrete manifestations of these structuring factors. . . . (Weis, 1995, p. 164)

We are arguing, therefore, that class, race and gender differences are not analytically separable. Pursuing a class/gender/race analysis involves viewing social relationships and, in our case, life in and around post-compulsory schooling as interdependent and multiple, rather than discrete and independent.

Class as a Site of Identity Formation

Another theme that resonated strongly in many of the interviews was the influence of families on young people's decision-making about staying on or leaving school. The word "family" might be placed in parentheses to indicate that families, like young people, need to be understood as heterogeneous. Invariably, parents or care-givers wanted their children to be happy and were also keen that they work towards their own economic independence:

> two weeks after I left and like, mum said to me you know, you just can't leave school and just do nothing. You just can't, like, be on the dole. (#008)

Young people reported that they were trying to develop and realize their own goals with whatever resources they had available to them, often drawing heavily off their own families. It sounds so obvious! One way of interpreting this is that they were defining their own identities and aspirations in terms of available resources. What was clear, was that young people vary enormously in the resources that are available to them to do this work:

> [K]ids [come] to school with histories of value and with different repertoires of social and cultural resources that they could use to create the value of the subject, self or identity. But, within the intense life of the school organization, some personal resources [are] ignored, while others [are] seized upon, used and affirmed as collectively valuable—building up in the process their possessor's image of identity. (Wexler, 1992, p. 7)

Wexler (1992) argues that social class is a category that enables us to talk about this issue:

[c]lass difference is the overriding organizing code of social life that sets one school apart from another. Against the background of a seemingly shared mass youth culture, what students struggle for in becoming somebody and how they engage that interactional life project during high school—the "best years" of their lives—is different depending on where their school is located in the larger societal pattern of organized social differences and inequalities. The ideal and the route to becoming somebody in the *suburban white working class* is not the same as becoming somebody in a high school in a *professional middle class suburb*. (Wexler, 1992, p. 8)

Early school leaving does not, therefore, impact on all schools in the same way. Early school leaving is not seen as a problem for elite private schools. Neither is school leaving seen as a problem for well-off public schools—well-off in the sense that the school population, comparatively speaking, comes from financially well-off and tertiary-educated families. Nor is early school leaving a problem for those interested in university entrance. Early school leaving is not a problem for those groups in society for whom schooling works well. In reviewing the available literature (Teese, McLean & Polesel, 1993; Williams, Long, Carpenter & Hayden, 1993; National Board of Employment, Education and Training, 1995; Teese, Davies, Charlton & Polesel, 1995; Dwyer, 1996; National Youth Affairs Research Scheme, 1997; Dusseldorp Skills Forum, 1998; Lamb, 1998) on socio-economic status and schooling we find overwhelming agreement that "[s]ocio-economic status is a strong indicator of the likelihood of young people not completing 12 years of schooling" (Freeland, 1991, p. 173).

It seems that in Australian society (and we suspect elsewhere), there is a pervasive myth (aided and abetted by the mainstream media), that we live in a class-less society—one in which poverty is almost non-existent. This point was made poignantly by Fitzgerald (1976) in one of the reports written as a result of the Henderson Royal Commission into Poverty in Australia:

> In conclusion, we argue from the evidence contained in this Report that people who are poor and disadvantaged are victims of a societal confidence trick. They have been encouraged to believe that a major goal of schooling is to increase equality while, in reality, schools reflect society's intention to maintain the present unequal distribution of status and power. Because the myth of Equal Opportunities has been so widely accepted by Australians, the nature of unequal outcomes has been largely ignored. Thus *failure to succeed* in the competition is generally viewed as being *the fault of the individual rather than the inevitable result of the way our society is structured.* (p. 231, emphases added)

Schooling is clearly not working well for those in the community who have the least wealth. Early school leaving is tangible evidence that schooling still contributes to the inequitable reproduction of society and, as such, many young Australians are navigating a transition to adulthood upon terrain in which "class formation operates between abstract structures and concrete specifics of everyday life" (Skeggs, 1997, p. 8). Skeggs summarizes this process as follows:

> The social space we occupy has been historically generated. If the transmission of capital over time, hence in families over generations, is introduced we can see how when we are born we enter an inherited social space from which comes access to and acquisition of differential amounts of capital assets. From being born into gender, class and race relations we occupy the associated social positions such as "women", "black", "working class". (Skeggs, 1997, pp. 8–9)

In asserting the need to reinsert a class analysis into Australian schooling Connell and White (1989) argue the following:

> First, class inequalities in education (measured by a range of outcomes from school progression to secondary retention to tertiary entry) persist on a massive scale in contemporary Australian education. They are not an issue of the past . . .
> The second unambiguous conclusion from the research is that these inequalities are not a minority problem to do with pockets of poverty in a landscape of affluence. Study after study shows a gradient of inequality that stretches right across the class structure . . . There are indeed some findings that suggest the distinctive minority in education are not the poor but the privileged. (p. 89)

In reinserting class as a category for analysis, we are reminded that identity formation actually happens within a struggle around material conditions. In our society this struggle is around the nature of capitalism and its imperative of capital accumulation. Class, as Williams (1976, p. 59) reminds us, is a complex category inferring a form of social organization that implicitly sets up an antagonism between those who own the means of production and those who have only their labor power to sell. Importantly, "in the day-to-day running of capitalist economies, the capitalist pays labor as little as possible and labor organizations fight to improve wages and conditions" (Weedon, 1999, p. 136). There is a struggle or antagonism over who gets to extract the surplus value from labor power. The capitalist system sets up structural inequalities which produce class differences which are manifested in different economic positions (or classes). The present arrangements, characterized by a dismantling of the welfare state, are leading to a further concentration of wealth in fewer hands, those in the capitalist (ruling) class having much more control, not only of the means of production, but of access to institutions that control the distribution of wealth and information, the power to shape the nature of society, health, leisure, safety, high paying work and educational opportunities not available to those who cannot pay.

Notably, a number of informants in this study themselves used class as a category of analysis, and demonstrated their own class consciousness. The first extract below outlines how young people took notice of the way schools often misunderstand the effects of poverty:

But, I mean, Hillside High isn't a private school, it's only public and this teacher, he was . . . assistant principal or something, he was real big and bossy and everybody just like sort of wore what they want. You know, you can't force students to wear a uniform, if it's not a private school. That's what I thought anyway. So, and, like some of the students they are not very rich, or, you know, and there was this one kid who would wear the same pants nearly every day, and then they started to really fade and lose color. And he said to him, you have to get some new pants, you can't wear them any more, and he was, like, can't afford it sort of thing, and he had to like scrape for the money otherwise he'd, you know, get detention or get suspended or something, so he had to scrape around for some money and buy some new pants for school. (#008)

Likewise, the extracts that follow offer very insightful analyses of just how important class location was in young people's view of their schools:

They didn't see people for who they were, they took everyone on face value, and I didn't like that very much. That was probably the aspect of [private] school that I despised the most. It was an incapacity for people to take them on good nature and generosity and all the aspects that you appreciate a person rather than he drives a good car, like a Commodore or his dad owns a bakery or something, makes heaps of money. (#018)

'Cos all the people, I've been to school with all, like, everybody in my class, I've been to school with them since, like, reception. And like, they still treat you like shit, because my dad's only a truck driver whereas their dads are farmers or big businessmen. They don't realize how much is involved in our business. Probably more than what theirs is. (#114)

I can mix, like, we're all poor, and we all have the qualities that we can go mix with the rich, but we prefer hanging around with the poor. (#120)

It's full of snobs you might as well say like this town like with all the businesses and shops and stuff like that it's mainly for the people that's got the money not the lower people. . . The ones that put 100 percent in, the ones that are not that, not the ones like feel like putting the 100 percent in, it's the ones that have to put 100 percent in to please their parents. Mainly the snobs, the "richies", the ones that had good primary school bringing up like strict school like [Country School] and stuff like that. They're the ones that went there to primary school or wherever. The ones that had a really good, you know, childhood. (#197)

Yeah, there's like a systematic thing of putting people in, like you've got the upper class, you've got lower class, you've got the "ferals", and you've got the um poor people, and you've got the "yuppies" and you got the "townies" and you got a whole list of people that just fit in to that categories and it's and you've also, even in schools you've got, which one's the "yuppies" cos they all wear the latest clothes and baggy jeans and all this kind of, and you've got the "ferals", there with the dreadlocks and um sitting there listening to Yani and shit and then you've got the upper class that are real snobbish and like prissy looking clothes and stuff and cars (#198).

Some young people astutely recognized the classed nature of the way their teachers worked:

Ah huh. The teachers always go for the slightly younger, smarter, richer people, it's just always the case. The girls I was talking about and another three guys in my class that are all fairly short, fairly smart but really rich. They always got the whole report card, all distinctions, and it hasn't happened very often in [Country High]. It's pretty ridiculous, actually. (#107)

To reinstate class as a category of analysis means understanding that young people are navigating their transition to adulthood in terrain in which experience is organized around class location.

I mean, [I'm] just another blue-collar worker. I mean, I can't . . . like, if you want to be respected in this world, you have to have a good job, good money, a family so to speak . . . and just have a perfect life. And not everyone has a perfect life. I guess I'm one of them. (#024)

Seen in these terms, young people are making decisions about whether school is a part of their project of becoming somebody in relation to what "capital" they have available for pursuing their aspirations. What's essential here is to remember that not everyone is living a middle-class, "perfect" life.

The work of Bourdieu over the past twenty years is a powerful resource for understanding the complexity of class, through the way he conceptualizes the notion of "capital". Central to his work is a view of the role of schools in (re)producing social and economic inequality. The following quotation gives an idea of how Bourdieu understands the ongoing role of schooling as a site of social formation:

> It is difficult to anticipate fluctuations on the stock exchange of scholastic value, and those who have the benefit, through family, parents, brothers, sisters, acquaintances, and so on, of information about the formation circuits and their actual or potential differential profit can make a better educational investment and earn maximum returns on their cultural capital. This is one of the mediations through which scholastic—and social—success are linked to social origin. (Bourdieu, 1998, p. 25)

One of the informants in the study put it somewhat similarly:

> Sort of feels like the whole place is going down the whole time and you start wondering what, 'cos everyone in your street starts losing their jobs and my dad lost his job . . . whatever. And you start to wonder what's going on. Like, is it really worth what I'm doing, or should I just bum around. You don't know what to do. (#059)

Bourdieu is clearly referring, in the quotation to cultural capital—a term now widely used by educators. His theory of capital, though, is somewhat more complex and involves economic, cultural, social and symbolic capital. These might be summarized as follows:

1. *Economic capital:* This includes income, wealth, financial inheritances and monetary assets.
2. *Cultural capital:* This can exist in three forms—in an embodied state, that is, in the form of long-lasting dispositions of the mind and the body; in an objectified state, in the form of cultural goods; and in an institutionalized state, resulting in such things as educational qualifications. The discourses of femininity and masculinity become embodied and can be used as cultural resources. This is not to say that gendered relations are purely cultural, for they clearly are not. Cultural capital exists only in relation to the network of other forms of capital. Gender carries different amounts of symbolic capital in different contexts (Moi, 1991).

3. *Social capital:* This consists of the resources based on connections and group membership. This capital is generated through relationships.
4. *Symbolic capital:* This is the form the different types of capital take once they are perceived and recognized as legitimate. Legitimation is the key mechanism in the conversion to power. Cultural capital has to be legitimated before it can achieve symbolic power. Capital has to be regarded as legitimate before it can be capitalized upon. All types of capital are context specific. Thus people are distributed in the overall social space according to the global *volume* of capital they possess; the *composition* of their capital, the relative weight in their overall capital of the various forms of capital; and the evolution in time of the volume and composition according to their *trajectory* in social space. (Skeggs, 1997, p. 8)

Bourdieu's model pushes educators to think more expansively about the relationship between socio-economic background and educational success. That is, the educational disadvantage of those from low socio-economic backgrounds can not be understood only in terms of having enough economic capital. Bourdieu's model asks educators to be aware of the effects of other types of capital. In other words, social and cultural capital have to be considered as well. Social and cultural capital are being traded as young people navigate their way through schooling.

In the interests of brevity, we will limit discussion at this point to issues of economic and social capital. (Subsequent chapters will take up the issue of cultural capital.)

Many young people reported that they could not continue their schooling because of a lack of financial resources within the family:

> I decided to stop, and that was right at the beginning and then after I just needed money more than I needed to go to school, and . . . because my mum was sick as well, so I had to, like, I needed money more than I needed to go to school at that stage, so and I don't really have any ambition to go to uni . . . It was mostly the money, sort of like . . . I mean, you don't get enough, you don't get paid enough on AUSTUDY [government assistance scheme], especially when, 'cos my mum was sick and she can't work and so . . . I just, to support your mother as well, you just can't. (#004)

> I left round about last year—November, December . . . I was on AUS-TUDY and 'cos my mum's on a sole pension, she hasn't got [much money and] I have to pay her money to support me, food and board—and from that I've got $5 a week to live on, for myself. (#024)

There was a struggle by some young people to contribute to the family finances, and still go to school:

> I mean you see all these flashy cars with their kids coming through in private college I mean you know, and they've had that really good opportunity life-style and I'm not saying my mum has never given me good opportunities, . . . No, my mum had a few money problems and I decided that I was going to get a job. I had a rough time in year 11 so I said alright, I'll go get a job and that way I can help her out as well as get some money for myself. (#179)

For many, not having money meant significant problems socializing with others at school:

> Well basically I think it was because I was one year younger and everybody was like you know really cool and like that and I was never someone who had the money to be really cool, so I was kinda paid out [being harassed]. (#121)

> I've found like over the years at school it was harder having not quite enough money, yeah sort of like you get jealous of other kids that have all these good things that you don't and it's harder for a kid to be pushed outside because it's not their fault but they get pushed away because they don't have what the other kids do. (#179)

We found that there are many ways in which social capital gets played out, in the process of leaving school. In other words, it's not what you know but who you know:

> My parents. They have racehorses. I've watched the farrier all the time and I thought, well, I might as well do that . . . there's a TAFE [Technical and Further Education, or a type of Community College] course . . . you have to go for a couple of years and actually be with a farrier . . . it's actually an ap-prenticeship or traineeship or something like that. (#048)

> Yeah my dad he was a cabinet maker by trade and so I thought I would give that a shot. (#084)

> Yeah 'cos I play the cello and that—musical family. (#127)

> the manager lived across the road so like you get pretty friendly with your neighbors and everything and I told him that's what I wanted to get into and that, and . . . because mum works with a lady whose husband has a father who works at Skillshare [a job agency], so it's just, you know—it all gets there. (#137)

I kind of fell into the job. My father, he knew the manager at the time. (#144)

Many young people felt they did not have the benefit of coming from a family with the economic capital to enable them to remain at school for 12 years. Often the government allowances were also insufficient to enable them to live the life of a full-time student. Many also felt that because of family background, their cultural capital ill-equipped them to aspire to university, or to speak in a powerful dialect. Many did not have the social networks that opened up opportunities for a wide variety of post-school options.

The interview material from the study resonates with Bourdieu: that a school system that uses the "logic of competition of everyone against everyone" (Bourdieu, 1998, p. 27):

> maintains the existing order, that is the gap between pupils endowed with unequal amounts of cultural capital. More precisely, by a series of selection operations, the system separates the holders of inherited cultural capital from those who lack it. (Bourdieu, 1998, p. 20)

The way inequalities of "capital" get played out in the lives of students is through the silence surrounding the issue. Those young people who are living in poverty, and their number is increasing and substantial, can't speak about it in the context of the school. And if they do attempt to "speak", their voices are almost universally misunderstood in mainstream high schools. The reaction of the many young people living in poverty to the alienating experience of school is almost universally misunderstood because of the unexamined assumptions schools have about the lives of young Australians. The persuasive myths of equal opportunities—the belief that we live in an egalitarian and class-less society; the moral panics around "dole bludgers" or "welfare cheats"; the overwhelming view that poverty is a psychological phenomenon—all combine to produce a context in which the experience of poverty can't be listened to in schools. And recent changes in education policy only seem to exacerbate this issue.

While it may seem obvious that schools and education policy need to stay clear of blaming either the student, the student's family or the particular school, there is less than widespread support for the need to focus instead on exploring social processes. But pursuing such an emphasis does enable an exploration of the relationships between specific groups of young people and institutions (Wyn and White, 1997). In choosing such a perspective, what becomes significant is the different "experience and the meaning of everyday life" (Wexler, 1992, p. 8) that gets played out in this struggle to become somebody:

> It is not simply a question of deficits or deprivations and advantages, but of different lifeworlds and of the dynamic organizational economies that generate and sustain diverse understandings and aspirations. (Wexler, 1992, p. 8)

"Organizational economy" here refers to the way in which schools mediate the flow of social and cultural resources that students use to create a self or identity. In essence, schooling involves a complex interplay of multiple realities in which some realities get to be valued and others do not. Hence, life in schools is characterized by a powerful misunderstanding: that everyone attending schools is working from some commonly shared view about what is going on and that everyone has the same "opportunities". This is clearly not the case. Such misunderstandings get played out to the detriment of the most vulnerable—those living in poverty, or families struggling to make ends meet on a week by week basis.

One way to proceed, then, is to contemplate what gets valued in schools. Which identities get valued and which ones do not? How do the processes that schools use to value certain identities lead to misunderstandings and hence "trouble" for some groups of students? Perhaps the question "what is required of the student to be successful in acquiring the school credential?" is a good place to start. This next quotation gives a few clues as to what is required:

> all of the study and that, I just couldn't have hacked it . . . and they just didn't have any life. (#030)

Being a successful student, therefore, requires being able to accommodate to an almost unlimited expectation for commitment. A young person's, life needs to be able to accommodate the following:

- a space within one's life in which to geographically and emotionally concentrate on the demands of teachers;
- a willingness to comply with even the most appalling teaching, and in some instances, to learn in spite of the teacher;
- access to intellectual/cultural resources for dealing with the learning tasks set;
- access to computer resources with which to complete assignments;

- a space within which to fit a regime that may provide little capacity to negotiate deadlines and certainly little capacity to respond to circumstances of living, such as a death in the family, illness, having to work part-time, wanting to be a serious musician, sportsperson or artist, or even having many friends; and

- literacy and numeracy skills that might not have been taught explicitly during previous years at school, and that will need to be developed on the run.

This list is just the beginning of the demands on young people who make the decision to try and complete the post-compulsory years of schooling. If the ideal school-identity for young people means an almost unlimited expectation for commitment, then many young people are going to be unable to met this commitment because they do not have the "capital" needed to support such a life. If the ideal school-identity requires an almost unlimited expectation for commitment, then a whole array of obstacles will interfere with school completion.

The performance pressure (anxiety) caused by the requirements of the credential itself can act as a means of self-affirmation, but it can also threaten the identity of some young people. Wexler (1992) argues that students need to regulate the pressure of escalating and invidious performance demands. A crucial question here is: "[h]ow much emotion and self-expression is shut down and depressed in the course of forming a responsible, professional school self?" (Wexler, 1992, p. 139). A corollary is: what is the cost of self-dampening or depressing emotion? Possibly for some students the need to regulate the pressure of escalating performance demands results in one of the forms of alienation already mentioned. For some, this means violence, vandalism or running amuck in classes. For others it means apathy. Apathy regarding school is perhaps a "less violent expression of rejection of the school" (Wexler, 1992, p. 140).

To summarize, then, in the senior years of school, young people are making sense of themselves in a context of an almost unlimited expectation for commitment. There is an ever present and escalating performance anxiety as students make their way through school. They need to defend themselves against performance demands, which may mean either sabotage or silence. To defend the self against devaluation, some students put much store in peer relations. They go to school for their relationships with friends. Such "work" is an alternative to academic success.

Portrait #127
Georgia: Education and the Search for Meaning

I was on exchange in Europe last year for six months, and when I came back I realized I had just changed too much for the school sort of people I was with. That was one of the reasons why I left. I found that I had grown up a lot more and a lot faster than everyone around me and it just really got on my nerves to be around these people who, nice as they were, were just kids.

And that's what annoyed me about the teachers. Like one teacher was constantly complaining oh you're so immature, you're such children, you're so childish and everything to the whole class. And how can we as students mature and grow up and have some self esteem if a teacher is treating you like that?

Also I found that some of the things we learnt at school, some of it was pretty useless and year 11 was a joke. I would have thought it was much harder, much more challenging, and much more interesting. I was just bored out of my brain.

I was doing Business Maths, Chemistry, Music. Yeah and Australian Studies and French. I didn't do German because they didn't offer it. I did Music because I play the viola and that's why I'm at a music school. Chemistry? Well before I went to Europe I was thinking about becoming a vet. And I did Business Maths because I've always hated Maths. But in Europe in year 10 I did the standard Maths. The first two lessons I knew what was going on because I'd already done that, and then they sped along so much faster, and here I was, in year 11, stuck in the same type of Maths for three months.

So you can see that when I came back to school here it was literally driving me slightly insane. Some of it was too easy and some of it was just plain boring.

I'm not sure any more what I want to do with my life. I definitely want to travel first. I want to take off around Australia for a while, and when I've got the money take off and then come back and settle either in Europe or here and decide then what I want to do. I went away and learnt a lot about myself and I think travelling around would help me find out what it is in my life I actually want to do.

I did a course in tourism which the school counsellor helped me find once she came on side. Thought it might help me get a job as a tour guide or something. It turned out to be bullshit. Just skimmed over all the topics. I got the certificate. Yeah, we all passed. We all got the certificate. But no-one on the course got a job.

I was a very quiet little girl, very shy. Went to a private school. Started in kindergarten hardly speaking a word of English, so I had a hard time starting off and making friends. I was targeted by bullies. I was very self-conscious and couldn't defend myself and so they gave me more. That's the way kids are. Mainly verbal bullying and occasionally kicking and that. There was a lot of it at the school but the teachers just don't do anything about it. When I left there I had just one friend left. High school was better, but I figured, because I was used to being independent, that I would get along without many friends and without really close friends. I went to Europe because of that, you know, because I had to be even more independent there.

Then the host family was so supportive and I grew a lot more open. They had one daughter my age and we were the best of friends and we're still in contact. So I came back a lot more outgoing. Even so the friends I'd left behind at school were never really close friends, and after coming back I changed so I wasn't exactly one of the tight little group anymore.

So here I am and one day I thought OK I'm not going to just sit around knowing nobody, so I went out and walked down to the park on a Friday night and just met everyone because it's a small country town and everyone knows everyone and so the people are just a lot more open to new people.

It's just a little group. The adults hate us because we hang out at the park. Or we used to. We used to make a lot of noise I guess. We go to the pub nowadays. Some stay in the park but the police started hassling. And if someone new turns up people go and talk to them because new people are so rare. Yeah, the girls are about my age and the guys about 20 to 25.

I like going out with them. I find I have a lot more in common with them. I think they're probably the same as me in that none of us really know where we are going in our lives. Oh yeah some of them have jobs and two girls I am best friends with are just finishing year 12, but a lot of us don't know exactly where we're going.

There's a few extremes. There's one guy in the group, he's schizophrenic. He took a trip once and never came off it. That was about five years ago. So he doesn't have much of a life which is a real pity because he's a great person. He's a bum but we're all good friends and we try to support him as the person he is. And another great thing my dad says is there's nothing wrong with being a bum if that's what you want to do. It makes life very tough because you don't get any money but it's your choice and your life.

About school. You know I always hated school. Yeah that's part of the reason I left. I always felt trapped in school. Trapped in this one little stream where I had to go along and do it and I couldn't get out and live my life. In Europe it was better because they start at 8 and they go on to 1 in the afternoon, so you've got the whole afternoon to do your own thing.

Another thing is school uniform. I can't stand school uniform. Our principal, she's so proud of the school uniform. I always had a bit of a laugh at assembly when she's lecturing us about how to wear our school uniform and if you want to express your individuality do it some other way. But um none of the other students ever did.

Some teachers really got on my nerves. So I got on their nerves. Not disrupting the class or anything. I kind of told the teacher personally, sort of make them see what they were doing and the way it annoyed me. Just little comments and hints really.

The best teacher I suppose is someone who knows what they are teaching so they do have a certain authority, but someone who respects the students. Because if they treat us like idiots then I can't respect them. How would they show respect? If they acknowledge the sort of work I'm doing and they tell me what is good and what is not good and then I know what they're talking about and I know that they're trying to help me along. And they encourage each individual to learn in their own way. Some students work better if they are taught straight from the text book, or from a teacher handing out sheets, but some don't learn that way.

A lot of teachers, really, I don't think they really care. I think it's a pity, because it's obviously very hard for teachers to help you find who you are unless they're interested in every individual student. That's hard even if you do care. It's a pity because we do spend so many years at school, and these are the years when we should be learning about ourselves.

Gendered School Leaving

Because of the pervasive nature of patriarchy, early school leaving needs to be understood as profoundly gendered. Patriarchy can be understood as the "order of things" that subordinates women through a normalization of a hierarchical binary: male/female. Patriarchy, simply put, is a "gender hierarchy" (Smith, 1999) that gets worked out in the space between everyday experience, consciousness and social structures. As Ebert put it, capitalist patriarchy amounts to:

> a regime of exploitation that naturalizes socially constructed gender differences in order to deploy the social relations of production in class societies in ways that reproduce and legitimate the domination and exploitation of one gender by another. Patriarchy organizes asymmetrical, unequal divisions of labor, accumulation, and access to economic resources that guarantee not only the political privilege (domination) of male over female, but more important, the economic subjugation (exploitation) of the "other" gender as the very grounds of social arrangements. In other words, patriarchy—as a historically diverse ongoing system of gender differences for exploitation—is necessary to the very existence of class societies, including contemporary global capitalism. (Ebert, 1996, p. 4)

But "patriarchy" also infers a gendered system of social relations—gender relations; that is, the subordination operates relationally and hence is socially constructed, not biologically-given:

> Understanding of the process of gender construction is crucial if schools and systems are to work for equitable educational experiences for girls and boys. Dominant concepts of masculinity and femininity define males and females as opposites by highlighting their differences and assigning them unequal value, status and power. These dominant concepts limit, in different ways, expectations of girls' and boys' participation and post-school outcomes. (Ministerial Council on Education, 1997, p. 12)

Against some recent post-modern social theorizing, patriarchy might be regarded as a necessary "struggle concept" (Mies, 1986, p. 36) in confronting the ongoing and pervasive exploitation of women and girls. Patriarchy calls attention to a "system" of gender subordination that operates on and through our consciousness in all of the significant sites of identity formation in society, especially schools. That is, young people's identities as male or female are constructed within interpretive communities such as schools. Becoming somebody involves presenting oneself: in fact, enacting a performance (Walkerdine, 1989; Connell, 1991) in public as masculine or feminine. In other words, identities are constructed within the structures, practices and discourses that are available—it is through them that we make sense of what is going on. It is through such structures, practices and discourses that we learn to speak about who we are and how we relate to others. This is especially significant because the prevailing "common sense" about femininity and masculinity often limits young people's opportunities for their future lives. In the context of this study, some forms of femininity and masculinity interfere with completing school. In the next section, we will refer to some previous research which will provide a frame for interpreting the interview material.

Gender Difference and Schooling

Feminist research into the education of girls has placed the following concerns on the agenda for policy and practice:

> the subjects and books students studied too often failed to depict the range of contributions that women made; . . . girls were not given as much encouragement as boys to undertake a wide range of jobs and careers, not to continue with studies of mathematics and science; and . . . their experiences and pat-

terns of subject-choice in school were leading to marked disadvantage in their patterns of post-school study and employment. (Yates & Leder, 1996, p. 6)

These concerns have been elaborated upon in recent Australian research (Teese, Davies, Charlton & Polesel, 1995; Teese, Davies, Charlton & Polesel, 1997; Teese, 1998) which has revealed that a "curriculum hierarchy" does indeed operate in the post-compulsory years, and that it has had some marked effects:

- "boys do better than girls in high stakes, publicly examined subjects" (Teese, Davies, Charlton & Polesel, 1995, p. 105);
- "[girls'] superiority in English, though uncontested, has limited effect in promoting girls' access to higher education, particularly into high stakes courses" (Teese, Davies, Charlton & Polesel, 1995, p. 105); and
- traditional stereotypes around gender identity contribute to undermining post-school options, especially for girls.

Contrary to the current "what about the boys" backlash (Kenway, 1997; Lingard, 1998) in educational policy discussions, these concerns have yet to be properly addressed. The kind of issues still requiring attention include examining the construction of gender; eliminating sex-based harassment; improving the educational outcomes of these girls who benefit least from schooling; addressing the needs of girls at risk; reforming the curriculum; improving teaching practice; broadening work education; and changing school organization and management practices.

Research within a feminist theoretical framework has also recently turned to examining the interplay of masculinity and education. For example, Connell (1989) examines the ways in which schools are involved in constructing gender and negotiating gender relations. Of interest here, is how men and boys "learn to be male" (Kenway, 1995), or how they learn gendered identities. This was an idea continually affirmed in the interviews:

Oh yeah, it's more of a guy thing I reckon now. (#014)

Oh definitely, definitely, because being a kid they felt they've got to put on this some sort of, you know, macho attitude to like school, you know, not be classed as some little dunce or you know. (#016)

In rejecting conceptions of "natural" masculinity or "male sex role" views, Connell (1996, pp. 208–210) has developed the following framework to make sense of masculinities:

1. *Multiple masculinities:* within any cultural setting there are "different ways of "doing" masculinity" (p. 208).
2. *Hierarchy and hegemony:* usually there is a form of masculinity that is "culturally dominant", is "highly visible" and signifies authority in "relation to the gender order as a whole . . . It is an expression of the privilege men *collectively* have over women" (p. 209).
3. *Collective masculinities:* masculinities characterize the individual but are also defined and sustained in institutions including schools, as well as in the culture, as in sport and popular culture.
4. *Active construction:* "masculinities come into existence as people act . . . they are accomplished" (p. 210); that is, we do gender in everyday life.
5. *Layering:* the contested nature of masculinities is in part sustained through a "layering of desires, emotions, or logics" (p. 210).
6. *Dynamics:* "[t]here is an active politics of gender in everyday life" and hence "masculinities are composed, historically, and may also be decomposed, contested and replaced" (p. 210).

In seeking to make sense of masculinity, Connell therefore describes masculinity in terms of "a socially constructed form of life or project in time" (Connell, 1991, p. 143):

> This project is found in social space at several levels: in personality, in culture and institutions, and in the organisation and use of the body (e.g., sexuality). In any given society there are likely to be multiple masculinities. It is important to distinguish the *hegemonic* form of masculinity . . . , which is socially dominant (though not necessarily the most widespread), from subordinated masculinities which are discredited or oppressed (such as homosexual masculinity in our culture). (p. 143)

Hegemonic or dominant forms of masculinity are:

> seen to lock boys into narrow and restricting forms of being human which have negative effects on their health, their relationships and their perceptions of the value of different forms of knowledge and work and therefore their achievements. Further, certain masculine ways of being are said to limit boys' and men's emotional horizons and to tilt them towards aggression, repression, conflict and violence, and towards damaging forms of competition and control. (Kenway, 1997, p. 3)

This recent feminist (Mac an Ghaill, 1994; Epstein & Johnson, 1998) examination and critique of hegemonic masculinity goes to the heart of unraveling the way power works in patriarchy. It is the ongoing production and reproduction of hegemonic masculinity that sustains the hierarchy and is responsible for the continuing subordination of women and of other masculinities. When thinking about the dynamics of gender politics "[m]asculinity cannot be thought of apart from femininity . . . it cannot be fully understood unless it is seen in the context of historical patterns and relations of power between men and women" (Kenway, 1995, p. 62).

Contemporary analysis of gender in post-compulsory schooling is moving away from attempts to isolate gender issues from other forms of educational disadvantage. Instead, we are moving to understand how racial, class, and gender oppression function interactively:

> [R]eports since the mid 1980s have argued that cultural, geographic and socio-economic background variables should be included when schools' effectiveness in dealing with differences among girls and boys is considered. (Yates & Leder, 1996, p. 7)

For example, Teese, Davies, Charlton and Polesel (1997) argue that:

> Gender disadvantage is experienced unequally according to socio-economic status. Students from better-off households are least affected by gender disadvantage in curriculum choice or schooling outcomes. But as we move along the socio-economic scale the gender gap widens. Thus the real question is not whether girls as a group are more disadvantaged than boys as a group, but which girls and which boys? (p. 12)

We want to turn now to the following issues that emerged as the most significant in the interview material:

1. the fact that some young women appear to not be marginalized in their wage-labor identity;
2. the finding that (a) post-school options for some young people appear to be driven by a complex combination of gender and class location: and (b) some young people resist the traditionally gender segmented labor market; and
3. the fact that harassment in schools is often gendered and can be a potent interference to staying on at school.

The Wage-Labor Identity of Young Women

The interviews strikingly revealed that young women were keen to find a place in the labor market. They were taking their wage-labor identity (Weis, 1988) very seriously.

In patriarchal societies (like ours), gender domination and subordination is maintained, in part, through a sex-segregated labor market, and takes the form of convincing women of their place in the home. Patriarchy demands that a woman's place not be in the public sphere—especially the labor market—but be restricted to the private domestic sphere. One informant revealed this "common sense" very succinctly:

> Na. I thought I'd be like everybody else and just settle down with a white picket fence and kids. (#197)

In contrast, many young women interviewed spoke of their plans for entering the labor market, with few considering stereotypical futures at home looking after children:

> In this sense, then, they challenge a fundamental premise of patriarchy—that women's primary place is in the home/family sphere and that men will, in turn, "take care" of them. (Weis, 1988, p. 203)

That is not to say that some had not considered motherhood:

> I'll probably be divorced [laughing]. Divorced with three kids. Nuh, I don't know. No, seriously, I reckon I probably won't be working, because I'll be looking after my kids. And I'll probably get money from the government, because of that. (#013)

Some young women interviewed had become pregnant, and, as a consequence, had left school:

> Well I fell pregnant with Kerry, so yeah um I decided to keep the baby so I had to leave school . . . No I didn't. I didn't tell anyone at the school that I was pregnant . . . Um probably yeah if I had of told people because I told a few of my friends and they said oh well there was a girl at the school the year before that you know became pregnant at 15 and they all supported her and that yeah but I thought it wasn't worth saying anything because it was only like the last term, I only had a few weeks to go . . . 'Cos like I'd just moved over there like to go to school and that and I found out I was pregnant so it was just like a waste of time even going over there. (#189)

A significant theme to emerge from such lives was the difficulty these young women had in finding a place in school in which they could even speak about being pregnant, let alone contemplate staying at school after the birth. There were some schools who had programs for including young mothers, but these were extremely rare.

A number of young women rejected the idea of settling down to have babies as a "crazy" thing to do and were instead contemplating futures apart from motherhood:

> they think I'm crazy doing what I'm doing and I'm saying no I'm not, you're the one that's crazy for staying here in Country Town and having babies. I mean my best friend, she just had a baby. She's only 19, same age as me. (#197)

Others envisaged having a family, but considered a career as a first priority:

> I mean 'cos I wanted to learn, I wanted my education which is, both of my sisters have children, they have children, they had children at the age of like, 17, and I don't want to be like that. I want to have a career, have a life and then have children and stuff. And I wanted my education to do that, but I couldn't get it. (#025)

What seems evident here is a rejection of the separation between the public and the private by young women and certainly a rejection of traditional patriarchal views of a woman's place. This tension between domesticity and employment has been a key focus in recent feminist research (McLaren, 1996). The results seem to be divided between those who report that "girls and young women in Western culture continue to assume that their employment will be secondary to their domestic responsibilities" (McLaren, 1996, p. 293) and those who believe that girls and young women are increasingly rejecting patriarchal positioning. Weis highlights this tension:

> They may have the leverage to attempt to negotiate the conditions of family life, division of domestic tasks, financial arrangements [and recognize that in the present de-industrialization of the economy] the family needs her paid labor in the same way that the family needs male labor . . . This is likely to be even more the case since traditionally well-paid working-class jobs are being eroded. (Weis, 1988, p. 204)

Young women appear increasingly to be pursuing the opportunity to negotiate their own lives and the potential bargaining power that comes with paid labor.

Post-school Options: Aspirations for Their Future

While many young people interviewed talked about their aspirations for their future, they also indicated signs of gender segmentation. For example, girls spoke about "careers" in child care, secretarial studies, business, beauty therapy and hairdressing, and boys were interested in trade occupations, electronics and engineering. Despite changes in the labor market, a few young people were actively resisting gender stereotypes.

Aspirations were repeatedly framed in terms of positioning in both class and gender relations—class and gender being intimately intertwined, as the following three quotations demonstrate:

> Well I was hoping to become like my dad is. He lays irrigation, so, like sprinkler systems and I want to gradually go through the grades, which is grade 1 and whatever grade you can get up to and I want to get up to the irrigation level. (#032)

> Yeah, I want to be a truck driver. We done work experience last week and I worked for my uncle for work experience, . . . No, I ride on the property, Dad's property. I haven't got a licence . . . My sister reads but my brother, me and Dad don't read. I get my sister to do mine, she does my Maths, like the bits I don't know how to do . . . She knows all the Maths and everything. (#077)

> My dad taught me a little, helped me a little bit because he used to go to the gym and he used to do massaging and I think he did a training course and all that, he used to do body building and that, so he used to know a fair bit so he used to teach me a little bit, but I could never really grasp heaps of it. I remember him saying a good job would be a sports medicine person because there's like heaps of jobs around and that, and it's not that hard, but. . . . (#082)

On occasions, young people gained access to language, experiences and aspirations with which to resist traditional gender stereotypes. As one girl put it,

> Well I still, even now, I want to become a mechanic, automotive mechanic . . . The only reason I've been into mechanical engineering is since when I was five I started, my stepdad sort of took me out to the car. My brother wasn't really interested in cars so he took me out, he said well this is this, this is that, and I just got the hang of it then and even the work experience I went to automotive places—I really enjoyed it . . . I mean most of my life I had a bit of a, because I was a little bit weird I enjoyed doing things more

different than what most girls like doing. I was sort of a little like an outcast
. . . I didn't really care what everyone else was doing I just wanted to do what
I wanted to do . . . My family wasn't very wealthy and I was just sort of, I had
what I had—I was happy with it . . . I was the only girl out of, like there was
five other boys, I think, and me that did Tech [Technical Studies] . . . most
of the other girls went and done Home Ec. because it was sewing and cook-
ing and stuff like that but I found that was pretty boring. (#179)

Yeah, and I'm not going to do something I don't want to do because I don't
see why anyone should spend their life working doing something they don't
want to do because it just makes you unhappy . . . It used to be really low and
I've just, I learnt a real lot from my mum, she reads a lots of books and she's
done Women's Studies and she's done a lot of alternative learning. (#087)

What is revealed here is the importance of the mother in identity formation and future planning, and in helping her daughter think about
working against patriarchy. The mother introduced her daughter to "alternative" discourses, and hence important conceptual resources with
which to envisage a life outside of the gender hierarchy. But there is much
more to resisting patriarchy than working on an alternative vision, as the
next quote from a young woman indicates:

My poppa was a fitter and turner and I was the grandson he never had sort
of before my brother was born. Anyway he took me with him fishing and
men's stuff and then before he died he told my dad he wanted me to carry
on the tradition of the family doin' metal fabrication trade so I went and sat
this test at TAFE and to my surprise I got in and done it. I got a certificate
for it. But um I got too many knock backs [not successful] so I didn't worry
about it. (#197)

This case also indicates that gender hierarchies operate in the labor
market, with the latter undermining the non-traditional choices of some
young people.
Resistance to stereotypes requires a lot of careful planning—it does not
come easily. Having an aspiration is one thing, but feeling comfortable
enough in the school context to actually find a pathway in the existing curriculum is still very difficult for many young women who are trying to access the non-traditional curriculum:

I've been mainly brought up with all boys. My Dad used to be a mechanic
and spray painter, and panel beater by trade . . . I couldn't choose. I could
have done Tech Studies but I've never done Tech Studies . . . Well I put my
name down to do Tech Studies and I was the only girl in the class so that's

why I pulled out. So yeah . . . Ah yeah. I wanted to do Tech Studies 'cos hands on kind of thing um but then I would've been just in with all boys. I get along with the boys and that all right but I changed to Australian Studies then I think from Tech Studies. (#195)

Not only do young women experience difficulties in pursuing non-traditional post-school options in the school curriculum, but young men also encounter problems:

Alright, . . . they came around to the Home Economics room to see what I've got. It was like, the whole thing was, I don't know, bumped into the idea that if you want to be a chef, they think you're gay or something but now it's more like no one really cares. More guys at it than girls, a lot more guys . . . At our school there was, I think, I was one of three guys in the high school in Home Ec, and then when I actually went out and got the apprenticeship, it was like, all my chefs are largely all males. All my chefs except for the two at high school are all males. Most kitchens I went to are just males. (#014)

Boys studying Home Economics still experience sex-based harassment, or more specifically, homophobic insults. The harassment in the above instance was rationalized away in terms of "like no one really cares".

In this section we have provided examples of young people aspiring to some labor identities outside of traditional gender stereotypes. Family experiences were riven with class difference. But, in all instances these young people were imagining their futures in terms of what they knew, what they knew was possible, and what they could speak about confidently. All were envisaging futures in ways that were highly consistent with the class location of their family. Very few young people interviewed were imagining a future that was a long way removed from their present experience. Of some note were those who were interested in making a life out of music or other forms of artistic endeavour, such as dance. Often, such aspirations had little to do with what was happening in their family.

What these examples point to is the importance of considering gender and class location as significant in helping shape young people's aspirations for the future. In this way, many young people are developing aspirations that work against staying on at school. What is also significant, however, is the profound effect that "alternative" discourses had on some young people's thinking about their future. For example, feminist concepts provided some young women with ways of thinking past the gender stereotypes that are still working on and through many young women. Many young people were aware of changes in the labor market and were working to position themselves advantageously within these "new" possibilities.

Harassment: Disciplining Gender Identities

Understanding how gender relations operate in high school also involves making sense of the way identities are disciplined and maintained in the everyday life of schools. Student identities are normalized in schools through the use of repressive forms of power, in the form of harassment:

> And I was so humiliated. When I was a kid I used to come home crying every night because I was so upset that everyone was paying me out and calling me stupid. (#176)

> I used to stay home a lot because I used to get harassed . . . And sometimes I just run out of the classroom crying sometimes. I tell the teacher where I'm going but. . . . (#140)

> Sort of generally making me feel like an outsider. (#006)

Normalization works through the discourses that young people have access to. That is, people speak themselves into existence though the discourses they have available to them. But certain discourses get to dominate. "[S]ome positions are made more likely, others more difficult" (Grant, 1997, p. 105). Young people often do significant identity work in schools with and against forms of coercion from other students. It was clear from the interviews that class/gender/race were the foci upon which most of the harassment was centered. For many young people, the relentlessness of this form of disciplining, and sometimes its violent nature, often proved too much for them, and early school leaving was their only possible recourse:

> Well yeah, at high school there is, yeah because like, they say like if you don't have a boyfriend, then you must be gay. And if you have got a boyfriend, then you're a slut, so you can't win! (#040)

What came through strongly in the interviews was the connection between doing gender identity work, that is, performing gender in schools, and harassment. Young people were constructing a gendered identity in a context in which certain performances were disciplined—in some cases, so severely disciplined that many found school unbearable. School felt like a "gaol" or even a "living hell":

> I knew someone at [school] who was driven out of school by students basically, with this, you know, if you don't leave we are going to keep beating

you up every day, so I thought, and even if you have the parents come in talk about it and then it will stop for a week and then someone will start it up again, and . . . back into it. So, it's almost like being in gaol you know, if you're . . . that treatment. It's like gaol, yeah. (#001)

I think the classes were a bit bigger and there were just girls—they were bullies, and they used to pick on everybody and the teacher used to get frustrated with them and they used to get sent out of the class all the time and we all thought it hilarious. But in year 11 and year 12, there's like one girl that's top dog in certain classes, like she always used to turn up in my classes; and she'd single a few people out and they were her main target. Like, she wasn't just disruptive; she was mean to those people—I used to be one of them—and it just makes your life a living hell, like, she's just picking on you and . . . saying things behind your back, writing things on the blackboard and stealing things, throwing them in the bin, throwing them downstairs. She used to pick on the teacher too, like, if the teacher seems weak then she'll have a good go at 'em and they'll get all frustrated and send her out of the class and then all her friends will cheer her on. And, because she's such a bitch she'll have popular friends that like, I don't know, try to be like her, like, I don't know, and she loves it, like. And the more she teases people the more her friends think she's great. (#009)

The connection between being harassed and leaving school was very clear for a large number of the young people interviewed:

Kids. I'll say, kids can be cruel, very cruel. And I had to put up with it most of my life. And when I got out of school, mate, phew, best thing I thought I'd ever, ever done. (#114)

Because I wasn't doing too well at school and I was always getting picked on. Sometimes I was getting bashed up in the afternoon and I just didn't feel like going to school that much. (#196)

The main reason I left school was, I was being picked on most of the time and the fact that I couldn't, I thought I had got as far as I could. (#032)

It's just like if you've got one little flaw, people just pick at it and pick at it for a long, long time. Yeah, for about a month straight, flat out and I wasn't— mum was wondering why I was staying home so much because at least two days a week I was at home . . . Yeah and before I left school it was getting up to like going four days a week, and then just going there once. It just got worse and worse. (#107)

Other young people were able to make sense of their harassment at school in terms of not being able to fit in because they didn't have the "money to be really cool":

> My brother still goes to high school and he can't like, the family can't afford to get him Adidas jackets, like this, which isn't even mine and you know all that sort of brand clothes so he gets picked on at school because he hasn't got that so he tries to, because he wants to be like everybody else because he thinks that they're cool, but they're really not. (#040)

Often the harassment was around body shape. In the following case, not being thin was the reason for being picked on:

> Well sometimes it makes you feel really down because like everybody's picking on you, and calling you names and stuff and you know, you feel, but in some ways it's good because it makes you a stronger person when you leave, and it makes you realize what people are really like . . . Mm, I reckon, in grade 8 and things like that, like they said, "if you come to school tomorrow then we'll bash you" so they don't come to school and that makes their education even lower . . . Like sometimes it might cause people to become suicidal because they don't feel accepted and they don't feel like they're good enough and stuff like that. Yeah because they're not pretty enough, they're not thin enough . . . Probably grade 8. If you're with guys it's alright to be like pretty fat, but with girls there's some huge thing, it's just not allowed. It's stupid. (#040)

Many young people reported being the target of disciplining from their peers because they had actually taken up the academic identity being promoted by the school. This seems again to be organized through gendered and classed power relations. In some schools, doing well and being a boy came at a cost, as the following example indicates:

> I always thought that if someone was going to give me a hard time for being successful or for achieving we'd just see later in life—if I'm successful and living a happy fulfilled life because I'm doing what I want to do, that makes me better off than copping a bit of a hard time . . . Oh, only by certain people it was OK. The sorts of people who go to school just to muck around and don't really take it seriously it wasn't OK but all my friends, it was OK to be successful and then on the other hand you have your other friends who are maybe a little smarter or maybe just tried harder than you at school who said, "You don't try hard enough, lift your game". (#033)

Various forms of name calling were also common and were often combined with forms of physical violence. The old adage, that "sticks and stones will break my bones but names will never hurt me" just didn't seem to work for some young people:

> Got called every name under the sun. I'd have school bags chucked at me in the hallway. I'd have things stolen from my locker. (#066)

> Like, I used to get crank calls all the time at home. And like, they'd change my phone number over. (#066)

> I used to get harassed anyway. And then they'd all start rumors and then all my, like when I did make friends, all my friends would believe them and you know, it would just go around. Like you'd walk through the school yard and you'd be called names and just picked on and you know. (#025)

Rather disturbing also was the prevalence of sexual harassment. Not only that, but many girls rationalized sexual harassment as "just practical joking":

> Yeah it went for 12 months. It was a pretty good course I mean I was the only female in the class and got a lot of crap put on me but I handled it . . . No because I never complained. Like it wasn't harassment it was just practical joking around. If it had got any worse then I would have complained but I mean I've got a sense of humor. It can take you so far but yeah. (#197)

Often young people reported that they were the target of "stupid rumors":

> So the harassment takes the form of rumors. Like, other girls telling stories, that sort of stuff. (#048)

> another big part of it was the kids at school, because I'd had, you know, stupid rumors that they've, like, for about four years about losing my virginity to a sausage or you know, something stupid like that, you know. And in the end. . . . (#070)

For many young people, the daily experience of harassment meant having to find strategies to use when not in the classroom. Many young people reported their tactics for protecting themselves at school:

> I never went to recess or anything. I was the sort that would study. (#007)

Because nothing was being done about it, it all became one big game and like, just more and more people joined in, 'til it wasn't funny any more. Like, you know, I'd leave it to the last minute before I'd leave the classroom and then go back to classroom early. Like, there was one part of the oval over where we went out and sat and, like, most of them didn't come up that way, so it was fine. (#066)

Not "feeling safe" at school emerged in the interviews as a significant interference to completing schooling. Feeling safe at school for many young people involved adequate supervision from teachers. At times this supervision did not work, and resulted in a loss of confidence in the school:

I had a group that I went to primary school with, that we did not get along at all and I was actually in the year above them, and going to [high school] they met some others and formed like a group that you know, picked on certain ones and I happened to be one of them, and it came to a situation where like I was like grabbed around the throat trying to defend one of my friends. Like I just asked this girl to leave, like, I said just go and sit down, leave us alone, and it actually ended up in like, she picking a fight with me and there was no teachers or anyone for about five minutes but I didn't fight her back. So we, we pressed like charges, like my family like made me like go down and press charges because she got sent home half way through that day at school. The teacher drove her to the train station and put her on a train, she got off at the next stop, came back and waited for me after school because she thought she'd been like humiliated so she came back and I had marks on my neck and the inner part of my leg because that's where I blocked like her kicks and so forth. And I guess kind of that's really where like they just thought I was a trouble maker 'cos I was like where were the teachers, where was anyone, you know, and . . .

I said well where was anyone. You know, there was no one there, and she had about a group of about 20 of them and I was just waiting for them to all jump in and that's why I just didn't react to her fighting me I guess.

I got yelled at by the teacher straight after it. I was shaky as anything and one of the teachers yelled at me because I asked where were any of the teachers.

So, and I had to live with that, like the rest of the years I was there as well. You know, oh, you know, she's easy to beat up, you know, pick fights with her and I think it's where a lot of her friends started just little comments here and there, walking down the halls and I really don't like that sort of thing.

I went down hill in year 11, very much. I got worse and that's when like half way through, probably half way [through] year 11 I just didn't bother doing anything any more. It was just like, I hated the place, didn't want to be there, couldn't be bothered doing the work, saw no point in it any more. It was, lost the whole initiative and you know. (#016)

When students sensed that their feelings did not matter, or they felt that they had been treated unjustly, then this cascaded into a lack of interest and finally early school leaving. The previous story highlights, again, the need to consider the "emotional labor" that young people are doing at school.

In summary, this discussion about gendered school leaving seems to have raised more questions than answers. It seems appropriate to finish this section with a set of questions that could be used to examine this issue in schools and to examine educational policy:

- in what ways do "boys learn to establish their masculinity in opposition to femininity?" (Martino, 1997, p. 6)
- what forms of femininity and/or masculinity interfere with school completion?
- what characteristics of hegemonic masculinity are oppressive for those boys who do not fit into school life?
- in what ways are hegemonic masculinities homophobic? (Mills, 1996)
- in what ways are hegemonic masculinities based on a system of abuse and violence?
- how might we theorize about femininity and masculinity in ways that do not cast all girls and boys into a similar mold, and thereby treat them as belonging to a homogenous group (Martino, 1997, p. 21), or treat them as victims?
- how might schools productively engage girls and boys in examining the politics of gender with a view to enhancing their achievement at school?

Dealing with Racism

The statistics tell a grim story. Aboriginal and Torres Strait Islander students had the lowest school completion rates of all monitored groups in South Australia in 1994 to 1996. As Dwyer (1996) put it "Aboriginal young people have the highest likelihood [in Australia] of becoming early school leavers" (p. 17). The interview material exemplified what the figures conceal—that there is a high level of systemic racism in schools in some parts of Australia.

Australia's Indigenous community, in collaboration with others, including both state and federal governments, have campaigned actively (Moore, 1993a) for ways to improve the educational outcomes for Indigenous students. This campaign has been based on the view that being educationally disenfranchised seriously undermines the opportunity for human, social and economic development (Department of Employment, Education and Training, 1993, p. 1).

This unsatisfactory situation has been widely recognized in recent royal commissions (Johnston, 1991; Human Rights and Equal Opportunity Commission, 1997) and other inquiries. All highlight the need to recognize that the cultural reasons for Indigenous students' failure in education are situated in a historical and socio-political context characterized by "a troubling inheritance" (Pearson, 1994), dispossession and marginalization, leading to poverty, ill-health and homelessness. Influences on student achievement transcend the classroom, and they are deeply embedded in the institutional structures defining the relationship between the school community and the larger society. For example, Indigenous Australians, no matter how well educated, have to deal with racist practices in the job market itself; these, not surprisingly, lead to the lowest rates of labor force participation and the highest rates of unemployment (McClellans, MacDonald & MacDonald, 1998). There is thus an inter-relationship between educational inequality for Indigenous Australians and white racism. White racism is "the process of 'racializing' social formations", such as the economy, the political system and public social institutions such as schools, "in such a way as to impoverish, de-power, disenfranchise, divide, silence and exclude black people and to ensure that they receive minimal services" (Moore, 1993b, pp. 5–6).

The interviews revealed a number of recurring themes. Paramount among these was evidence of sustained forms of racist harassment from other students towards Indigenous Australians, some of it quite vicious:

> No but I mean if you're a different color, if you're larger than someone else, you always get the finger pointed at you. I went through that quite a bit. I mean some people don't take it to heart, others do. (#146)

> Oh, they called me "nigger" and "black" all day but they never like, oh most of the people, like wouldn't say it to you very much, but my friends did, my immediate friends and that.

Yeah, to my friends it was a joke, you know, call me black or whatever [?], but other kids around the school that tried to call me that, some I did, but some I didn't mind, but some I'd give shit to and pay them out, gave them crap back about their race. But mostly just my friends so I didn't really care. So it didn't really bother me. (#082)

I went to high school in year 10. Like first ever I got there the teachers just picked on me straight away. My brothers and my cousins or whatever were split up and so I was in the same class as John and they just picked on us from day one and like we'd get hassled out every day . . . Oh they was just splitting us up straight away, didn't even know us and like, you know, didn't even give us a chance to sit next to each other and that's why I got real fed up with it and getting hassled out and I started losing my cool and calm and that and started taking it out on the teachers and that's at the time I started to get suspended. I just didn't worry about going back there and they said, "You come back a week later" but I just didn't worry about it. (#154)

I was just getting harassed by young boys that was going to school and like I could say "Na, I don't like yous boys" and they wouldn't take no as an answer and they kept on harassing me and other than that it was like some non-Aboriginal girls, boys coming up calling me a black and everything, you know. So that's what that was. (#173)

There were reports of Aboriginal students being shamed, humiliated or embarrassed by teachers in front of other students:

The teachers here don't drill it into you like they do at high school. Like in high school if you don't know something, the teacher would make a point out of it, and humiliate you in front of the whole class. (#042)

Teachers not supportive. Friends left school. Teachers yelling at me in front of other students. (#043)

If you get a question wrong they'll just have a big stress about it. They say you don't try hard enough, or you don't do your work, something like that. They just put you to shame. The teacher doesn't pull you aside, they just tell you straight out in front of everyone. (#0153)

Many young Aboriginal students reported having trouble obtaining assistance from teachers:

I started year 12 but wasn't trying harder. Really wanted to do an Art course. School was good but they kept changing teachers. They gave you heaps of work. It's hard to keep up. The teachers, they don't really help you. (#017)

Because the teachers don't explain it to you properly. They explain bits and pieces and then you put your hand up and ask [and] they say, "Weren't you listening, you should listen". So you get into trouble and then it's like well I was listening, they just go off their head at you and it's like, what a waste of time, why am I here and then you just give up and walk out, go home, forget about school. (#153)

The "trouble" for Aboriginal young people seems to come from being harassed by racial slurs, feeling shame in classrooms, and not being able to get help. Having to do the extra emotional labor required to cope with the dissonance, misunderstanding, fear and anger came at too high a cost for many Aboriginal students.

Interactive Trouble in Post-compulsory Schooling

In this chapter, making sense of early school leaving has meant reading the interview material as descriptions of doing "identity work" (Snow & Anderson, 1987; Fraser, Davis & Singh, 1997)—defined as "the range of activities individuals engage in to create, present, and sustain personal identities that are congruent with and supportive of the self-concept" (Snow & Anderson, 1987, p. 1348). Whether young people stay at school or not depends in part on the sense they make of themselves, their community and their future, and in part on "the adaptive strategies they use to accept, modify, or resist the institutional identities made available to them" (Fraser, Davis & Singh, 1997, p. 222). In this sense, doing identity work involves a complex negotiation to maintain "one's overarching view or image of her or himself as a physical, social, spiritual and moral being" (Snow & Anderson, 1987, p. 1348). This involves struggling to sustain a working compromise between the meaning individuals attribute to themselves, and the social (or institutional) identities made available to them. In this sense, many young people are living multiple consciousness—living in one reality at home, in another reality with peers, and then negotiating another reality at school. Many young people negotiate their lives through consciously taking on different identities in these different contexts (Gilroy, 1993).

Below is an instance of one young person who spoke about having to be different at home. This "choice" was a "survival strategy", not a lifestyle choice. It was about avoiding fights and negotiating a place at home:

So I figured out a self-plan. As soon as I walk home through that door I change, I go to what they [my parents], want. (#028)

This kind of insightful comment suggests that certain young people have theories about the system not working well for them, and of having trouble "getting through".

Succeeding at school, for many students, meant having to suppress their own personal identities and act within a narrowly defined and institutionalized view of what it meant to be a "good" student. For many young people, going to school involved a particular and difficult type of identity work—negotiating/suppressing their own identities. But schools offer possibilities for future independence and also offer conceptual resources that can contribute to some identities. The struggle over identity at school, however, can become too difficult to negotiate for some. For the majority of the young people interviewed in this study—those who left school early—school had lost its potential to contribute to their life plans. Schooling was no longer seen as a viable place to do identity work.

Rather than blaming social structures or "blaming the victim", we have argued that early school leaving needs to be understood in terms of an "interactive trouble" that gets played out in the relationship between many young people and schools. What seems to be happening, as young people negotiate their lives in and around post-compulsory schooling, is a clash of frames of reference. The school operates with one frame of reference, or maybe more, but students bring their own frames of reference. Often schools assume a high degree of shared understanding of their frame of reference, an assumption that is often way off the mark. This misunderstanding is what we are calling "interactive trouble".

Freebody, Ludwig and Gunn (1994) describe interactive trouble as situations in which there are breakdowns in communication. Such breakdowns occur when there is a lack of understanding by students of the cues within teacher talk, a failure by teachers to hear cues in student talk, an application of overly subtle criteria by teachers and a possible mis-reading by either the teacher or the students about what is going on in the context of the classroom. Interactive trouble names what is going on in the relationships between students and teachers. Freebody, Ludwig and Gunn developed this idea of interactive trouble as a way of understanding what was going on in literacy learning for disadvantaged students. We want to borrow and enlarge the use of this category as a means of understanding what is happening for young people in the later years of secondary school. The idea of interactive trouble resonates strongly with cultural discontinuities theories. Cultural discontinuties or interactive trouble are expressed when the everyday experiences of any discourse community are either absent, muted or misrepresented in the school curriculum. If we think about culture in terms of class/gender/race then we have a complex constellation of possible misunderstandings. Interactive trouble comes about, in part, because of unexamined or implicit assumptions carried by the teacher about the lived experiences of students and their identities. It often leads to the alienation of those students whose class/gender/race is absent, muted or misrepresented in these assumptions.

What many of the informants in this study described as early school leaving looks very much like resistance to the discursive and pedagogical practices of post-compulsory schooling:

> [A]ll discursive practices are pedagogical, in the sense that they propose a theory of reality—a world in which those discourses are "true". For the proposed world of these discourses to be "obviously" *true*, people need to be "instructed" so as to find them true. The goal of the dominant pedagogical practices is to situate people at posts of intelligibility from which the reigning economic, political, and ideological social arrangements are deemed uncontestably true. This is another way of saying that we conceive "pedagogy" to be a means, in ideological practices, of constructing and maintaining [identities] that are necessary for reproducing existing social organizations. (Morton & Zavarzadeh, 1991, p. vii)

What young people experience in schools is a struggle over identity. They are creating a pastiche, often without much adult assistance: a view of themselves, their relationship to others and the world in general, and a view of a possible future. This identity, as we have argued early on in this chapter, is a becoming: it is always in process and is being constructed through young people's interactions with media culture, their families, their friends and their school.

Too often school is presented as always empowering to all young people. What the informants in this study reported, instead, was an alienating experience characterized by practices of selection, and exclusion and the maintenance of an academic or school identity that was foreign to them, impossible or even stupid. The stakes were high, of course. On the one hand there was a recognition that school had the potential to lead somewhere, to offer possibilities of making it in life. Exactly what the possibilities were, though, was very much moderated by how a young person was positioned in a matrix of class/gender/race power relations. And competing with the possibilities were the almost infinite work demands made on young people during the latter years of high school. What we expect young people to do in those two years seems almost inhumane. The expectations are ones that many young people cannot possibly fulfil because their lives can't accommodate to the demands, even if they want to. Because the dominant view, the view promoted by government policy, by the universities, by the community at large, supports such an unreal set of expectations for young people, many of them are left with no other option but to find a way out. And with the collapse of the youth labor market, this "pathway" is both treacherous and disrupted.

CHAPTER 5

THE MAKING OF YOUNG LIVES
WITH/AGAINST THE
SCHOOL CREDENTIAL

This chapter takes as background the increasing perplexity with which young people experience their lives in the post-compulsory years of schooling. That we should be surprised at all about this is of even greater concern, because it points to a policy incoherence that is located in a myopic view of what is occurring inside schools. Looker and Dwyer (1998) locate the issue in the problematic linear pathway trajectory for young people:

> This linear assumption may have had some justification up until the 1960s, prior to the collapse of the youth labour market . . . but its perpetuation within policy settings . . . is much more problematic. (p. 6)

It is remarkable that this kind of policy setting persists despite warnings against "tying the school qualification to the single pathway of university study" (Ministerial Review of Post-Compulsory Schooling, 1985, p. 41). According to Looker and Dwyer (1998) this persistence can be explained only because of the continued prevalence of "instrumentalist", narrowing views on how to respond to continuing high levels of youth unemployment. These views continue to have currency because they are given legitimacy by organizations like the OECD (Organization for Economic Co-operation and Development) that have a powerful influence in shaping government education policy in countries like Australia.

What is needed instead, Looker (1997) argues, is to start with the altogether different presumption that "young people experience and exercise a sense of agency" (p. 8) in the way they make decisions that affect their educational lives. For research this means starting out with "a set of questions that focus on how youth describe the influences on their educational decisions" (p. 8).

In this chapter we want to attempt, therefore, to move considerably beyond the debates about the "overlaps, zigzags and shuffles that are now far too common to be accounted for by notions of linearity" (Looker & Dwyer, 1998, p. 8), and to pay serious attention to how young people actually negotiate their realities, particularly around the issue of acquiring a school credential.

We want to advance some of the theoretical arguments rehearsed by Wyn and Dwyer (2000) around "new patterns of transition" and examine what these mean for polices and credentials based on "old linear categories". (p. 153) In doing this, we will need to tangle with some of the "multi-dimensionality" of how the young informants make decisions and choices, and how their voices speak back to the increasing incoherence and inadequacy of such linear policy explanations as those embodied in the credentialling process. To put it in its sharpest form, the struggle seems to be between a dominant policy thrust for a more skilled, efficient, effective and globally competitive economy, and young people themselves who are not completely convinced of the linear pathway notion, and who are more inclined to endorse multiple forms of transition.

While we want to focus particularly on how we saw the credentialling process operating on young people's lives, at the same time we want to show that this was far from a "deterministic" structural process. Our evidence suggests that young people were in fact making complex decisions that gave them feelings of "autonomy" and "agency" that were quite at variance with the way the credentialling process was designed or enacted.

Rudd and Evans (1998) capture this tension, between policy imperatives and the space young people are able to create for themselves, in terms of the "propulsion" analogy. The policy presumption is that young people will be propelled through the education system in pursuit of a credential, and as a consequence, emerge out the other end able to both enjoy the individual benefits of their education and contribute usefully to the economy. But the problem with this technological model is that it seriously underplays the part young people themselves actually play, as Rudd and Evans (1998) note:

> The almost deterministic macro-sociological perspective of "propulsion" into career trajectories and their associated occupational outcomes, with very little control over these processes on the part of young people themselves, involves a rather minimalist view of the input which young people can put into these processes. (p. 60)

The reality in our instance was that, like Rudd and Evans (1998), we found that young people "operate at a relatively optimistic and self-confident level and enjoy [a] degree of freedom" (p. 60).

It would be inaccurate, therefore, to regard the young people in our study as being in the vice-like grip of the their high school credential, even though it appeared to be founded on a set of outmoded, two-dimensional "old linear categories" (Wyn & Dwyer, 2000, p. 153) around study and transition into full time permanent work—which in reality amounted to a "foreclosed option". Credentialling was only one of a number of dominant features identified by Wyn and Dwyer (2000) as playing a part in the recent trends in youth pathways to adulthood. The dominant features include the following:

- overlaps between study and work;
- the decline of opportunities for the uncredentialled;
- the increasing deferment of career outcomes;
- an increase in part-time employment outcomes for graduates; and
- a growing mis-match between actual credentials and employment outcomes. (p. 151)

At the heart of the mis-match, as Wyn and Dwyer describe it, is the failure of human capital theory, upon which credentialling is based, to connect in any meaningful way with the unregulated, deregulated, unpredictable circumstances in which young people live their lives.

What we want to do, therefore, in this chapter is give "active voice", through the credentialling process, to this "increasing disparity between the rhetoric of youth and education policy, and their own experiences of its outcomes" (Wyn & Dwyer, 2000, p. 149) In other words, rather than pathologizing either the experience of schooling or the personalities of the young informants, we need to look at the way in which young people were giving expression to their lives and aspirations at the same time as they were living the incoherence of the credentialling process:

> It seems ironic that in the face of the uncertainty that characterizes the nature of life in the 1990s, education takes refuge in the artificial construction of highly abstracted measures of educational achievement . . . To put it another way, schools are marketing the production of a false certainty for young people and their parents through these ritualized educational mechanisms which appear increasingly out of touch with the ways in which young people are actually "using" education. (Wyn & Dwyer, 2000, p. 157)

There are four related questions we want to pursue here:

- how did credentialling construct young people in this study?
- how did young people contest and negotiate the credential?
- how and in what ways did the credential constitute an impediment?
- whose knowledge and skills were celebrated, and whose excluded?

How Did the Credential Construct Young People?

The popular view that school credentialling is a neutral, objective and value-free activity is a sham, and the voices of the young people in this study show how and why that is the case. Broadfoot (1996) indicates the nature of the deception and the way in which the process of silencing occurs. It is framed around "the idea of *competition* or selection [and the idea] that individuals should be allowed to compete on an equal basis to demonstrate their claim to competence" (p. 10). According to Broadbent, the rationale is as follows:

> The provision of competition which is apparently open and fair suggests that those who are not successful in achieving their aspirations will accept the rational selection criteria being applied, and, hence, their own failure. In so doing they acquiesce not only in their own defeat but in the legitimacy of the prevailing social order. To this extent the provision of an apparently fair competition controls the build-up of frustration and resentment amongst the least privileged. (p. 10)

It is a little more complex than that, but before we examine this in more detail, it is important that we say a little about how the credentialling process works.

One place in which to start this discussion is in the changing nature of the transition being experienced by young people in the pathway through school—because credentialling is a crucial part of that. As Rudd (1997) argues, what is happening is a dramatic shift away from "socialization theories" as an explanation, and towards theories of "resistance" and "accommodation":

> [W]hen employment prospects for young people were relatively favorable, sociological and educational writers tended to take the view that there was *one*, reasonably straightforward, transition from the school to the workplace

. . . The model of the young person used in frameworks based on socialization theory was nearly always passive and often manipulable. Society, via the family, the school and, later, the workplace, would *mould* the young, impressionable individual into appropriate roles . . . These roles were based upon conformity, social expectations and social control and there was no real possibility in this perspective of young people having a say in how their behaviour and attributes should be shaped or in what outcomes they desired. (p. 259)

The inadequacy of this line of explanation became clear in the early 1990s when "simple unitary models of transition" (Jones & Wallace, 1992, p. 10) were no longer defensible because it was increasingly clear that "young people were not compliant, conforming, passive beings" (Rudd, 1997, pp. 259–60)

If the credential at the end of secondary education had never worked in the past for those young people least likely to acquire it as a ticket for life, then in more recent times it was in serious danger of becoming totally obsolete.

Teese (2000) provides us with some insights into how academic success, and the credentialling process upon which it depends, actually works. It is on the basis of "social power":

The academic curriculum reaches through the cognitive architecture of the school subject . . . which it then shapes into a scholastic identity. (p. 5)

Put another way, there is a "curriculum hierarchy" operating in secondary schools, with a "monopoly access", and those without the requisite social capital are exported as "failures". It works something like this. Because the beneficiaries of secondary education have been defined historically, there is a process of harnessing advantage that is highly dependent upon student family background, accumulated cultural expertise, and a curriculum that is organized, structured and reported upon in terms of grading, a process that permits this hierarchical sorting and selection to continue. As Teese (2000) put it:

The social beneficiaries of secondary education protect their collective interests by assuring the capacity of the strongest individuals to compete among themselves. The requirement that talented students be free to demonstrate their strengths in open competition imposes on the curriculum a series of academic mechanisms—specialized subjects, a hierarchical order of options within subject areas, external examinations, homogenous, reliable assessment measures and finely scaled grading of results. (pp. 196–197)

What is occurring here is the building up of "scholastic advantage" in subjects like Mathematics, the physical sciences and languages, often inter-generationally, and in ways that are quite exclusive:

> The subjects in which the most intense competition occurs are distinguished not simply by their use in university selection, but by the scholastic and cultural attributes of the students who take them . . . Competition becomes progressively restricted in social terms, with the bar being raised high against groups new to upper secondary education. (Teese, 2000, p. 197)

Teese points to the "strong cognitive architecture" of these subjects which act to hold their exclusivity in place. He says they all have "systems of concepts in an ordered relationship that is pedagogically well defined" (p. 197):

> [T]heir pedagogical aim is to master this interior space of fundamental ideas, arguments, laws, principles and rules, or at least be proficient in the operations that depend upon them . . . Precocious and continuous success enables children to master the formal operations involved in intellectual abstraction . . . Success also builds self-confidence, openness to new challenges, risk taking and creativity, helping to establish school learning as a source of interest gratification and social identity. (p. 199)

What we have, then, in this inequality of access is a stratified curriculum in which "success . . . [is] concentrated in one [sector] and failure [is] . . . driven into the other" (p. 208). What goes on is a kind of academic herding as those who have the capacities and attributes to inhabit and exploit the most profitable "academic compounds" (p. 209) of the curriculum do so unashamedly, while the less able remainder are relegated to squalid and "unfortified sites" (p. 208), academically and physically. But of even greater concern, Tesse says, is that this is not a self-perpetuating system—such structural inequality "depends on continual political action" (p. 209).

The way the scam is perpetrated in this particular instance is that the credential is publicly proclaimed as doing one thing, while it is actively working to do something quite different. The assertion in the case of the informants in the study was that the credential was purportedly "within reach of all" with the not insignificant proviso, "given their serious application to the tasks" (Gilding, 1989, p. 30). The evidence from the 209 young people interviewed was that far from the credential being within their reach, in an unacceptably large number of instances, they considered the credential as being irrelevant to their current and future lives. In point of fact, the credential was working for less than 30 percent of the school population—the ones headed for university—and not at all for the remaining 70 percent. The credential seemed to bear down upon and have a profound effect on shaping school polices, making them hostile and the instrument by which exclusion operated.

This situation is further complicated by the way in which young people position themselves according to a classed view. Ball, Davies, David and Reay (2002) argue that university choice is a "classed concept". Drawing from Hutchings and Archer (2000), they argue that working-class students position themselves "outside" of university, "potentially able to take advantages of the benefits it can offer, but not as owners of it" (quoted in Hutchings & Archer 2000, p. 25).

If we are honest about what is going on here, to use Gillborn and Youndell's (2000) terminology, there is a fairly blatant process of "rationing education". In other words, there are forces actively constructing the way things will be. We want to turn to some of those forces now.

While there might be some limited appeal in trying to "privatize" a "public issue" (Fine, 1989) by blaming individuals who are educationally unsuccessful, in the end this is not a very sophisticated way of analyzing the issue—it is far more complex than that.

In the case of the cohort of young people we interviewed it was not insignificant that 84 percent of them came from economic backgrounds and circumstances that qualified them for government support (in the form of school cards), and this needs to feature in any attempt to analyze how the school credentialling process was working for them or not.

As Ball and Vincent (2001) and Reay (1998) argue, the analysis of class needs to feature much more prominently in the attempt to understand education and schooling, particularly in a context where the wider economic circumstances are revealing "an increasing middle-class policing of class boundaries " (Reay, 1998, p. 265). It is not that class relations have been unimportant in education in the past, but rather that "the changing labour market context and policy context have encouraged and made possible" (Ball & Vincent, 2001, p. 193) resort to strategies and tactics ensuring that positional advantage is not undermined. The reason social class is so relevant in the educational responses of the "fearful" middle classes, is that the:

contemporary educational perspectives and practices of the middle classes are shaped and informed by a set of fears and concerns about social and economic reproduction. (Ball & Vincent, 2001, p. 183)

Brown (1997) located the genesis of this fear when he wrote:

The declining faith in the ability of employing organizations to offer secure long-term employment, to meet their [employees'] expectations of career advancement, will lead to an increasing emphasis on academic and professional credentials as an insurance policy in the same way people insure themselves and their homes against adversity. (pp. 740–741)

The comments about the perceived irrelevance of the credential and the school curriculum and practices that flowed from it, by the young people we interviewed, really amounted to a way of expressing disdain and scorn for a class-based set of educational experiences that were both alien and alienating. Within this there is an element of "schooling the discouraged worker" (Raffe & Willms, 1989) as young people who would otherwise have left school at the minimum leaving age somewhat reluctantly decided to stay on. Dwyer (1994) describes this phenomenon as "forced retention", brought about by the "collapse of the youth labour market . . . and the foreclosing of alternatives outside school . . ." (p. 59). We heard many comments in this vein, which all amounted to the same thing:

[T]he main thing was basically just I didn't think I was going to get anywhere. (#002)

I'd just say it [school] wasn't right for me, and I wasn't learning anything. So I just thought I'd get educated somewhere else. (#104)

[No-one has suggested I need the credential] Not for the work what I want to do. I just wanted to work. I wanted to do things with my hands and that. (#142)

But now that I'm in the army I don't really care now because I don't need [the credential] now. (#190)

I don't need my [end of year 12] certificate to get into the course I want. They only require year 11 [at] a TAFE college on interior decorating. I don't need to have year 12. I need to pass an English exam and a Maths exam—and that's about it. (#035)

Sometimes these young informants were quite articulate as to what they saw as the mis-match between the curriculum and credential on offer, and what they needed to advance their lives. For example:

> I think that you need something under your belt other than school—and you've got to get that stuff under your belt early, and not necessarily stay to year 12. (#027)

> [T]hey should be teaching them more about life and about things that you actually really do need [to] know to be able to be successful in life as a person. Like—it's hard to explain what I mean—health lessons and stuff. They talk about health and your body, like Biology and everything—but they skip out all the like the important stuff, like about, you know, how to deal with different things that happen in your life and about, you know, what things are open to you to help you along. (#087)

What they wanted was something to equip them to deal with real-life experiences:

> There was nothing at school that taught me that one day the boss is going to say, "You're out of work. There's a letter—and the door." (#146)

For these young people, the delayed gratification that was necessary to complete their secondary education was simply not outweighed by what they saw as the advantages:

> I thought that if I could get into it now, and get my four years [apprenticeship] over, then that's like more of a thing. Get out there quickly, sort of thing. I didn't like school a lot, but I was doing all right; just passing. Just wasn't interested. . . I reckon it's just mainly for that—just that bit of paper just to say you've done it. It gives you a heaps big advantage over everyone else. Just that you've completed SACE [the credential]. Yeah. (#014)

How Did Young People Contest and Negotiate the Credential?

The fact that young people were taking responsibility, actively making deliberate decisions and choices about their lives that involved rejecting the credential as a valued entity, was indicative of a situation in which they were not passive victims.

Fine (1989) argues that institutions like schools operate to silence "the subversive, the trouble maker" (p. 168) and that silencing "masks asymmetric power relations" (p. 166). She says "silencing . . . constitutes the practices by which contradictory evidence, ideologies, and experiences find themselves buried, camouflaged, and discredited" (p. 154) and that this more intimately "shapes low-income, public schools than relatively privileged ones" (p. 154).

The antidote to silencing is "naming"; that is to say, pursuing a "critical conversation about social and economic arrangements, particularly about inequitable distributions of power and resources by which these students and their kin suffer disproportionately" (Fine, 1989, p. 157). Not naming is a particular form of silencing, and institutional survival depends on not naming social problems. Schools, therefore, work in ways that maintain the school "as a fortress for mobility" for some, with pedagogical and administrative techniques that "sooth students, and smooth social contradictions" (p. 159). For many students involved in this smoothing over, "the price of 'success' may [be] muting one's own voice" (p. 163). Teachers become caught up in distorted individualistic games like the one reported by Fine (1989). As one teacher said:

> These kids [trouble makers] need to be out. It's unfair to the rest. My job is like a pilot on a hijacked plane. My job is to throw the hijacker overboard. (Fine, p. 167)

Students respond to such silencing in different ways depending upon the school context—some by "mute isolation", others by fleeing before completion, and others by replacing schooling with creative alternatives in which their "strengths, competencies and voices [can] flourish on their own terms" (p. 168).

When students chose the last-mentioned alternative, they are in effect interrogating the conditions of their lives and making often quite complex decisions about schooling and its credentialling processes, and where these fit in their lives.

Contrary to the collectivist responses described by Willis (1977) in his *Learning to Labour*, the cultural responses to schooling, the labor market and the decisions about life provided by young people in the present study were much more akin to the increasing forms of individualization reported by Biggart and Furlong (1996), who noted an ambivalence and tension about the pursuit of qualifications:

> While some young people who drift through the upper secondary school manage to collect qualifications which may subsequently provide them with

advantages, many are torn between the conflicting pressures which arise within peer and family groups. (p. 265)

Evidence from our interviews went some way towards confirming what Du Bois-Reymond (1998) refers to as the negotiation by young people of life "projects" that show "a tendency towards synchronicity instead of linearity" (p. 63). Linearity in this context might be seen as the clear and persistent pursuit of a credential, and the cultural logic following from that. It was the efficacy of this model that the young people in this study were calling into question. The value of the credential to them was only one among many considerations they were struggling with, and it often ended up as a consideration of subsidiary importance.

Young people are, therefore, constantly developing life concepts with which to handle complexity and respond to the fluid situations surrounding them. Du Bois-Reymond (1998) draws on Beck's (1992) notions of "choice biographies" and "normal biographies" as a way of explaining the changes underway:

> "Choice biographies" are by no means purely based on freedom and own choice, but are determined by a paradox which is typical in modern life . . . [Young] people are forced to reflect on the available options and justify their decisions. They might also get frustrated because they realize that there are many options available; perhaps they do not feel ready to make a good choice, or perhaps they would like to make a choice but are prevented from doing so. It is the *tension between option/freedom and legitimation/coercion* which marks "choice biographies". (Du Bois-Reymond, 1998, p. 65, italics in original)

This is in contrast to "normal biography" with its "relatively traditional sequencing of status passages" (Du Bois-Reymond, 1998, p. 68). There is a giving away to alternatives that are more contingent, open and even reversible. Du Bois-Reymond gives an example:

> The life course of modern young people does not necessarily follow the model of finishing school, completing professional training, getting engaged to be married, and then beginning an active sex life; instead, a sex life may commence while at school, and then a trial marriage may take place rather than an engagement. (p. 66)

So too with schooling; the pathways and choices are far from straightforward. Often the axis of choice for the young people in this study hinged around the perceived relevance of schooling to the rest of their life, and by implication, the value they were prepared to attach to the possession of a credential. Sometimes that was a simple as looking for confirmation of choices already made:

> They didn't encourage me to leave—but they didn't encourage me to stay, sort of thing. Like, they just said, "It's your decision". (#002)

On occasions young people also received affirmation that the school's agenda was not consistent with their own:

> Just like real subtle ways, I think—well that's the way I saw it—just real subtle ways of getting me out. (#026)

As another person put it, it seemed the school had worked out what it wanted, and they didn't fit the model:

> Um. . . . if you haven't been putting in a top effort. They've been trying to get rid of all the trouble makers. Keep just a class of kids that want to go straight on to uni, straight on to TAFE. They've got it all organized. (#059)

Choices were sometimes precipitated by student failure to understand the incoherent way schools handled and failed to understand the nature of transition between schools:

> [I] left at the end of year 12, about two weeks before the actual end of, the official end of the school year. . . I left because, there is very, very bad lack of understanding, between the [rural] school up there, which was public also, and [City] High School. Near the end of year 12, they told me I basically had to repeat three or four subjects because they were different to what was up there. And that really got me angry so that's when I decided to look for something else outside of school, like a job. (#003)

A major point of continued and vexatious contention concerned the way schools were regarded as inflexible and unable to intersect with or accommodate to individual students. As one young person, perhaps rather too simplistically, put it:

> [Years 11 and 12 should be organized] on the individual student. Not have like, a set; like, you have to do this, you have to do that. I think it should be styled to the individual student. I mean not all students are gonna be good at Maths. Not all students are gonna be good at science, or Art . . . your education should be styled to you. OK, yes, you have to do a Maths, but make sure that the whole—all of the whole is, of your education—is styled to you.

So if your interest is in Maths, or in Science, or in Dance—but yes, it is based around that—but with the bits and pieces of everything else. But a big chunk of what you want to do. (#064)

The feeling of being pushed along a pathway to nowhere was the way it was often put:

I figured here's what I want to get into. If I continue to finish right through SACE I'm basically wasting a year because I don't really need all of my SACE to get the sort of job I want and have. (#033)

Um, . . . the main thing was basically just I didn't think I was going to get anywhere. (#002)

There was a thoughtfulness about the decisions they were taking that reflected a weighing of options, and not simply inertia:

Since I've started working especially, I've always thought that—that's after my first year of working—that you see a lot of people that have gone to uni, and haven't got jobs for up to two or three years after they finish a degree, and so I mean I suppose I know I'm pretty much always going to have a job, something to fall back on if I want to go further. (#030: second interview)

The drudgery, boredom and uninspiring nature of school featured prominently in the decision of some young people to jettison the pursuit of credentials in favor of alternatives:

sit down on your arse in front of your desk. . . writing that's all you ever did. . . it was always, you got to do this or else. (#198)

Just it's better here [at TAFE], 'cos you have a set time to do the work and nobody's pressuring you to do, and like, you do it in your own time, stuff like that. Where with school, they're always on your back. Do this, do it now. And it's one thing you're not gonna do is, you're not gonna say, oh well, I'll do it. I'll do it now. You're just gonna say, well if you're gonna talk to me like that, I'm not gonna do it at all. That's what I was like at school. (#068)

What schools had on offer was not what many young people wanted or valued, either. They were looking for connections they often couldn't find:

majority of stuff that you learn. . . you don't need it and you know you're learning all this stuff and it's like, OK, I'm learning this, OK, I have an understanding of it, but where am I going to use this in real life, you know, everyday life? (#002)

it's like I couldn't do theory, as much theory. When I was going to TAFE it was more practical and the same with working. Like, that is to me more practical than being at school. (#203)

There were also major questions about the value employers placed on the credential:

As long as you're the right person for the job—you've got the skills needed, you've got the experience and you can prove you're a worthy person for that job—I don't think they [employers] even bother [about the SACE]. (#171)

What many of these young people were saying effectively was that the curriculum they were studying was a version of what Ball (1993) has cryptically labelled "the curriculum of the dead" (p. 210)—which is shorthand for a curriculum which is oblivious to issues of class, race and gender, based upon "temporal disengagement", "suspicious of the popular and the immediate, and made up of echoes of past voices, the voices of a cultural and political elite" (p. 210).

How Did the Credential Constitute an Impediment to Completion?

The central argument is that the "game of truth" (Foucault, 1980) here is being played out around an ideology of allegedly fair competition that is neutral and based on meritocratic performance, and where success or failure is argued to be based on "academic ability and industry" (Broadfoot, 1996, p. 32). Following this logic, failure to succeed in acquiring the credential must be due to a lack of industry, the absence of innate ability, or personal disorganization—or a combination of these.

Listening to the young informants we get quite a different picture—one that sounds more like structural features within the credential that present themselves as barriers to completion. But this is not a simple and straightforward process—it is actually quite complex.

There can be no denying the profound and pervasive effect of the way the individualistic ethos is being constructed and used as a mechanism of social control in the case of this credential. It is played out in terms of the constructed legitimacy of the "individualist rationality of personal talent, personal responsibility, personal endeavour and personal reward" (Broadfoot, 1996, p. 79). Foucault's (1977) notion of "disciplinary power" is helpful here. The argument, as summarized by Sarup (1982), is that "disciplinary power co-exists with democratic forms" (p. 24). The credential is used as a form of social control through the twin principal themes identified by Foucault of "commodification of time and the use of surveillance as a form of social control" (Broadfoot, 1996, p. 97). The credential is given legitimacy by appearing to have democratic intent in the sense of success being dependent on personal effort; but at the same time standards are upheld by carefully ensuring admission only to those who demonstrate themselves as being worthy.

The construction of the problem in terms of "workload", "keeping pace", "meeting deadlines", and the perception that satisfying the requirements of the credential was all about being able to handle the "pressure" meant that "the student [was] controlled through a system of 'micropenalties'" (Broadfoot, 1996, p. 99), the effects of which were forms of "self-control" (p. 100) in meeting the requirements of the credential. In Foucault's terminology, there was both "hierarchical observation", in the sense of permanent and continuous surveillance, and "normalising judgement", in which individuals could be sorted, sifted and compared "as the basis for categorization" (Broadfoot, 1996, p. 97). The problem under these conditions was not, therefore, located in the credential itself or what it was doing, but in certain categories of students who had deficiencies that were all too demonstrable.

Students, in effect, policed themselves by deciding that they didn't have what it took, and therefore had no choice but to leave school.

Sometimes this self-policing took the form of students making the normalizing judgement that they were not as smart as their friends:

> if I'm seeing friends who I know are a lot smarter than any, whatever else, who are having a lot of troubles and, you know, really finding it hard to keep up and doing homework 'til all hours of the morning and all that sort of stuff, how was I going to keep up and even if I could keep up, how was I going to get good grades? (#002)

At other times students acknowledged finding it near impossible to handle the intensification of their workload in out of school hours as they moved into years 11 and 12. They often spoke of the seemingly exponential explosion in moving from year 10 and mentioned being forewarned of this by their friends:

> I don't know, if they make it [so] they don't give us so much work; like we just do one assignment after another, it just constantly becomes a hassle. If they slow down a bit there it would make it a lot easier, a lot easier to get

[the credential], less homework, I suppose. People have got their own jobs and stuff. Sometimes I don't go to work or anything just because I have to do homework. (#181)

The workload really, it's like . . . assignment's due, in year 11 they have to be on that day, in year 10, it doesn't really matter. I don't know it was just so different . . . don't know, you've got more time to do things in year 10; in year 11 you don't have any time to spare, there's lots and lots on. Unbelievable all the homework. It just got too much. Yeah, and it was like every subject would have homework that night and in year 10 you used to have like a set thing like this subject you could have this homework for tonight. But in year 11, it was like just every subject you have homework. It wasn't like a planned thing. Oh, I had people in older years that were always saying, have fun now in year 10 because otherwise in year 11, it's too hard. (#168)

This could involve not only the intensified volume of work, but also the type of work required:

there's this thing called WBLA [Writing Based Learning Assessment] . . . that you've gotta do, and it was a whole heap of things and you start stressing about it. Each stage that we'd get an assignment we'd have six at once, all different subjects and then as soon as you finish another one you get another one palmed on top of you . . . It's too much at once. (#194)

Some students saw this as an insurmountable obstacle:

There's this WBLA crap. Four pieces for writing! Like, just say you didn't get it in. You're doing heaps well in your subjects and everything. End of the year you fail because you didn't get four pieces of these pathetic pieces of writing in. And like, it can stuff up your whole bloody career and life, just for four stupid stories, assignments. (#114)

Rather than actively engaging them in a series of meaningful learning tasks, the abstraction and individualization of responsibility that came with the hidden agenda of having to prove that they were able to manage their time was simply too much for some students, and they capitulated:

That was the only thing we used to hear. Deadlines, objectives and SAs [Satisfactory Achievement] and RNMs [Requirement Not Met]. That's the only thing that I used to hear. And it didn't help much. It didn't help me at all. Like them pushing me made it worse. Um, the ones that really like stunted me was the ones like due in 13 weeks, they were huge and I would just come to it about two weeks before it was due. And I'd think, oh oh, I haven't started this yet and like, I'd just run round in a mad rush to try and get it finished and it wasn't what it could have been if I had've started on time. (#203)

We just got [assessment tasks] given to us one at a time. Yep. Bang, here's your assessment, I want it back next week, that's exactly right. [Deadlines], they're pretty well not negotiable. Unless you've got a serious reason for it, the deadline stands. (#171)

[Assignments] just pop up. Like you'd have one and then while you're in the middle of doing that one they'd say you've got another one due in two weeks time. And they'd pop up wherever. Yeah we didn't have dates or anything. Sometimes you'd get assignments where um you'd have to finish it but they wouldn't give you a finish date. And then when you'd have to finish it, they'd say, oh, it's due in two days and you might not have that extra bit you need. And then they were really inflexible about . . . If you needed just a bit of extra time they wouldn't. . . . (#194)

Beck (1999) refers to the situation described by these young people as the "transformation of institutions for *overcoming* problems into institutions for *causing* problems" (p. 51). Putting this another way, institutions "create and intensify the problematic situations to which they are supposed to respond" (p. 52). The contradiction according to Beck and Beck-Gernsheim (1995) is that individuals are both made responsible for their actions at the same time as they are made "dependent on conditions which completely elude [their] grasp" (p. 7). Bauman (2001) sees this as a device for shifting blame "away from the institutions and onto the inadequacy of the self" (p. 5). The effect is a defusing of anger towards the institution and a re-casting of it as forms of "self-censure and self-disparagement" (p. 5) that take the form of narratives of retribution against the self.

This is precisely what happened as the young people in this study took upon themselves a disproportionate share of the blame because they found themselves unable to meet the demanding schedule of the credential. They explained their difficulties in terms of the volume of work, finding it hard to keep up with the pace, trying to balance study with the demands of outside employment, and, by implication, a lack of intellectual ability to achieve what was required. In a sense they were able to "name" the impediments, but only in a way in which they "owned" the problem.

On occasion some young people were able to see through the meritocratic charade being presented to them and pinpoint with uncanny accuracy the way in which the institution of the credential was operating to select, sort, sift and categorize them:

Brains. Yeah the brainy ones stuck at it—and the dumb ones dropped out, I suppose. I'm not saying that I'm dumb. I mean, I know how to write my name; I know how to count to 10. Brainy—the ones that can, um, really do the work, I suppose. It's the ones that have to put 100 percent in to please their parents. Mainly the snobs, the richies, the ones that had good primary school bring[ing] up, [at] like, a strict school. And stuff like that. (#197)

Whose Knowledge and Skills Were Celebrated, and Whose Excluded?

At this point it is appropriate to return to Wyn and Dwyer's (2000) arguments about the breakdown of the traditional notion of a linear "transition" that has dominated educational policy thinking and research around youth for more than two decades. In the case of this study, the pathway is from primary school, to high school, to university—but as Wyn and Dwyer (2000) argue, in recent times:

> there has been an increasing lack of "fit" between these ideas of development and a reality of events in which traditional life events become less certain markers. (p. 148)

The uncertainty and unpredictability of contemporary times means that young people have a heightened sense of agency and a much greater range of options and choices:

> The emphasis is on what young people themselves are making of their lives—not what policy makers assume they are (or should be) doing. (p. 147)

The mis-match became particularly evident in this study, where the credential could be seen as predicated around a set of aspirations that the young people interviewed said were out of kilter with their own. The way they gave expression to this was in terms of the credential being on offer "for uni"—meaning that they saw it as a ticket for university entrance, and they were not among the 30 percent of students headed down that particular track.

In effect what these young people were saying was that the "normal biography" (Rudd & Evans, 1998), based upon a sequenced educational pathway to university, might be "normal" for policy makers, for school systems, and even for teachers at the level of the school—but for them, it was more problematic. They seemed to be endorsing Rudd and Evans' (1998) "choice biography", regarding their lives as involving a great deal of negotiation rather than foreclosure on one option only—that of securing a credential for university.

> I'm leaving because [this school] is aimed at university. Um, if you don't do pure Maths, like, hardest English, hardest Science, then it's just not worth going here. (#187)

> A lot of the teachers there were hoping that most people were doing year 12 and going to uni and whatever, so you didn't hear much about other stuff. (#030)

> I think the teachers that have gone to school, gone all the way through school, gone to uni, teachers' college, whatever, and then they've gone straight back to a school, and they've never seen outside of that. . . . (#030)

> I was at high school and I was in year 11—did about the first term of it—and I just felt it wasn't based on the trade that I wanted to be in. I felt that it was for children going on to further education, on to university and that, and so my father set me up a job as an apprentice with a boiler maker. (#058)

> Dad was . . . I was supposed to be the son that's going to uni . . . It's always put in me since I was, you know, year 7. Going to uni, you're gonna get a degree. So . . . He says, you know, there was no pressure, but there always has been. He'll deny it till this day . . . So . . . And then half way through I decided I didn't want to do that. (#001)

> I knew I didn't want to go to university, and I knew I just wanted to work. It's all I ever wanted to do was go into the office and work and make my way up through the company. Um, so I really didn't like the subjects cause I had to choose out of certain areas . . . and that made it really hard . . . I had to choose it anyway, then I wouldn't be happy doing it. If they changed—like, I know they wouldn't change it—but I think by making the subjects compulsory, like all the areas compulsory, makes it really hard, cause then you think "I don't want to go to school". (#006)

> If you don't want to go to uni at all, then none of the subjects there are really relevant to what you want to do afterwards, except maybe a computing subject, or something. (#014)

> So, people finish school, they get their year 12, they go to university and this whole time they've been learning how to get a career and how to be successful in their life. But they haven't, you know, learnt any stuff. And then they think about what sort of person they are, and they don't have a clue. (#087)

I decided to leave because I really didn't feel I was accomplishing anything. I had no intention of going to university so—at that time—so I didn't really feel year 12 would benefit me in any way. I'd go to class. It would be an effort to do work because I really didn't have my head in it. So I didn't really feel comfortable at school. My teachers—I didn't like many of my teachers because they were giving me all this stuff I found to be sort of a waste of time. So, they were considered bad people. So, I didn't see it as benefit on my behalf. (#018)

This understanding by young people that there is widespread support for the school credential being for university but "not for people like me" (Looker, 1997, p. 8) is a particularly good illustration of the fact that early school leavers were able to make choices for themselves "which enable them to maintain their aspirations despite the persistence of structural influences on their lives" (Wyn & Dwyer, 1999, p. 5).

It is increasingly clear from the comments of these young people that there is some support for Furlong and Cartmel's (1997) notion of the "epistemological fallacy" (p. 2), the idea that:

[A]lthough social structures, such as class, continue to shape life chances, these structures tend to become increasingly obscure as collectivist traditions weaken and individualist values intensify. (p. 2)

Put another way, there is a "growing disjuncture between objective and subjective dimensions of life. People's life chances remain highly structured at the same time as they increasingly seek solutions on an individual, rather than a collectivist basis" (Furlong & Cartmel, 1997, p. 4).

While most of the young people interviewed in this study certainly did not discount the structuring effect of their class location and the effect it had in terms of the playing field being tilted against them, they were also sufficiently pragmatic to realize that they had little real alternative but to negotiate the realities of their lives at a practical level—and that meant thinking through what were often complex and messy alternatives.

But at the same time, as Wyn and Dwyer (1999) note, "it is important not to romanticize the choices they are trying to make" (p. 18), because to do that would be "to obscure the real effects of social divisions on people's lives . . . [and] gloss over questions of power and disadvantage" (p. 18). Nevertheless our interactive study has attempted to take up Looker and Dwyer's (1998) challenge of asking young people how and why they made the complex choices they did. In the end, it seemed that young people were not prepared to have their identities totally "ignored or subordinated within the dominant discourse or policy framework" (Wyn & Dwyer, 1999, p. 19).

CHAPTER 6

SCHOOL CULTURE AND STUDENT VOICES IN EARLY SCHOOL LEAVING

The aim of this chapter is to examine the notion of school culture as it is constructed by young people as they struggle to make sense of their decisions around early school leaving.

We want to pursue this aim against the broader backdrop of the whole project of early school leaving. There are some important themes emerging here that connect back to themes from earlier chapters, especially around alienation, transition to the labor market, and the operation of the credential. In a sense, then, this chapter draws on all of the preceding chapters and reflects on the study as a whole.

The chapter commences with an explanation of the contested nature of school culture. It also considers what this might mean from the vantage point of constructions put on school culture by young people, as we interpreted what they told us.

We then present a reading of the cultural geography of schools and the impact of this on the decision making of young people around leaving school. While none of the possibilities we present were found to exist in a pure form, they nevertheless represent pronounced tendencies that emerged out of the voices of young people as they positioned themselves among other key actors in living out their school lives. We make the important point that these understandings are necessarily partial, but they were profoundly real to the young people who experienced them.

In the final section, on school culture and youth identity formation, we revisit themes from earlier parts of this book and advance interpretations of how the notion of youth intersects with school culture. We provide indications that youth voices on school culture amount to scripts of what schooling is about, and show that this is often at variance with official interpretations and aspirations.

School Culture as an Orienting Theory

Anecdotally, we know that the cultural politics of the school has a powerful effect on how young people make sense of schooling, on the spaces that exist for them to be listened to, and on how they work to shape schools as places. As an "orienting theory" (Carspecken & Apple, 1992), "school culture" has been largely neglected in the literature and debates about early school leaving.

In this chapter we are searching further for interferences with regard to school completion that are located in the ways schools think about themselves and the ways they position themselves when they sort and sift students through curriculum and pedagogical practices. Since some students are clearly provided with more appropriate pathways than others, schools are not innocent in this process. Some schools operate in ways that include students; others appear indifferent; and some have postures that are inhospitable and exclusionary. Each of these possibilities represent school practices, policies and actions that are qualitatively different, and we want to address some of those differences here.

None of this is to suggest, of course, that within a particular school the culture is fixed or monochromatic; it may be more accurate to speak of cultures and, even then, to see them as highly contested notions, rather than unitary or always agreed upon. Various groups within the school struggle to fashion the culture of the school so as to make their view the "norm" for what "school" is. There is a dominant culture in schools and we spell out what that looks like in more detail as this chapter unfolds.

It is important at the outset to make it clear what we are attempting here and what lies outside our scope. In many respects, this is a pivotal chapter because of the way in which it provides a crucial linkage between student voices and early school leaving, and how both relate positively or negatively to the culture of the school. Having said this, we must note that school culture is one of the most elusive, difficult and complex notions in the educational literature. Positioning schools in relation to what effectively amounts to the failure of large numbers of students is likely to be a hotly debated issue. In a sense we did not observe school culture as such, but rather have inferred it and constructed it out of what young people told us.

Because there is considerable scope for misunderstanding on an issue like school culture, we want to try and make our position on this complicated issue as clear as possible.

School cultures are produced through a complex interweaving of socio-cultural, political, economic and organizational factors, together with a constellation of class/race/gender factors. School cultures are not the prerogative or domain of any one group—teachers, students, parents, politicians, the business community or policy makers. Rather, school cultures emerge out of and are continually constructed and re-constructed through the ongoing struggles between and among each of these groups as they vie to have their particular view of schooling represented. School culture, therefore, looks quite different depending upon whose vantage point is taken in any attempt to represent it. Because of the dynamic and shifting quality of school culture, any attempt to capture or represent it is necessarily a fraught process because of what is included and excluded.

At this point we offer an important caveat. The vantage point we take in representing school culture here is partial and unapologetically that of the young informants in the study, for that, after all, was the avenue through which we chose to collect our data. Written from this standpoint, school cultures can sometimes appear to be somewhat uncompromising because of the way students, especially those who have been "failed" by the institution of schooling, appear to construct school cultures as bearing down on them. Simultaneously, students are pushing to resist the more oppressive aspects of those cultures through their own counter-narratives.

There is a decided risk here, but one we believe is worth taking: that in providing a reading of school culture from a student or young person's vantage point, some aspects will be under-represented while others will be over-represented. Voiced research of the kind we are dealing with here clearly has within it the capacity to portray school culture antagonistically, which is not to say that it is necessarily blind to those elements which are virtuous in schooling. But we do need to be aware that student accounts, around their decisions to leave school, of something as controversial as school culture, can appear to be somewhat harsh and uncompromising on schools and teachers.

One way around this problem is to see teachers, at least in part, as often being the public face of the much wider educational system and its reforms. This is often the way students see teachers. To that extent, teachers are bound to be seen as relayers or carriers of the wider globalization agenda of which educational policies are a part, far more than they possibly deserve. Sometimes it can be even more complex than this. If we take the case of the credential, discussed in the previous chapter, the intentions of teachers and an attempted egalitarian educational policy manoeuvre appear to have been overridden by wider considerations of competitive individualism driven by the global market agenda.

Our point is not to position teachers as entities to be blamed for early school leaving, but rather to portray them as being implicated, in part, by the wider ways in which schools are increasingly being constructed by wider sets of forces in contemporary times. To put this another way, teachers are not so much to be blamed for students who leave school prematurely, but rather to be seen as co-constructors, along with students, parents and the wider community, of the way schools are. Seen in this way, the role of teachers in students' representation of school culture needs to be viewed as a part of students' active construction of aspects of that culture.

None of this is intended as an excuse, of course, for poor teaching, and in this chapter we have not held back on presenting it as it was presented to us through the voices of the young people we interviewed.

We want, therefore, to focus discussion of school culture on our fundamental concern here: how does the culture of the school contribute to or interfere with early school leaving? Put another way, how are the practices of the school constructed, organized or scripted so as to include or exclude some categories of students? We turn to these matters now.

The following portrait begins to give us a sense of how the aspirations of at least one young person were in tension with the way she was required to live her life in school. It seemed, at least from her vantage point, that there was not much attempt on the part of the school to understand her aspirations and her need for independence. Neither was there much evidence of the school trying to explain the options and flexibility available to her. This rests in marked contrast to the maturity of outlook which such young people are forced by circumstance to display.

Portrait #093
Sophie: Independence

Ever since I was 10 years old I wanted to be a lawyer. Like when I was young, I wanted to be a cop like my brother, because that's what he wanted to be. And that's what he is now. I just love the law, like Legal Studies just comes so natural to me, it was really easy to learn. I've always tried to cut things fairly, make sure everything was equal. And I have a lot of debates with my brother. I had three older brothers and they were always bullying me. Then starting high school I was starting to become a lot stronger, sort of find my own identity.

In year 12 a lot of my close friends had either dropped out or were coming only now and then, and they were doing other subjects so we hardly got to see each other. And it was a really small group, and everybody was just emotional and bitchy. Even the guys were just as bitchy. It was really pathetic. You know you'd be talking to a person and then they'd talk behind your back. They just didn't value friendship. Like the groups were separated in the younger years. Then in year 12 they all combined like some from each group. And the main group were the more popular ones who are called "sluts" and "bitches". You know, they'd go around to parties, sleep with anyone, keep scores.

My two best friends dropped out I think because they couldn't stand the people at school. That's the combination of students and teachers. Half the teachers, they refuse to let you grow up. You are treated like a child so you just act like a child, like muck around and don't do any homework. Like I didn't do any homework from year 8 to year 11.

And then they took away our year 12 center. We could only sit there during our frees and study. We protested, but it didn't help. They still treated us like year 8s. I think it was the new principal. The school went downhill after he came. It got worse and worse. You even caught the teachers saying something about it. Nothing went smoothly any more. Like it's just impossible to find a teacher through lunch or recess. And the people in reception, even in the library, are real bitches. Like if you go in there, they tell you off. No matter the problem, they'll tell you off for not wearing a uniform or for having sneakers on. Then they brought in a new uniform with a logo everyone has to wear. Like year 12s have to buy a uniform for three terms.

But the real problem in year 12 was the Maths. Like I couldn't do Art and Maths 2. They were in the same room even. Even in year 11 I'd been begging the deputy principal to change it. So I had to go to an adult campus one night a week for three hours to do it. And I just couldn't do it. I needed a lot of help because Maths 2 is a really hard subject. And my Maths 1 teacher at school wasn't any help. He had lots of other jobs around the school, and he wasn't much of a teacher anyway. I mean I'd go see him at lunch time, and he'd have students that would show up about uniform or something, and I'd have to come back. So basically I'd sit outside his office all lunchtime which is forty minutes, and get five minutes worth. And then he'd make mistakes all the way through the problem. And if I asked help from other teachers they'd refer me back to him. So I was just pretty much depressed, and I was unhappy going to school, and I was just skipping more and more days.

I went to see the principal. He couldn't understand it because I didn't really want to tell him what was going on. I suppose that was because it was basically the Maths 1 teacher. I couldn't stand him. And when I told the principal that and he told me not to say anything bad about teachers. And when I told him about the Maths 2 problem it was like, "I told you so". Like in year 11 the Maths teacher was really emphasizing that Maths 2 is really difficult, and he was really putting me down saying, "I don't think you have the brains to do a subject like that", which really annoys me. I wanted to shove it in his face. I guess, when I did drop out, I gave him the satisfaction of being right.

And it was all for nothing. I found out this year that I only had to do 4 PES [Publicly Examined Subject] subjects and 1 SAS [School Assessed Subject]. So there were other options. Anyway I half dropped out half way through last year and had some time off. I was going to continue some subjects but had an injury at work and stuffed up my knee. Went back to work too soon and strained it even more. So had to drop out completely.

Now I'm at this adult center. The people there are a lot more mature and the teachers are there to help you. It was a big class but now there are only about 12 people. It's a much better environment. None of that bitchiness.

I'm doing very well in Legal Studies, Art and English. In Politics I didn't do well. I did it with a friend and we'd just sit in class and chat. Didn't listen too much. He's not very clear anyway. After we failed we made a pact we'd listen more. And I do Business Maths and it's really easy.

I'm really well organized. Mondays I have two afternoon lessons so I just sleep in and go to school. Tuesday is a full day. Wednesday I only have the last lesson, so I have a little bit of sleep in, I either get up and so some homework, or go to school and do it. Thursday is a full day and then Friday I only have a morning subject, so most of the time I just stay at school, work in the library and do homework. That's when I get most of my research done. The librarians are really willing to help you, whereas I never found that at my school.

I'm OK for money. I work at Fastfoodtown and live off the money I earn and save like $30 a week. Then I save my youth allowance except for $100 a fortnight my mum takes out for board. I knew the only way I'd save was if money gets directly taken out of my pay. It was like the homework. I looked at my situation and just got organized. Like I started to get behind, and the teacher said reward yourself when you do something good. So I do a couple of hours homework and I'm a chocoholic, so I have it stashed in the top drawer, all ready. And it works.

The whole situation and environment is better now. It's like being independent and not being treated like a child. Like most kids at school are there because they just don't know what else to do. And the school just doesn't allow that independence. But now I'm here for myself.

This portrait reveals the lost opportunities, the confused understandings on the part of the school, and a young person who has embarked on a new stage in her life in which she is having a set of alternative experiences, which for her highlight even more clearly what it was that was so unsatisfactory and lacking in the experience of schooling.

Through portraits of the kind obtained from Sophie, we can begin to obtain some indication of the general shape of the school culture, at least as she experienced it.

Complex portraits of students' lives around the time of deciding to leave school, therefore, have the potential to provide a fascinating window into the kind of school culture that shaped these decisions. Put another way, fragments of the accounts of early school leaving, revealed by the young people we talked to, enabled us to construct a cultural geography of school. We turn to that now.

Cultural Geography of the School around Early School Leaving

At this point in our account it is important that we try and provide a way of making sense of the kinds of school cultures that are reflected through the voices, experiences and aspirations of the students, as we heard them.

There were a multitude of ways of representing the conflicting and confounding cultures that seemed to be embedded in the narrative accounts of the lives and experiences of the young people we interviewed. But, keeping in mind the caveats about school culture that we noted at the beginning of this chapter, three quite distinct archetypes of school culture seemed to keep presenting themselves to us throughout the project, as demonstrated in Table 6.1 although they did not actually exist in a pure form:

- the "Aggressive" School
- the "Passive" School
- the "Active" School

Fragments of each of these cultures could exist simultaneously in any one school, faculty or class; that's what made the interpretation interesting as well as complex. For example, in some instances related to us by young people, it was clear that the school could change dramatically from one archetype to another.

It also became increasingly clear that while these archetypes represented useful categories, they also needed to be treated with some caution—there was certainly some fluidity within and around them. In other words, rather than appearing definitive, they appeared more as a constellation of tendencies or trajectories, including school climate; inclusion/exclusion; curriculum construction; students' lives/emotions; behavior management; flexibility; pedagogy; and pastoral care. There were many

TABLE 6.1 The Cultural Geography of the School around Early School Leaving

Dimension	"Aggressive"	"Passive"	"Active"
School climate	• fear, silence, resentment • some students speak back • treated like children	• benign attitudes • habitual actions • struggling to come to grips with changing nature of youth • some students' lives are written over • culture of dependence • treated indifferently	• student voice • agency and culture of independence
Inclusion/ exclusion	• "trouble makers" removed • students" own sense of justice not welcome	• "ease out" those who don't fit	• those who traditionally fit the least are the most welcome!
Curriculum construction	• hierarchically determined • streaming undermines self-image	• an intention to deal with the relevance to students' lives, but this is not translated into the curriculum	• negotiable around student interests and lives • connected to students' lives • respect for popular culture • a socially critical dimension
Students' lives/ emotions	• no space for dealing with student emotions	• acknowledges student emotions, but deals with them immaturely	• students are listened to • atmosphere of trust

more dimensions we could have pursued, but for reasons of manageability we restricted ourselves to these.

These archetypes of school cultures derive from of our wider reading of the stories told to us by the young informants in the study and, to that extent, they emerge from the totality of the 209 interviews, and not just the instances we cite below. In the section that follows we will offer some examples of our informants' voices, informed as well as shaped by the evolving typology of school culture.

An observation that repeatedly presented itself to us throughout the interviews was that, generally speaking, the average high school tended to be characterized by dimensions that position it more towards the *aggressive/passive* categories, while the re-entry high school showed features po-

TABLE 6.1 *continued*

Dimension	"Aggressive"	"Passive"	"Active"
Behaviour management	• policies and guidelines adhered to and enforced • compliance demanded	• attempt to operate equitably, but the school gets caught in the contradiction of wanting to operate differently, but not having the underlying philosophy, self-fulfilling prophecy	• behavior management generally regarded as a curriculum issue • student participation in setting the framework
Flexibility	• compliance demanded	• gestures towards flexibility, but interpreted by students as inconsistency and lack of understanding	• respectful of student commitments and need for flexible timetabling
Pedagogy	• condescending way of treating students • over-reacting and paranoid teachers	• uninteresting classroom practice and boring curriculum • lots of misteaching (mis)management of learning processes	• enlarges cultural map for many students • students treated like adults • negotiation of content and assessment
Pastoral care	• no way of acknowledging harassment, sexism, racism, classism	• pastoral care but of a deficit kind • inadequate time, skill, structure and commitment	• actively connects with student lives • acknowledges importance of re-entry and alternatives

sitioning it more towards the *active* category. Again, while certainly not applicable in all instances, this interpretation held up remarkably well across a large number of the interviews.

Another way of interpreting this tendency is in terms of the way power is was seen to be exercised in the various school cultures: in the *aggressive* case, it was largely within the administrative structure and apparatus of the school; in the *passive* case, in large measure, both teachers and students appeared to be relatively powerless (although, by default, there was is some deference towards traditional notions of power over students, but this occurred largely unthinkingly) and, in the *active* instance, there was a pronounced attempt in the direction of negotiating power with students.

We turn now to examine each of these in a little more detail, before we show something of how these archetypes of school culture arose out of the student voices.

The Aggressive School

The aggressive school, as described to us through the accounts of the young people in this study, distinguished itself by its emphasis on a climate of fear, silence and resentment, usually embodied in a "strong discipline policy". To put this another way, there was a pervasive absence of a sense of trust and respect for young lives. There was a tendency for the school to frame success in terms of the middle-class norm of students pursuing an academic curriculum leading to university entrance. Students who opposed this norm were labeled "trouble makers". Often these were the same students who had a robust sense of justice, or who were prepared to take a stand against the school policies or practices that they regarded as disrespectful of them. This action invariably brought them into sharp conflict with the school authority structure. And it was often students from low socio-economic backgrounds who failed to meet expectations, because their cultural capital was not adequately recognized.

These were also schools that affirmed the "Competitive Academic Curriculum" (Connell, 1998), often through processes of streaming [ability grouping] that served to further undermine the self-images of particular students. Behavior management policies and guidelines were enforced in ways that left little doubt as to the consequences of failing to comply. The outcome was often self-fulfilling. This was especially notable in relation to the possession of prohibited substances. Students who got caught up in the implementation of these policies were left in no doubt about their authoritarian nature. Such a culture was not especially good, either, at dealing with student emotions; indeed, young people were treated in ways that preferred to assume that all such matters reside outside the classroom door.

This kind of school did not have caring ways of dealing with students who "speak back", and teaching approaches were often enacted by teachers who appeared condescending, over-reacting and even paranoid. Issues of harassment, sexism, racism and classism were rampant in these schools, with an attitude of indifference on the part of the school, which regarded such matters as not being the purview of the school.

The Passive School

The passive school presents itself as much less strident, almost benign in its attitudes. Underneath, however, it is struggling, with limited success, to come to grips with the rapidly changing nature of contemporary youth. Symptomatic of this is an overall failure to understand the importance of curriculum relevance to the lives of students. Looked at superficially, it could be said that these schools appear to be "nice places" on the surface. But the odds of succeeding with large numbers of students are strongly stacked against these schools.

Students find these schools have curriculum, teaching and assessment practices that are boring and uninteresting, and what passes as teaching often more accurately amounts to "misteaching" because of the multitude of lost opportunities for connecting in any real way with young people's lives. Many of the students in these schools describe themselves as having been "eased out" by a school trying to present itself as acting in their best interests, while denying that it still bears allegiance to an elitist curriculum that is satisfying only for the minority of students heading for university. In other words, these schools still teach to the competitive academic curriculum.

A further illustration of this is an incapacity to operate flexibly, for to do this would require a more mature and sophisticated understanding of young people, which is absent. There are pastoral care programs in these schools, but they handle problems as if they were caused by the deficiencies of individual students, rather than by systemic or social pathologies. Thus there is an acknowledgement that students have emotional needs, but these are dealt with immaturely by the school.

The overall lack of understanding of young people's lives ultimately produces a culture of dependence in these schools for those who remain there. At worst, there is a process of writing over the lives and experiences of students who fit the self-fulfilling prophecy of appearing to be ill-suited to the competitive academic curriculum. At the same time, there is also a fundamental failure to challenge the glossed over or covert manipulative power relations that clearly exist in such schools.

The Active School

While it was not one of our deliberate objectives to uncover schools that were working well for students, it was inevitable that conversations with young people would reveal some elements of such schools, and although not quite clearly articulated (because of the fortuitous way it was acquired), we have come up with a tentative archetype of the culture of an active school—active in the sense of reaching out to the lives of young people, and not merely responding to them.

An active school presents itself as stepping out and working reciprocally with students to create an environment in which, regardless of background, all students have the opportunity to succeed. Student voice is the pre-eminent theme in such schools, and it is used to construct a rigorous curriculum and pedagogy around the lives and experiences students bring with them. Rather than deny popular culture, or relegate it to the realm of "outside of school", these schools see this as an important factor around which curriculum is actively constructed.

Instances of student behavior management are regarded not so much as requiring discipline, but as instances of students disengaging with a curriculum that is inappropriate or propagated in unthinking ways. The curriculum in these schools includes both content and process and, as a consequence, necessarily engages with power relations between teachers and students. The negotiable nature of the curriculum and pedagogy flows over into the flexible way these schools approach timetabling and the scheduling of student commitments, which is important in the way it acknowledges different forms, styles and paces of learning, as well as the complex lives students lead beyond the school.

There is a mutually respectful tone within such a school that winds up producing agency and independence in the way students own their learning and the curriculum. Above all, students are listened to respectfully, and there are high levels of mutual trust between students and teachers. The consequence is that students in this kind of school have enormously rich experiences, and the school is also enriched; the cultural map is enlarged for both school and students.

As we have indicated, the mapping of school culture outlined above emerges from the project as a whole, but it is important to obtain at least some glimpses of the young informants' voices in this construction. These are at best partial, in the limited way we are able to present them here, and we do not try to be exhaustive. Rather, we want to give a taste of what the young people were saying, and how this led us to the conceptualization of school cultures that emerged.

Voices of Students on School Culture

In moving to show the connection, it might be helpful to think more concretely of how students' voices represent some of the more specific factors contributing to the larger picture of schools as we have just presented them.

Students who left school before the end of the post-compulsory years, wanted their voices to be heard in multiple areas. They wanted the following:

- to be treated with respect and be encouraged to develop workable relationships with teachers and other students;
- to have a say in matters like school uniform;
- to be listened to and have their wishes/interests taken into account in choice of subjects and scheduling of assignments;
- to be treated fairly and consistently in respect of discipline policies;
- to have issues of harassment by teachers and students taken seriously; and
- to be empathetically listened to and heard regarding the complexity and individuality of their lives.

During our discussions with young people, a number of themes concerning school culture emerged as contributing to early school leaving. These enabled us to construct Table 6.1. These included the following:

- making students responsible for their failure;
- handling "kids" who "speak back";
- falling through the cracks;
- uninspiring pedagogy; and
- being treated like children.

While each of these themes gave us a clearer fix on the features of the aggressive and passive schools, the students were also remarkably articulate about the antithesis. For this they were able to draw sometimes from their high school experiences, but more often the revealing information came from post-school experiences, like TAFE, re-entry high schools and even the workplace.

Making Students Responsible for Their Failure

In school cultures that had an aggressive or passive predisposition, there was a strong tendency towards a culture that regarded issues in individualistic ways—behavior, attendance and progress were invariably construed as the individual responsibility of the student. Deviations invariably invoked retribution that resulted in predictable consequences, which were always couched officially in terms of failure on the part of the student to take personal responsibility. This frequently came across in ways that made it appear as "common sense", in which the (in)actions on the part of the student justifiably provoked the response by the school.

This is typical of the responses students gave:

> nothing's followed up . . . it's your problem . . . you are in a big place, and basically nobody gives a stuff. (#001)

After absences, for whatever reason, students in the aggressive and passive schools spoke of the difficulties of re-connecting to school:

> the teachers would be supportive, but you have to catch up. (#009)

Students frequently mentioned the piling-up syndrome:

> once you let yourself get behind . . . it all just piles up. (#009)

"Freaking out" was also another common expression of this phenomenon:

> The first couple of weeks seemed alright then I started getting more and more projects to do . . . I freaked out . . . rushing stuff, wouldn't get it in on time, not getting the marks I should have. (#014)

On the other hand, the orientation of the active school culture was also apparent on those occasions when teachers construed student responsibility less harshly:

> some teachers were really good . . . if you wanted help they'd counsel you . . . encourage you. (#014)

But in those school cultures that were not favorably predisposed, often it was those young people who most needed assistance who saw themselves as being left floundering:

the people who were good at school, and who wanted to go to uni—they could do it without much trouble, so they didn't need much encouragement from the other teachers 'cos they already knew how to do it without getting help. They could just sit down and do it. (#013)

In these cases, students were being given the message that success or failure were individual attributes, and that non-compliance with the peda-gogical regime of the school would have its own predictable conse-quences. Education, under this regime, was seen to be largely a one-way relationship—the school and the teacher had a diminished responsibility towards students.

As we saw in chapter 4, schools are important sites of youth socio-cultural identity, and what we have seen above is an instance of "interac-tive trouble"—young people are being prevented from fully participating in the school curriculum because of a failure to understand the cues of the teacher, while teachers are seemingly unable to make sense of student talk. It is a classic case of mis-communication at the cultural level of the rela-tionship between the lifeworlds of students and teachers.

Handling "Kids" Who "Speak Back"

In the case of the aggressive school, demands for student commitment are pretty much undivided—the school is insistent on adherence to the ver-sion of school culture it constructs. In Coser's (1974) sense such institu-tions are "greedy". The passive school is similarly characterized, although this is more by default than by deliberate and forceful intent. The active school, on the other hand, regards student commitment as much more partial or provisional, and, while such a school may not have totally re-solved the issue, it is at least better positioned to negotiate the intersecting affiliations students bring with them.

If a school promulgates an atmosphere of fear, silence and resentment, then it is going to be harsh in its treatment of the students it feels are "de-viant" and who are prepared to argue with it or interrogate it. This feature can give such a school an adversarial and inflexible appearance, and this is one of the defining hallmarks of the aggressive school culture:

it's basically "them and us", like there's teachers and there's students and a lot of the friction in the discipline that they try to give us. Like, our school didn't use to have a school uniform and they brought in a school uniform, well that was that. And they just took it way out of proportion . . . it's just little things that teachers do . . . Like I mean, you're allowed to wear plain blue tracksuit pants but if they've got a little Nike or something, you get detention. (#027)

The distance between the school's and the students' constructions of culture in the aggressive school were sometimes expressed in terms of the school having "nothing to do with your life" (#062). Or, as another student put it: "I think it is better to leave school . . . school's over now . . . You can get on with the real stuff or whatever" (#059). The interviewer put it back to the student in terms of "You mean, getting on with real life? School is the place *before* the real stuff?" (#059).

The aggressive school this was said to be "cracking down on you", "monitoring your effort", "having you carded" (referring to the official behavior management strategy of school warnings prior to suspension/ exclusion/expulsion). The interactive sequence went something like this:

> you are getting looked at . . . you get a bit more angry and a bit more angry with heaps going on . . . At first they just talk to you about it. And then . . . all the teachers start talking with each other, then you start getting put on, like a card, where you have to get it signed if you put in a good enough effort in each lesson, and stuff like that. (#059)

What this student was saying was that in the aggressive school, you are under scrutiny, under surveillance, and if you don't shape up, then you are on the ropes and out of the game! One student saw surveillance as so extreme that the school even went to the length of installing a smoke detector in the girls' toilet to stop the students smoking (#008). At another school, the students believed the school uniform had been introduced so that "if you wandered off, they can spot you" (#027). What was seen to be missing in this case, according to the student, was any opportunity to be part of the decision-making process: "They might have had good reasons, but they didn't discuss them with the students first. It was basically, we've got a school uniform coming in and you've got to wear it" (#027).

Some students saw this as a convenient way of "easing them out" for the aggressive school:

> Oh, they didn't care. No. No, they didn't really care at all. It was just like, oh well, you know. There's one case off our hands sort of thing, you know. They really didn't care. (#016)

Capturing the same sentiment in another way, one student said:

Instead of making it fun to be there, they made it hard for me. In the end I just told them to stick it because they made it too hard for me to be in their system . . . They wanted me out of school when I was 15. (#028)

Students were also able to quickly see the price of compliance:

It was a very nice neat school if one got A's in everything and particularly if it was in Maths, Chemistry, Biology, Physics. (#007)

Students often portrayed the aggressive school as a place where "teachers are continually yelling this and that at us" (#087). The way the process was experienced was captured by this student:

you don't learn anything if you don't make mistakes . . . And I would probably have been a pretty difficult student . . . I'd have a teacher, you know, yelling this and that at me. I'd like, well you know, say, you can't . . . I've never been able to just shut up and not say what I think . . . I know I have to accept rules but I'm no good at accepting the ones that I find unreasonable. (#087)

Another student put it in terms of speaking up for herself:

I'm the kind of person that says what I feel and the teachers don't like that. (#023)

This was not an uncommon experience. It would seem that teachers sometimes feel uncomfortable with students reversing the power relationships, as the following incident illustrates:

We can come in like, with makeup on our face or something. She'll pass you like, a tub of moisturising cream or something, and she'll say go and get that crap off your face. And I'll say no. If you're allowed to wear it, I'm allowed to wear it, you take it off. (#005)

In some schools that fitted the aggressive typology this sounded like a systematic process of purging, of "cracking down" as the students called it:

they wanted people that had a goal to go somewhere . . . If you hadn't been putting in a top effort, they would be trying to get rid of all the trouble makers. Just keep a class of kids that want to go straight on to uni or TAFE. They've got it all organized. (#059)

It is important that we comment briefly on the preponderance of negative comments by students so far, which ought not to be surprising since the project was, after all, pursuing interferences to young people completing schooling. It would have been most surprising indeed if it had been otherwise. What was surprising, however, was the large number of positive stories (often interspersed with the negative ones), based around post-school experiences, of how young people would have liked school to have been for them.

The following portrait neatly illustrates the way in which a young person was able to articulate the contrasting features that positioned two high schools as being aggressive, and another (an adult campus) active. In the end, the lack of structure in the adult campus seemed to work against this young person, just as too much structure inhibited him. Yet there is still an optimistic tone about the educative experience in the adult campus that was lacking in high schools he attended.

Portrait #039
Robert: Getting Fitted

There was just this one teacher that I really didn't get along with and I ended up getting suspended for getting a record sheet. It's like if you muck around in class, they write out a sheet and hand it to the deputy principal. I can't remember what it was, but it was really minor, and then they suspended me for five days for it. I was already at school for that day so they suspended me for one day internally and four days externally. Then I was out at recess and this teacher that I just didn't get along with, she came out and she said "You shouldn't be out here with everyone else", and I said, "every other time I've been suspended I've come out here", and she goes, "You shouldn't be here", and I said "Crap", and she didn't like that too much and she goes, "Alright then, come up to the front office with me," and I said "I'm not going anywhere". She goes, "Alright then, you're disobeying an order, I reckon we can get you another five days for that", and I sort of told her where to go and I didn't call her a very nice name and I walked off and that was my last day there. I wouldn't say it's her fault I left, but she sure contributed.

So I just walked off and got a job for six months car detailing [preparing cars for sale]. I had three or four weeks break first and went down to the school a couple of times. Basically they were trying to get me to leave. The last day I went back, I had to take this leaver's form and get all the teachers to sign it. When I went to her she goes, "Oh I knew this day was coming". And she goes, "I'll probably see you in a dole queue in a few years". And I didn't appreciate that much, so I told her to get fucked again. I didn't like high school. You don't get any respect from the teachers. And the school always sides with the teacher.

People talk about counsellors, but I don't think it's about someone in to help. I think it's the teachers who have to change, so it doesn't matter if you've got someone to talk to. I mean it would help you at the time if you're angry or whatever, but it's still going to happen the next time you get into the classroom. Like in year 8 I was having problems with this teacher and he called me a dickhead, and I said "You can't say that to me", and he said "I can do whatever I want". And I went to the counsellor and he said to me "Oh, you must have done something wrong", and I said, "Well, that's not the point, he shouldn't be saying that sort of stuff to me". And he said to me, "We'll speak to him about it". But nothing happened.

I remember a meeting I had with the deputy principal when he suspended me, and he said, "You're going to end up like all of your friends. We're going to get rid of you all". Most of the people in my year level, we were just one big group of trouble makers. So I said, "So you are getting rid of everyone, are you?" and he said, "Yeah, and you're going to be the next one". And a lot of them did get suspended and expelled or just left. So I reckon they purposefully planned to get rid of all the trouble makers before year 12. It's fair enough in some way for the people who actually do want to learn. It's pretty annoying for them. But I don't know, they just don't have control over the classes any more, and I reckon it's because they don't respect anyone.

The senior group at this high school was sort of weird because there wasn't really a group, like everyone was friends with everyone. Everyone sort of looked after each other. Once this guy went to hit a girl because she was really hitting him back, and all the guys we sort of chased him around for a while and he ended up leaving the school. He was scared. So no one got out of control. Everyone was in the group, so nobody had to be told twice, if you know what I mean.

The other high school I went to was different. I hated that school from when I started in year 8. I only managed to stay there for two and a half years because I was in the top group. You were in the group basically because of the sort of clothes you wore and the way you spoke and that. There was lots of bitchiness. Bitchy boys and extreme bitchy girls. Lots of he said this and she said that. If you looked at someone wrong in the group they'd start a rumor to get you back for it. And if you'd done something that was sort of uncool then that meant war. Like I was in that group but I used to go and speak with all the other groups as well. And a few times someone would have a fight with someone in another group and then I'd go and speak to someone in that group and there'd be trouble. Like they'd say, we don't want you to hang around with us anymore. So yeah, there used to be fights within that group all the time. Real fights. Fists and stuff. But no weapons. All that group stuff, you know, and being young, that's what it's all about these days. Some people reckon I've got high self esteem. Funnily enough I think it's from being in the right group most of the time. I mean like having a lot of friends and having that sort of confidence, walking around school and stuff.

But with teachers you can't win at high school. Like if you're having an argument with the teacher about something. Because I was pretty good at arguing and I used to love winning. So I'd say something and just stump the teacher and he'd say like, "Get out, you're disrupting the class". I mean, with some teachers we might joke about it. But people who are doing a power trip on you, you play the power game, so you look for mistakes, and they can't handle it.

It gets personal. I remember when I used to muck around in most of my classes and if we'd get assignments, like I was never usually expected to hand anything in, but when I did hand in stuff, I knew it was good work, because I know what's good and that. And other kids, they got like 18 out of 20 or something, and I'd think, mine's much better than this, and it's a lot more informative and stuff, and I'd still get failed for it.

Anyhow, I worked for six months, and I just kept thinking I don't want to be doing this for the rest of my life and how am I going to get a job in the future. When I was younger I wanted to be a lawyer and that's sort of faded away now, so I'm either going to do Psychology or if I get the marks I'd really like to do Medicine.

So I came back to this adult campus and got pretty good marks last semester. It's more relaxed here. Like when the teachers treat you with respect you actually want to learn. At school when the teachers say shut up and get out and stuff, it just makes you want to disrupt the class more. When they react I used to think, "We've got her", and then see how many times I can get told off. But here everyone is quiet. This school is different because of the older people. In the group we sort of hang around with older people and twenty year olds, and everyone is on the same level.

A lot of younger kids as well would abuse the system. I think they'd take advantage of the freedom that we get. Like today in Australian Studies I hadn't finished my brochure and I was stressing it because it's the first work I haven't finished on time and I said to him, "I haven't finished, can I finish it in another lesson?" And he said, "You can have until Tuesday if you want". In High School it would be like, "Hand it in now. And stay in until lunch".

12 Months Later

I left about three months ago. It just sort of wasn't working out. I got a bit slack and got too far behind in my work. So I got a job at a car yard and quit there on Monday. Like most of the time I'm pretty placid and laid back, but my boss, he just pushed me too far and I told him where to shove it and walked off. So yeah, now I'm doing telemarketing.

I did half a year of year 11 at high school, and then last year I finished year 11 at the adult campus. It was really easy and I was just flying through all my subjects. I suppose I got used to being slack. Then once year 12 came they just started piling on the work and I started getting behind and finally it was just too much, because there was no chance of me catching up. There's no authority there between teachers and students, which is good. But I suppose it would have helped if they'd pushed me along a bit.

The age range was good in year 11, but in year 12 it got out of hand because the older people were just like they thought they were teaching the class as well, and there were a few people that just knew everything about everything and that was really distracting. One teacher in particular only talked to a few people, and there was a general feeling around that the younger people are not so important.

The career goals? They weren't real. It was more like a dream and the more I went on at school the less of a reality it became. And I always sort of wanted to do sales. That's linked into the Psychology a bit. And yeah, I'd still prefer to go to the uni and that, but I do enjoy talking to people and selling stuff. My dreams now? I've got a job. I've got a car. I've got a relationship. I just want to be happy and try not to worry about anything.

Falling through the Cracks

In schools where the active culture predominated, there was a more flexible approach to negotiating the curriculum and pedagogy with students: "They'd help you work out a plan so you wouldn't fall behind" (#014). By way of contrast, in the passive schools, the culture was much less proactive: "they didn't encourage me to leave, but they didn't encourage me to stay. They said, it's your decision" (#014). For another student, "I think they called me to return some books or something. I just went in and did that" (#004). Another typical response indicative of the indifference of the passive school was this:

> they just said, if I wanted to leave, to get a note from my parents . . . and get the teachers to sign the leave form. (#062)

Young people who had experienced life in aggressive and passive school cultures, and who had also been in active schools, were able to show how the teachers in the latter were genuinely grappling with issues in ways that amounted to trying to understand the lives of young people.

Flexibility is a major axis around which school culture rotates. It can take multiple forms. For example, scheduling dates for assignments, so that students are clear about their commitments and can feasibly plan and handle both heavy school commitments and the rest of their complex lives outside of school, seems to be a logical thing to do. However, in many cases we heard evidence to the contrary, often amounting to refusal (especially in aggressive schools) by teachers to listen to students' perspectives:

> They'd say, "No way, you've had plenty of time like, four weeks, three weeks, and you've left it to the last minute, that's not acceptable". . . . Why can't they just give it all to you at the start . . . so you know what you're looking at in advance? (#009)

Another flexibility issue often centered around the issue of how the school handled the possession of prohibited substances, and the school cultures differed remarkably in their response to this.

A typical story, usually from the aggressive or passive school, would center around a student, who had previously not had a history of suspension, being suspended for the possession of marijuana. Suspension brought with it immediate difficulties for students maintaining their studies, but it also had tangible consequences upon the later return to school:

> some [teachers] were really nice and understanding and did their best to try and help me catch up, but one teacher held it [my suspension] against me and called me a "waste of space" and [said] that [I was] "taking up space in the classroom". (#015)

The same student indicated that, while the school offered her counselling, re-entry meetings, and behavior plans, in the end the teachers just didn't "have the same respect for me . . . I didn't really feel part of the school when I came back" (#015). What this student was saying was that the school culture of playing it by the rules was setting her up for almost certain failure because of the way the suspension process worked and the stigmatization that accompanied it:

> [They laid] lots of emphasis on working out your time management [but] missing out on five weeks stuffed that up . . . messed all my time lines and this stuffed up the rest of the year. (#015)

There seemed to be a fairly well-defined slippery slope for students who engaged in "running amuck". One student reported having been "suspended nine times . . . [but not having been] into smoking or drugs . . . just misbehaving, not doing schoolwork . . . in trouble for talking in class" (#070). He went on to say that he "used to muck around in class, get sent to the focus room, and when you got four focus rooms, you got suspended" (#070). It is not hard to imagine how infractions like this could easily escalate, especially where students "couldn't see the point to [what they were learning]" or who "found some subjects boring" (#059)—a frequent response from students who had made the decision to leave school early.

Yet even here, questions about consistency of treatment were never far away, especially around the issue of uniforms—a constant source of interactive trouble, as discussed in chapter 4. Indeed, so salient was the issue of school uniforms that young people raised this in 65 of the 209 interviews, generally in relation to the way it impacted on their sense of identity. There seemed to be different forms of treatment for different students, depending upon their previous "record of being in trouble":

> There was one incident where I got in trouble for my uniform . . . I had to go home, change my uniform and then go back to school and there were two other students in the class who basically had the same thing wrong with their uniform, but they didn't get into trouble for it and I thought that was unfair. I could never understand why I'd get in trouble for something but yet someone else would have the same thing wrong and they wouldn't get in trouble for it, then you'd try and say something to the teacher, "how come I'm getting in trouble and that person's not" and they turn around and say you're back-chatting. (#025)

> Different rules for different students, different rules from different teachers. You get a strict teacher, you tend [to] get into a lot of trouble; you get an easier teacher, you get away with murder, but, yeah, I think so. If you're one of these goodie goodies getting straight A's and stuff you can pretty much wear what you want as far as [you can?] go, but if you're one of these people that tries to stand out a bit and you wear the slightest thing wrong, that's it, "Go to the detention", "Go and get expelled" and stuff. (#027)

From another student, there was a very clear picture of how the detention process worked:

> I got suspended and put on probation. I used to give the teachers a hard time. I was horrible, a complete bitch. I know a lot about the school's detention system. I was always getting it for minor things, like not wearing the correct uniform. You'd be told to pick up papers or go to the detention room. I used to love going to the time-out room because I could go to sleep there. It was often packed. Sometimes it was so full I had to sit outside in the corridor. You get pushed out of class into the time-out room for even looking sideways. (#083)

It is hard not to be left with the impression of a suspension, exclusion and expulsion policy that was putting these young people on a fast track out of the school.

Uninspiring Pedagogy

The young people in this study were quite articulate about what uninspiring (and inspiring) teaching looked like. In the words of one:

> Like Maths. Instead of teaching the class he would actually like write up on the board and as he was writing he would be talking to the board and teaching the board and we'd be sitting there like, yeah okay, and you'll go through it and the next thing you know you're lost and . . . too late, he keeps going so you just, oh. So that's when you start talking to your friends because he's actually like talking to the board. He's got no eye contact with you so you just lose him and then if you don't understand a problem you put your hand up and he can't see you so he just keeps going so you miss that part, miss that part, you just give up. You just don't worry about it. . . .

> I got along with some of the other male teachers like the PE [Physical Education] teachers, because they actually, they actually talked to you and teach you the skills instead of like throwing it up on the board and it's so boring . . . Teachers treat you like you're a child and like I wasn't allowed to do nothing and like if you're late they would spew at you and it was just full of pressure . . . Like when it comes down to it, I can do the work but I need someone to go through it with me, like a couple of times, to understand it. The teacher will say it on the board but I need extra help to go through with it, to understand it. (#083)

What students like this and many others were saying to us is that schools in the aggressive category produce "dickhead behavior" (#151). They were conveying the idea that certain school cultures set up antagonistic sets of relationships between teachers and students, the culmination of which provided no other apparent option than to leave school—even when this meant giving up on getting school credentials. It seems that for many students school is not worth the aggravation, a notion that Aggleton (1987) describes in terms of "symbolic challenges which are directed against fundamental power relations that act pervasively throughout society" (p. 124). It seems that the way in which the context of the school itself is structured, especially the enactment of pedagogic relationships, can be highly predisposed to pushing targeted students out:

> Yeah, because the teachers, they don't explain it to you properly. They explain bits and pieces, then if you put your hand up and ask, they say, weren't you listening? You should listen . . . It's like, well, I was listening [Interviewer: but you don't get a chance to say], but I still don't understand. So,

they go off their head, and you say, what a waste of time, why am I here, and you just get up and walk out, go home, and forget all about school. (#153)

As another said:

Teachers just chilled me out . . . and the school just gave up on me in the end . . . When I left, they just said "see you later". (#152)

On the other hand, good teaching (embodied in an active culture) was represented by teachers:

who would talk to us . . . not just write on the board, or say, do this page and finish it by the end of the lesson . . . I need things explained again . . . with Maths, do an example for me, then I understand. When I don't understand, I just leave it behind. (#151)

Students often made comparisons with primary school. The following was a typical comment:

at primary [elementary] school they're still focusing on having a primary class, and being interactive with the lesson. Whereas at high school, it's written and set; it's a set method to follow, you have to learn certain things. (#028)

In an example of the active school culture, a young person related the flexibility introduced by a substitute [replacement] teacher:

We had this substitute teacher who came in one day. And we were sitting at the back and were talking and that, and we just turned around and he said, "This is ridiculous. Let's get outside and actually do sport instead of sitting in here learning about sport". It's like, yeah. Wicked, let's go. We had a great day, and everyone felt a lot more respected, because we went out for most of the day and actually did physical fitness out in the sunshine. Then we came in and did Maths and stuff in the afternoon. You know it was still balanced, but we weren't sitting there staring at little black and white lines for nine hours a day, you know. (#028)

It seemed that young people who self-deprecatingly described themselves as "having an attitude problem" or "getting shitty really easily" could not handle the fact that the school treated them like children.

Most people hate getting told what to do, and that's what teachers do, just tell you . . . [I would] just snap and couldn't handle being told what to do. (#151)

This particular student claimed that during her frequent absences from school she:

> still did [my] work, even if I wasn't at school . . . I preferred to work at home . . . I get distracted very easily at school. I had more chance when I worked by myself. (#151)

In a case of sexual harassment, in which the student spoke of the teacher "feeling down my back . . . [while saying] 'you're a good student, aren't you?'" the student spoke of "slamming" (physically hitting) the teacher, out of frustration with the teacher's demeanor and her inappropriate pedagogy:

> I kind of slammed her a couple of times during the year to get her to wake up to herself, to actually teach a lesson properly before everyone else in the class ends up walking out. (#163)

This was from a student who described herself on one occasion as scoring 98 per cent in English, the third highest mark in all of the year 11 English classes. By the end of the year she had accumulated 30 detentions, none of which she ever went to. This student was articulate about what constituted good teaching:

> [Teachers who were] easy to talk to . . . [would] actually sit down with me and help me with my work . . . talk to you politely when you are not in lessons . . . someone you can turn to when you're struggling with your work. (#163)

As one student said, her decision to leave school was connected to her difficulty in Mathematics, along with a school and teacher culture she described as "falling apart"; "nothing ever goes smoothly, and it's impossible to find a teacher during recess or lunch". (#093)

Being Treated like a Child

We repeatedly heard of young people who had become caught up in the rules and structures of the school, especially in the case of the aggressive school. Again, invoking the voice of the young person in the portrait, they resented being treated like children. In the words of another student, "in high school you are treated like you are a child, so you act like a child" (#093). Students held strong views about how they were treated, in terms of both the theory and the practice. Sometimes, as in the case of one student, these views were tempered by the retrospective realization that "I didn't actually realize the work I had to do. I've looked into it more, and now I've realized I've got all this homework to do"(#093). For this student, and others like her, there was the added complication of an inherent contradiction of being told that, as a year 12 student, she had the freedom "to do whatever you want", although in reality the school wanted to "keep a firmer clasp on you, treating you like you are a year 8, saying, you can't do this, do that" (#093):

> Like most kids at school are there because they just don't know what else to do. And the school just doesn't allow that independence. (#093)

On the other hand, when they had the opportunity to experience the active school (usually an adult re-entry high school) responding in a helpful and constructive way to the issue of how to treat them respectfully, students were in no doubt:

> Um, [the school] was really good just because they treat you like adults. If you don't want to go, you don't have to, basically, as long as you keep handing your work in on time. (#004)

Students who had left school and gone into employment also had a good basis upon which to make judgements, and often their current workplaces (exploitative as they were) provided a good reflective opportunity, as the following student revealed:

> I was only 6 months off of being 18 but I'm treated so different at like my workplace. I'm treated like an adult whereas they treat you like little primary kids and I couldn't go back to that environment where they like tell you what to do and treat you like little tiny kids. I just couldn't do it now. I just, I mean, I'd go to an adult re-entry but I wouldn't go back to like a normal, you know, high school. (#016)

For this student the situation was summed up in these words: "I don't think they actually focus on the students' needs enough. They don't understand" (#016). Another shrugged her shoulders philosophically and said: "It's just school" (#015).

Being treated as a child and without respect was a point made repeatedly and powerfully by the young people in the study. The following portrait furthers this point.

Portrait #104
Hannah: Being Respectful

I just decided to leave because the teachers were always picking on me and all the kids were naughty and always talking and I wasn't learning anything. I wanted to go to TAFE but I was only 14. So I left and started going to Second Story [youth drop in center] and talking to a counsellor there. She was so understanding and helped me through everything, like situations with my mum and family as well.

Like in term 2 I just wagged it for the whole term. My mum suspected but the school never rang up or anything, even though my home group teacher told them. I met this girl who was 15 and she was looking for a job because she didn't want to go to school any more. I said, "I don't want to go to school today", and she goes, "Neither do I", and it just started off like that. So every day we'd meet and like put on another top so it looked like we didn't go to school. And then we'd go anywhere, like to friends' houses, shopping, wherever we could. But it got boring, because we were running out of places to go. So I told my mum and left officially at the beginning of term 3.

At school I guess year 8 was all right. Like I passed all my subjects. But it started to get worse towards the end of that year, because I didn't have very good teachers or anything. Year 9 was much worse. Like in the Maths lesson everyone would just back-chat the teacher and chucking papers and rubbers and swinging back in the chairs and running around. Most classes were like that. I'm good at Maths. In primary school I was always entered in the Maths competition and got distinctions, like 100 percent. But here I wasn't learning anything. No one liked Science. I hated it. It just didn't interest me. It was boring. The German teacher was a bit of a dog and nobody is nice to her and they're all mucking around. Well she used to make us stand up when we went in and then she'd sit down first and then we'd sit down. But really it was the way she talked to us and everything. She talked to us like we were really low. Everyone seemed to be good in Home Ec and Tech Studies. They had fun in it so no one was really noisy in those classes.

English was alright with one teacher because he was really nice, but then he left to go to some other school and we got this really stupid teacher. That was like closer to when I started to wag and I didn't like him because he always used to blame everything on me. Like if me and my group of people were talking he'd always blame it on me and say it was my fault and I was making them talk and make me sit next to him for a whole lesson or whatever. Then he started to make me sit out in front all the time whether I talked or not. I didn't like sitting so close to him, like at the same table. At first I used to speak to him nicely but then I started to talk to him rudely. I think he hated me. And then I just stopped going to English. Then they said I could be in his class but if I start to get aggravated with him because he's saying stuff to me, I can just walk out and go to the counsellor.

So first term in year 9 I really hated it, and I didn't want to go, but I thought I just can't quit now because I wouldn't be able to get a job or anything. But then I just got totally sick of it and I just didn't want to go anymore. The school wasn't doing anything for me, like they weren't helping me with my work. I'm pretty good at my work and all of it was really easy, and so most of the time I'd just sit there doing nothing because I had no work to do because I'd done it, and they wouldn't give me or help me do more. But really it wasn't the work, it was the teachers. They didn't treat students like anything. They were just the biggest and we had to look up to them. And if you tried to correct them they'd just turn it against you and blame it on you. So they were always right and we were always wrong. Like if I went up and said, "Oh I can't seem to get it all down because everyone is too noisy, and my concentration wasn't there", they'd say, "That's no excuse, you should get it done". Now I think that maybe that was partly a hearing problem.

I tried to speak to the counsellors about it. I told them I didn't seem to be learning anything and I couldn't concentrate with the noise, and I was so bored. But they didn't seem to be doing anything. My favorite teacher this year was my drama teacher and she was my home group teacher. I used to talk to her and everything and she knew I was having problems, and I didn't like the school. She just really listened and she'd go, "Well, what do you think is best?" And she'd say, "You know you're the only one who can make the decision."

I'm not 15 till next July, so I can't get into TAFE till then. For now I go to work experience on Tuesdays and Wednesdays, and to a girls' personal development group on Mondays and Fridays. There's only six people in the class and you really talk about what you want to do, and goals, and they help you in your careers and everything. It's been for 15 weeks and really built up my confidence.

I want to be a beautician or a hairdresser, or even have my own shop, like a fashion shop, or something. That's what I've always wanted to do. It's the sort of job where really you just need to be a friendly and a nice type of person. I don't think I'll have a problem getting a job. My next door neighbor's sister's a hairdresser and I always watch her and she teaches me how to do some hairstyles and everything, and I like doing that. And I did a week's work experience at a small hairdresser's and I learnt a lot and got a good report. And because of all the support I've been getting, I'm enrolled in the beauticians' course in July at TAFE. And I've already got enough money for the first two semesters, that's $3000, from my grandma's inheritance.

I don't think leaving school at year 9 will be a problem later on. If people ask me I'll just say school wasn't right for me and I wasn't learning anything, so I just thought I'd get educated somewhere else. My older sister, she says I'm stupid leaving school. But my oldest brother, he's 27, and I just talked to him and he said it was up to me, and if I wanted to leave I would just have to work hard for what I wanted to do. My mum's supportive so long as I carry on with some education. My older brothers, they just like taught me to be more mature maybe than other kids my age, because people would respect me more and I'd get more in life.

I don't really keep in contact with friends from school because a lot of them were bitches. Like somebody was away, they'd bitch about them, like criticize the way they dress, or act, or just spread stupid rumors. Then when they came back then they'd be friends. I can do better than that. The friend I used to wag with lives in xxx now. She still comes down and rings and we write every week to each other. We're close friends and she ended up living with me for a month, and we got really, really close.

I don't think I'll ever go back to school. I mean, the teachers have got to learn to treat you fairly. If you're going to respect them, they've got to respect you. Like they need to speak to you properly like you're not dirt or trash. They need to let you give your opinions on the work. They need to understand you and not turn their back on you.

At this point we want to draw together the material that has emerged from the various voices of students, to illustrate the nature of the boundaries around each archetypal school culture, and the contradictions and complexities that come with them.

Cultural Geography and the Crossing of School Boundaries

When school authorities talk generally of their students, they usually have a particular group of students in mind: it is this group that determines the contextual boundary of the school's geography; it is this group that the school's discourse about students implicitly refers to; it is this group that gives meaning to how the school thinks of its purposes and its activities; and at this deep level, it is this positioning that makes other groups invisible or superfluous.

Such a view can help us make more cohesive sense of the characteristics of the three school "types" described earlier.

The boundary around the aggressive school, with its traditional and elite characteristics, is provided by the concept of the competitively successful and structurally docile student. Examinations provide quality control over the meaning of "successful". The client of such schools is the would-be academically successful student (and/or parent), with their accompanying characteristics of conformity and conservatism (embodied, for example, in the school uniform). Because the structure and ideology of the school is focused on the successful student, the morality of the school (that which conserves its structure) and the ethics of the school (that which conserves its ideology) are compatible. Such schools are thus stable and strong, and are quite easily able to justify the exclusion of both non-conforming and non-successful students without compromising the integrity of the school. The boundary conditions make such students, and others like them in the community, structurally redundant, and thus personally invisible. Such schools will defend the current assessment and credentialling processes because both are compatible with their positioning, and thus with their interests. Credentialling, thus conceived, is about maintaining the status quo.

The boundary around the active school, with its inclusive and responsive characteristics, is provided by the concept of educating as well as possible all the young people who attend the school. The ideology of such schools stresses attributes such as diversity and flexibility, and attention is given to the complexities of individual students. The traditional school structures (both power structures and physical classroom and timetabling structures) have to be modified. All unsuccessful students, whatever the reasons, are seen as losses. They remain visible as failures of the school. As with the aggressive school, such schools contain few internal contradictions between ideology and structure, and so they have considerable stability. However, they exist in a larger societal context where strident and powerful voices extol the virtues of elite schools, even as they mouth platitudes about inclusivity and equality. So the aggressive school maintains the much stronger gravitational pull, and the inclusive school must expend considerable energy to hold its social position generally, as well as in relation to specifics such as the supposed flexibility in the credential, and non-punitive behavior management practices.

Most schools exist precariously balanced between aggressive and active types, and so the passive school is passive because it is confused, and is trying to balance contradictory forces which are only dimly perceived. Structurally, passive schools remain tied to tradition, and thus to the social relations and physical containments of the aggressive schools. Ideologically, they accept most of the principles of inclusion and equality that pervade the credentialling and system rhetoric. The most vocal parent groups and some teachers pull them towards the classic vision of the elite school, a direction supported by the cold political reality of economic rationalism, with its fundamental assumptions of individual merit, competition and the money-happiness equation. Their professionalism and the inclusive values and compassion of some of their teachers and students move them towards the ideal of a much more responsive, humane and equitable system. They make the best choices they can in the light of their confusion.

School Culture and Youth Identity Formation

We are trying here to give a picture of how schools position themselves and the way they talk about and relate to youth. This is of crucial importance in the context of the complex reading of youth identity formation and the construction of school culture. In this context, the notion of youth should not be seen as an abstract, categorical, undifferentiated or homogenized concept.

One way to proceed is to continue to regard the concept of youth in terms of "identities [that] are shifting and fragmented, multiple and contradictory, displaced and positioned . . . across the various discourses which historically and currently constitute their lives in and out of school" (Kenway, Willis, Blackmore, & Rennie, 1994, p. 192). The view of Kenway, Willis, Blackmore, and Rennie (1994) frames youth "as complex human beings and as active readers of their cultures . . . " (p. 192), capable of embracing complexity and ambiguity (which are often created by schools and other social institutions).

The intersection of young people's identity formation with the entity we call school can best be understood from Bourdieu's (1991, p. 384) notion of schools as "spaces of regulated confrontation"—that is to say, from a position in which schools are seen as places where teacher and student (counter)scripts intersect in often less than authentic forms of interaction. It is within this "social space" (Gutierrez, Rymes & Larson, 1995, pp. 446–453) that the power relations of teachers' official scripts and students' unofficial scripts are "constructed", "co-constructed" and "re-constructed" in the way teachers and students live out their school and classroom lives.

We will run with this notion for a moment, because it is central to school culture. We are using the term "script" here as a metaphor for the way the social practices of the school are played out, by whom and with what effect. If we start from the position that the school and its classrooms are "scripted" places (Gutierrez, Larson & Kreuter, 1995), then we are more likely to see the culture of the school as "not so much an area of social life where people share understandings, as that area of social life where people struggle over understandings" (Quantz, 1992, p. 487)—or as Fraser (1995) put it, "the struggle for recognition" (p. 166). According to Gutierrez, Larson and Kreuter (1995):

> The notion of script is useful in the discussion of classroom life insofar as the classroom script characterizes a range of social, spatial, and language or discourse patterns constructed by participants in the course of everyday classroom activity. (p. 413)

While most teacher scripts are dominant and restrictive (as in the case of aggressive and passive schools), with the primary emphasis being upon social order and "the physical control of students' bodies . . . that is, their movements, whereabouts, and silence" (Gutierrez, Larson & Kreuter, 1995, p. 413), students also construct their own "counterscripts" in the "underlife" that clearly exists in the context of classrooms. How these tacit agreements, or "scripted pacts" are observed, maintained and played out at the level of the classroom and the school is interesting:

> The scripted pact . . . is maintained by the teacher and the other students in order to preserve their own roles and status. This pact plays a role in maintaining the power configuration in the classroom by excluding voices that do not follow the same unspoken conversational and procedural rules . . . [T]he teacher agrees not to teach anything too difficult and the students agree to sit quietly and follow directions. Thus, in the context of the larger school culture both teacher and student are constructing and affirming the school's valued script. (Gutierrez, Larson & Kreuter, 1995, p. 418)

Yet, despite "the seeming rigidity of the teacher script" (Gutierrez, Larson & Kreuter 1995: 418), "multiple counterscripts" (Gutierrez 1994) still exist in the form of a "contained underlife" (Goffman 1961) lived out and experienced by students.

Putting it another way, Giroux (1996) uses the term "fugitive culture" as a colorful way of explaining the conflicting and dynamic set of experiences of everyday life of many youth of low socio-economic backgrounds who constantly attempt to "push against the grain" in shaping their identity within/against/outside of schools. Through their curricular structures, schools often end up producing what can only be described as a set of oppressive pedagogical relationships between students and teachers (Ng, 1995). For example, on a daily basis students are tested on how far they are prepared to push against the institutionally sanctioned (Stanton-Salazar, 1997) discipline policy of the school. The disruptive responses students make to what often amounts to "alienative learning" (Woods, 1994, p. 123) are an indication of the extent to which aspirations have been subjugated and made to "disappear from the social surface" (Bannerji, 1987, p. 11) of schooling. Put another way, students are often placed in situations where they have to consciously place on hold their personal views about respect, authority, dignity and fairness.

There is a well-known school culture that works for students (and it looks very much like the active culture we have been discussing here). Goodman and Kuzmic (1997) portray it as looking like this overall:

- There is a marked shift away from individual, isolated, competitive norms of learning, to a "connectionist pedagogy" where students explore learning collectively within an anti-authoritarian context (p. 81);

- The rituals and organizational structures of the school emphasize and foster opportunities for promoting a "sense of family" within the school (p. 82);

- Teachers are at the center of curriculum decision-making in the sense that they are intellectually engaged with their professional fields and the theory and practice of pedagogy, as well as involved in it practically (p. 82);

- There is an orientation to a "socially conscious curriculum" that engages students in projects and activities that foster "compassion, altruism, civic responsibility and commitment to the welfare of our planet" (p. 83);

- There is a view that learning is not just for personal benefit but also for "the democratic well-being of our society" (p. 85); and

- There is an emphasis on "community building" rather than on simply getting children "to behave" (p. 84).

While there were glimpses of this cultural orientation in some of the stories young people told us in this study, sadly there was a preponderance of testimony that pointed in less optimistic directions, and in this regard there is much reclamation to be done within a more supportive environment in schools.

PART IV

CONCLUSION

CHAPTER 7

GRAPPLING WITH THE MIS-MATCHES: THEMES, QUESTIONS, ACTION

In closing we want to briefly revisit the major themes of this study that emerged from the responses of the young people interviewed. While the themes emerged only gradually as the research team immersed themselves in the student voices, it finally became clear that there were some major interferences to these young people's successful completion of secondary school.

The major theoretical explanatory category we have chosen in this study, in an attempt to move research in new and urgent directions, has been the notion of "interactive trouble", borrowed from Freebody, Ludwig and Gunn (1994). Our argument, informed by the set of conditions described by our young informants has been that the experience of schooling was alienating because of a significant mis-match between their struggles to "become somebody" (Wexler, 1992) and the narrowly defined identity that schools expected. To put this most crisply, in an unacceptably large number of cases they found that their post-compulsory schooling

- was irrelevant in terms of navigating a transition from school to economic independence, in a youth labor market that has almost collapsed;
- endorsed forms of assessment and a credential that was about going to university, and hence not inclusive of their needs; and
- perpetuated a school culture that actively contributed to and produced early school leaving.

What was going on here was a complex process of identity formation in which young people were working on generating and maintaining a sense of meaning and self-worth in the experience of being a person.

Whitebrook (2001) defines identity as primarily "a matter of the stories persons tell others about themselves, plus the stories others tell about those persons and/or other stories in which those persons are included" (p. 4). So identity entails the integration of two aspects: "'what the self shows the world' or 'what of the self is shown to the world' together with 'what of the self is recognized by the world'" (p. 4). Defined in this way, the construction of identity is a political project. There is an inevitability around "an absence of closure" (p. 5) that brings with it "instability", "disorder", "uncertainty", "fragmentation" and even elements of the "threatening" and the "dangerous" (p. 5). While there is surely an aspect of "the individual, autonomous, rational chooser" (p. 7) here, equally there is also "in part, at least, [a sense] of [this being done] in community" (p. 7)—in other words, identity is "negotiated".

"Identity" is not therefore something which already exists, transcending place, time, history and culture. It is a "production" that is never complete, and always in process. Viewed in this way, "identity" is a matter of becoming, and the term "becoming somebody" is a particularly useful way to think and talk about the process of identity formation of young people. If we are to understand the way young people deliberate about how schooling fits into their plans for living a life, we need a vocabulary with which to talk about this process of deliberation. The term "becoming somebody" names succinctly what students are doing in making a life for themselves. As we put it in chapters 3 and 4, seeking to understand young lives from the vantage point of those experiencing it generates an interesting set of questions:

- How do young people navigate a transition from school into adult life?
- In what ways do young people make sense of the role of schooling in their future?
- How do young people work the economic, cultural, social and symbolic capital they have at their disposal in navigating a future?
- In what ways does schooling ameliorate, or not, the inequalities of capital that young people have access to?
- How are youth identities constructed by the school/school credential?
- Which identities flourish and which ones wilt?
- Which youth identities get to be commonplace in and around post-compulsory schooling?

The experience of early school leavers is often misrepresented. In this research we were interested in why the perspective of early school leavers tends to be discounted when considering what is happening in schools. We started from the investigative position that the most disgruntled "clients" have the potential to offer powerful insights into what is not working well. If as a wider community we honestly want more young people to stay at school longer, then we need to listen to those who are finding school most unconvincing.

Proceeding in this way brings to the surface some important clues as to what might need to be done differently, or at least what might constitute an efficacious starting point for asking questions about measures to minimize the extent of interactive trouble around early school leaving. Below are some suggestions, grouped in five areas, that are highly derivative of what young people in this study were saying needs to be done. These are presented in terms of propositions that might need to be pursued, or "worked on", in schools (although not exclusively) around culture, policy and practice:

1. Minimizing the *interactive trouble* that gets played out between teachers and students, so that the school:

   • is knowledgeable about local youth subcultures;
   • is sensitive to the way poverty impacts on young people's lives;
   • develops forms of masculinity/femininity that do not undermine school completion, and in which there is a sensitivity towards the negative impact of homophobia; and
   • develops pro-active anti-racism practices.

2. Undermining the *various forms of harassment* that affect young people in schools, in ways that

   • acknowledge "feelings matter" and ensure that teachers are sensitive to class/gender/racist/homophobic harassment;
   • locate students as part of the solution;
   • confront teacher-student harassment by requiring a rethinking of pedagogy; and
   • change those school structures that work against the harmonious social relationships that are necessary for productive learning.

3. Assisting young people to navigate a *transition into the labor market* by

- acquiring a heightened sense of understanding towards those students who are already working part-time;
- developing work experience programs that enable young people to learn critically about the contemporary workplace and to expand their aspirations for work;
- crafting a curriculum that enables young people to learn about the changing nature of the labor market; and
- ensuring that all students have access to adults they can talk to about their plans for navigating their future.

4. Transforming the *culture of the school* so that it has a reputation for acting as an advocate for young people, and is a place that ensures all students experience success, as evidenced by structures and practices such as these:

- providing approaches to middle schooling practices for young adolescents that emphasize the relationship between teacher and students, where the curriculum is negotiated, and where authentic forms of assessment prevail;.
- providing school-based forms of professional development that privilege teacher-initiated forms of inquiry;
- encouraging student voice in school decision making; and
- introducing ways of connecting the educational experiences of young people into local community development projects.

5. Reducing the *policy rhetoric around the credentialling process*, by

- actively promoting curriculum alternatives that counteract the dominant and distorting effects within high school brought about by a curriculum that is preoccupied with selecting for university entrance;
- placing less emphasis on curriculum, assessment and credentialling approaches that sort and select, and more emphasis on ones that provide pathways for other educational options for young people; and
- ensuring that the rationale for curriculum and course requirements are easily understood and mesh with the aspirations of young lives, rather than *operate on* them.

These five proposals do not represent some unrealistic and unattainable utopia for schools; rather, they represent a set of contours actually found in many schools. However, what is required to make these strategies more widespread is educational leadership at the institutional level that supports the ongoing development of them within schools. Schools, and especially public schools, do not exist in isolation. Schools are not autonomous units, but rather are constrained or enabled within policy discourses and accompanying policy leadership. It is enablement that is required if we are to increase the numbers of young people completing secondary schooling. We need a policy framework that is courageous enough to reform the "system" in favor of the most disenfranchised students—not a regime that continues to defend the rights of the most privileged.

It would be foolish to underestimate the fundamental importance of courageous institutional leadership. The contemporary educational policy regime in vogue internationally at the moment seems to be headed in precisely the wrong direction. The tenets of neo-liberal policy actually strengthen hierarchical relationships in schools under the rhetoric of devolution, while abandoning working-class young people to intergenerational unemployment, or else diverting them to forms of vocational training that mostly fail to develop the critical consciousness required to make sense of our rapidly changing societies.

Policy responses to the kind of stories revealed in this book defend the present set of arrangements, even though such arrangements generally work for the already well-off. The voices of the most disenfranchised are filtered through an apparatus that is deaf to all but its own view of the way things ought to be. That more than half of the students in our part of the world are not successful in the mainstream certification process is both hidden from view and denied. It is difficult to see in these circumstances how the problem of early school leaving is to be "fixed". Continual denial of the issue of early school leaving can only lead to the eventual demise of the secondary school as we know it. The growing alienation in our high schools will eventually force changes with or without official support. It would be greatly preferable for those charged with the responsibility for policy around public education to operate pro-actively, rather than allowing their actions to undermine the legitimacy of public schooling.

NOTES

Chapter 1

1. The # number refers to a numbering system used for all informants who were interviewed, to maintain their anonymity.
2. The term "retention rates" in the Australian context refers to the rates at which students stay on into the post-compulsory years, that is, years 11 and 12 of high school.
3. In South Australia the "school card", which is an indication of low income and an entitlement to government assistance, is taken as a proxy measure of low socio-economic status.

Chapter 2

1. In South Australia, students move from primary school to secondary school at the end of year 7.

REFERENCES

Agger, B. (1992). *Cultural Studies as Critical Theory*. London: Falmer Press.

Aggleton, P. (1987). *Rebels Without a Cause: Middle Class Youth and the Transition from School to Work*. Lewes, UK: Falmer Press.

Anderson, G. & Herr, K. (1994). The micro-politics of student voices: moving from diversity of bodies to diversity of voices in schools. In C. Marshall (Ed.), *The New Politics of Race and Gender* (pp. 58–69). Washington, DC: Falmer Press.

Apple, M. (1986). National reports and the construction of inequality. *British Journal of Sociology of Education*, 7(2), 171–190.

Apple, M. (1993). *Official Knowledge: Democratic Education in a Conservative Age*. New York: Routledge.

Apple, M. (1996). Power, meaning and identity: critical sociology of education in the United States. *British Journal of Sociology of Education*, 17(2), 125–144.

Aronowitz, S. (1992). *The Politics of Identity: Class, Culture and Social Movements*. New York: Routledge.

Aronowitz, S. & DiFazio, W. (1994). *The Jobless Future: Sci-Tech and the Dogma of Work*. Minneapolis: University of Minnesota Press.

Australian Bureau of Statistics (2000). *Schools Australia*. Catalogue Number 4221.0. Canberra: Australian Government Publishing Service.

Ball, S. (1993). Education, Majorism and the 'curriculum of the dead'. *Curriculum Studies*, 1(2), 195–214.

Ball, S., Bowe, R. & Gewirtz, S. (1996). School choice, social class and distinction: the realization of social advantage in education. *Journal of Education Policy*, 11(1), 89–112.

Ball, S., Davies, J., David, M. & Reay, D. (2002). 'Classification' and 'judgement': social class and the 'cognitive structures' of choice in higher education. *British Journal of Sociology of Education*, 23(1), 51–72.

Ball, S. & Vincent, C. (2001). The new class relations in education: the strategies of the 'fearful' middle classes. In J. Demaine (Ed.), *Sociology of Education Today* (pp. 180–195). Basingstoke, UK: Palgrave.

Balson, M. (1995). *Becoming Better Parents*. Melbourne: Australian Council for Educational Research.

Bannerji, H. (1987). Introducing racism: notes towards an anti-racist feminism. *Resources for Feminist Research, 16*(1), 10–13.

Batten, M. & Russell, J. (1995). *Students at Risk: A Review of the Australian Literature 1980–1994, Australian Council for Educational Research, Research Monograph No. 46.* Melbourne: Australian Council for Educational Research

Bauman, Z. (1998). On glocalization: or globalization for some and localization for some others. *Thesis Eleven, 54,* August, 37–49.

Bauman, Z. (2001). *The Individualized Society.* Cambridge, UK: Polity Press.

Beck, U. (1992). *Risk Society: Towards a New Modernity: Theory, Culture and Society.* London: Sage.

Beck, U. (1999). *The Reinvention of Politics: Rethinking Modernity in the Global Social Order.* Cambridge, UK: Polity Press.

Beck, U., & Beck-Gernsheim, E. (1995). *The Normal Chaos of Love* (M. Ritter & J. Wiebel, Trans.). Cambridge, UK: Polity Press.

Biggart, A., & Furlong, A. (1996). Educating 'discouraged workers': cultural diversity in the upper secondary school. *British Journal of Sociology of Education, 17*(3), 253–266.

Blackmore, J. (1996). Doing 'emotional labour' in the education market place: stories from the field of women in management. *Discourse, 17*(3), 337–349.

Boomer, G., Lester, N., Onore, C. & Cook, J. (Eds.). (1992). *Negotiating the Curriculum: Educating for the 21st Century.* London: Falmer Press.

Bourdieu, P. (1986). The forms of capital. In J. Richardson (Ed.), *Handbook of Theory and Research for the Sociology of Education* (pp. 241–258). New York: Greenwood Press.

Bourdieu, P. (1991). Epilogue: on the possibility of a field of world sociology. In P. Bourdieu & J. Coleman (Eds.), *Social Theory for a Changing Society* (pp. 373–387). Boulder, CO: Westview Press.

Bourdieu, P. (1998). *Practical Reason: On the Theory of Action.* Cambridge, UK: Polity Press.

Brake, M. (1980). *The Sociology of Youth Culture and Youth Subcultures. Sex and Drugs and Rock 'N' Roll.* London: Routledge and Kegan Paul.

Broadfoot, P. (1996). *Education, Assessment and Society: A Sociological Analysis.* Buckingham, UK: Open University Press.

Brown, P. (1997). Cultural capital and social exclusion: some observations on recent market trands in education, employment and the labour market. In A. Halsey, H. Lauder, P. Brown & A. Wells (Eds.), *Education Culture, Economy, Society* (pp. 736–749). Oxford: Oxford University Press.

Burgess, R. (1988). Conversations with a purpose: the ethnographic interview in educational research. *Studies in Qualitative Methodology: Conducting Qualitative Research 1,* 137–155.

Burke, C. & Jarman, K. (1994). Disruptive and anti-social behaviour in the middle years of schooling: approaching the primary-secondary divide. *Unicorn, 20*(2), 52–57.

Cannon, J. (1998 December). Making sense of the interview material: thematising, NUD*IST, and 10meg of transcripts. Paper presented at the Australian Association for Research in Education Conference, Adelaide.

Carspecken, P. & Apple, M. (1992). Critical qualitative research: theory, methodology and practice. In M. LeCompte, J. Millroy & J. Preissle (Eds.), *The Handbook of Qualitative Research in Education* (pp. 507–553). San Diego: Academic Press.

Casey, K. (1995). The new narrative research in education. In M. Apple (Ed.), *Review of Research in Education* (Vol. 21, pp. 211–253). Washington, DC: American Educational Research Association.

Castells, M. (1989). *The Informational City: Information Technology, Economic Restructuring and the Urban-Regional Process.* Oxford: Blackwell.

Commonwealth Schools Commission. (1987). *In the National Interest: Secondary Education and Youth Policy in Australia.* Canberra: Australian Capital Territory: Canberra Publishing and Printing.

Connell, R. (1989). Cool guys, swots and wimps: the interplay of masculinity and education, *Oxford Review of Education 15*(3), 291–304.

Connell, R. (1991). Live fast and die young: the construction of masculinity among young working-class men on the margin of the labour market. *Australian and New Zealand Journal of Sociology, 27*(2), 141–171.

Connell, R. (1996). Teaching the boys: new research on masculinity, and gender strategies for schools. *Teachers College Record, 98*(2), 206–235.

Connell, R. (1998). Social change and curriculum futures. *Change: Transformations in Education, 1*(1), 84–90.

Connell, R. & White, V. (1989). Child poverty and educational action. In D. Edgar, D. Keane & P. McDonald (Eds.), *Child Poverty* (pp. 104–122). Sydney: Allen and Unwin.

Cormack, P. (1996). Constructions of the adolescent in newspapers and policy documents: implications for middle schooling. *South Australian Educational Leader, 7*(6), 1–12.

Coser, L. (1974). *Greedy Institutions: Patterns of Undivided Commitment.* New York: Collier Macmillan.

Cumming, J. (1996). *From Alienation to Engagement: Opportunities for Reform in the Middle Years of Schooling.* Canberra: Australian Capital Territory: Australian Curriculum Studies Association.

Cusick, P. (1973). *Inside High School.* New York: Holt, Rinehart & Winston.

Davies, B. (1993). Beyond dualism and towards multiple subjectivities. In L. Christian-Smith (Ed.), *Texts of Desire* (pp. 143–173). London: Falmer Press.

Davies, B. (1994). *Poststructuralist Theory and Classroom Practice.* Geelong, Victoria, Australia: Deakin University Press.

Debond, G. (1970). *The Society of the Spectacle.* Detroit: Black and Red Press.

Department of Employment, Education and Training. (1993). *Retention and Participation in Australian Schools 1967–1992.* Canberra: Australian Government Printing Service.

Dewey, J. (1966). *Democracy and Education.* New York: Free Press.

Du Bois-Reymond, M. (1998). 'I don't want to commit myself yet': young people's life concepts. *Journal of Youth Studies, 1*(1), 63–79.

During, S. (1992). Postcolonialism and globalization. *Meanjin, 51*(2), 339–353.

Dusseldorp Skills Forum. (1998). *Australia's Youth: Reality and Risk.* Sydney: Dusseldorp Skills Forum.

Dwyer, P. (1994). Participation or forced retention? some implications of improved school participation rates. *Unicorn, 20*(2), 58–66.

Dwyer, P. (1995). Pathways in post-compulsory education—from metaphor to practice. *Australian Journal of Education, 39*(2), 146–162.

Dwyer, P. (1996). *Opting Out: Early School Leavers and the Degeneration of Youth Policy.* Hobart, Tasmania: National Clearinghouse for Youth Studies & Youth Research Centre.

Dwyer, P. & Wyn, J. (1998). Post-compulsory education policy in Australia and its impact on participant pathways and outcomes in the 1990s. *Journal of Education Policy, 13*(3), 285–300.

Ebert, T. (1996). *Ludic Feminism and After: Postmodernism, Desire, and Labour in Late Capitalism.* Ann Arbor: University of Michigan Press.

Elmore, R. (1987). Reforming and the culture of authority in schools. *Educational Administration Quarterly, 23*(4), 60–78.

Epstein, D. & Johnson, R. (1998). *Schooling Sexualities.* Buckingham, UK: Open University Press.

Eyers, V., Cormack, P. & Barratt, R. (1992). *Report of the Junior Secondary Review: The Education of Young Adolescents in South Australian Government Schools.* Adelaide: Education Department of South Australia.

Farrell, J. (1996). Narratives of identity: the voice of youth. *Curriculum Inquiry, 26*(3), 235–243.

Fine, M. (1989). Silencing and nurturing voice in an improbable context: urban adolescents in public school. In H. Giroux & P. McLaren (Eds.), *Critical Pedagogy, the State and Cultural Struggle* (pp. 152–173). Albany: State University of New York Press.

Fine, M. (1990). Making controversy: who's at risk? *Journal of Urban and Cultural Studies, 1*(1), 55–68.

Fine, M. (1991). *Framing Dropouts: Notes on the Politics of an Urban High School.* Albany: State University of New York Press.

Fine, M. (1994). Working the hyphens: reinventing self and other in qualitative research. In N. Denzin & Y. Lincoln (Eds.), *Handbook of Qualitative Research* (pp. 70–82). London: Sage.

Fine, M. (1996). Introduction. In D. Kelly & J. Gaskell (Eds.), *Debating Dropouts: Critical Policy and Research Perspectives on School Learning* (pp. xi–xviii). New York: Teachers College Press.

Fine, M. & Rosenberg, P. (1983). Dropping out of high school: the ideology of school and work. *Journal of Education, 165*(3), 257–272.

Fine, M. & Weis, L. (1998). *The Unknown City: Lives of Poor and Working Class Young Adults.* Boston: Beacon Press.

Fitzgerald, R. T. (1976). *Poverty and Education in Australia: Commission of Inquiry into Poverty, 5th Main Report*. Canberra: Australian Government Printing Service.

Foley, D (1990). *Learning Capitalist Culture: Deep in the Heart of Texas*. Philadelphia: University of Pennsylvania Press.

Foucault, M. (1977). *Discipline and Punish: The Birth of the Prison*. London: Penguin.

Foucault, M. (1980). *Two Lectures, Power/Knowledge: Selected Interviews and Other Writings 1972–1977*. New York: Pantheon.

Fraser, J., Davis, P. & Singh, R. (1997). Identity work by alternative high school students. *Qualitative Studies in Education, 10*(2), 221–235.

Fraser, N. (1989). *Unruly Practices: Power, Discourse and Gender in Contemporary Social Theory*. Minneapolis: University of Minnesota Press.

Fraser, N. (1995). From redistribution to recognition? Dilemmas of justice in a post-socialist age. *New Left Review, 210*, 68–91.

Freebody, P., Ludwig, C. & Gunn, S. (1994). *Everyday Literacy Practices in and out of Schools in Low Socio-economic Urban Communities* (Executive Summary). Melbourne: Curriculum Corporation.

Freeland, J. (1986). Australia: the search for a new educational settlement. In R. Sharp (Ed.), *Capitalist Crisis and Schooling: Comparative Studies in the Politics of Education* (pp. 212–236). Melbourne: Macmillan.

Freeland, J. (1991). Dislocated transitions: access and participation for disadvantaged young people. In B. Finn (Ed.), *Young People's Participation in Post-Compulsory Education and Training* (Vol. 3, Appendix 2). Canberra: Australian Government Printing Service.

Freire, P. (1970). *Pedagogy of the Oppressed* (M. Ramos, Trans.). New York: Seabury.

Furlong, A. & Cartmel, F. (1997). *Young People and Social Change: Individualization and Risk in Late Modernity*. Milton Keynes, UK: Open University Press.

Furlong, V. (1991). Disaffected pupils: reconstructing the sociological perspective. *British Journal of Sociology of Education, 12*(3), 293–307.

Giddens, A. (1994). *Beyond Left and Right: The Future of Radical Politics*. Cambridge, UK: Polity Press.

Gilding, K. (1988). *First Report of the Enquiry into Immediate Post-Compulsory Education*. Adelaide: Education Department of South Australia.

Gilding, K. (1989). *Second Report of the Enquiry into Immediate Post-Compulsory Education*. Adelaide: Education Department of South Australia.

Gillborn, D., & Youndell, D. (2000). *Rationing Education: Policy, Practice, Reform and Equity*. Buckingham, UK & Philadelphia: Open University Press.

Gilroy, P. (1993). *The Black Atlantic: Modernity and Double Consciousness*. Cambridge, MA: Harvard University Press.

Giroux, H. (1991). Series introduction: rethinking the pedagogy of voice, difference, and cultural struggle. In C. Walsh (Ed.), *Pedagogy and the Struggle for Voice: Issues of Language, Power, and Schooling for Puerto Ricans* (pp. xv–xxvii). New York: Bergin & Garvey.

Giroux, H. (1993). Living dangerously: identity politics and the new cultural racism: towards a critical pedagogy of representation. *Cultural Studies, 7*(1), 1–27.

Giroux, H. (1994). *Disturbing Pleasures: Learning Popular Culture*. New York and London: Routledge.

Giroux, H. (1996). *Fugitive Cultures: Race, Violence and Youth*. London: Routledge.

Giroux, H. & McLaren, P. (1992). Writing from the margins: geographies of identity, pedagogy, and power. *Journal of Education*, *174*(1), 7–30.

Goffman, I. (1961). *Asylums: Essays on the Social Situation of Mental Patients and Other Inmates*. New York: Anchor.

Goodman, J. (1995). Change without difference: school restructuring in historical perspective. *Harvard Educational Review*, *65*(1), 1–29.

Goodman, J. & Kuzmic, J. (1997). Bringing a progressive pedagogy to conventional schools: theoretical and practical implications from Harmony. *Theory into Practice*, *36*(2), 79–86.

Gore, J. (1995). On the continuity of power relations in pedagogy. *International Studies in Sociology of Education*, *5*(2), 165–188.

Grant, B. (1997). Disciplining students: the construction of student subjectivities. *British Journal of Sociology of Education*, *18*(1), 101–114.

Green, B. & Bigum, C. (1993). Aliens in the classroom. *Australian Journal of Education*, *37*(2), 119–141.

Griffin, C. (1993). *Representation of Youth: The Study of Youth and Adolescence in Britain and America*. Cambridge, UK: Polity Press.

Grundy, S. (1994). Being and becoming an Australian: classroom discourse and the construction of identity. *Discourse*, *15*(1), 16–31.

Gutierrez, K. (1994). How talk, context, and script shape contexts for learning: a cross-case comparison of journal sharing. *Linguistics and Education*, *5*(3 & 4), 335–365.

Gutierrez, K., Larson, J. & Kreuter, B. (1995). Cultural tensions in the scripted classroom: the value of the subjugated perspective. *Urban Education*, *29*(4), 410–442.

Gutierrez, K., Rymes, B. & Larson, J. (1995). Script, counterscript, and underlife in the classroom: James Brown versus Brown and Board of Education. *Harvard Educational Review*, *65*(3), 445–471.

Hall, S. (1988). The toad in the garden: Thatcherism among the theorists. In L. Grossberg & C. Nelson (Eds.), *Marxism and the Interpretation of Culture* (pp. 35–73). Urbana & Chicago: University of Illinois Press.

Hall, S. (1990). Cultural identity and diaspora. In J. Rutherford (Ed.), *Identity* (pp. 222–237). London: Lawrence & Wishart.

Hall, S. & Jacques, M. (1990). From the manifesto for new times: the new times. In S. Hall & M. Jacques (Eds.), *New Times: The Changing Face of Politics in the 1990's (pp. 23–37)*. New York: Verso.

Harraway, D. (1991). *Simians, Cyborgs and Women: The Reinvention of Nature*. New York: Routledge.

Hattam, R., Edwards, J. & Cominos, M. (1997). The extent of the problem. A discussion paper for the Students Completing Schooling Project. Adelaide, unpublished.

Haywood, C. & Mac an Ghaill, M. (1995). The sexual politics of the curriculum. *International Studies in Sociology of Education*, 5(2), 221–236.

Herr, K. & Anderson, G. (1997). The cultural politics of identity: student narratives from two Mexican secondary schools. *Qualitative Studies in Education*, 10(1), 45–61.

Human Rights and Equal Opportunity Commission (1997). *Bringing Them Home: National Inquiry into the Separation of Aboriginal and Torres Strait Islander Children from Their Families*. Sydney: Stirling Press.

Hutchings, M., & Archer, L. (2000). *Higher Than Einstein: Constructions of Going to University among Working-Class Non-Participants*. London: University of North London, Centre for Higher Education and Access Development.

Jameson, F. (1981). *The Political Unconscious: Narrative as a Socially Symbolic Act*. London: Methuen.

Johnston, E. (1991). *Royal Commission into Aboriginal deaths in custody, National Report, Vol. 4*. Canberra: Australian Government Printing Service.

Jones, G., & Wallace, C. (1992). *Youth, Family and Citizenship*. Buckingham, UK: Open University Press.

Kellner, D. (1995). *Media Culture: Cultural Studies, Identity, and Politics between the Modern and the Postmodern*. London & New York: Routledge.

Kelly, D. (1993). Secondary power source: high school students as participatory researchers. *American Sociologist*, 24(1), 8–26.

Kelly, D., & Gaskell, J. (1996). *Debating Dropouts: Critical Policy and Research Perspectives on Leaving School*. New York: Teachers College Press.

Kelsey, J. (1995). *Economic Fundamentalism: New Zealand Experiment—A World Model for Structural Adjustment*. London: Pluto Press.

Kemp, D. (1999). *New Knowledge, New Opportunities: A Discussion Paper on Higher Education Research and Research Training*. Canberra: Commonwealth of Australia.

Kenway, J. (1995). Masculinities in schools: under siege, on the defensive and under reconstruction. *Discourse: Studies in the Cultural Politics of Education*, 16(1), 59–79.

Kenway, J. (Ed.). (1997). *Boys Will Be Boys? Boy's Education and Gender Reform*. Deakin West, Australian Capital Territory: Australian Curriculum Studies Association.

Kenway, J., Willis, S., Blackmore, J. & Rennie, L. (1994). Making 'hope' practical rather than 'despair' convincing: feminist post-structuralism, gender reform and educational change. *British Journal of Sociology of Education*, 15(2), 187–210.

Kincheloe, J (1995). *Toil and Trouble: Good Work, Smart Workers, and the Integration of Academic and Vocational Education*. New York: Peter Lang Publishing.

Knight, J., Lingard, B. & Bartlett, L. (1994). Reforming teacher education policy under Labor governments in Australia, 1983–93. *British Journal of Sociology of Education*, 15(4), 451–466.

Knight, J. & Warry, M. (1996 December). From corporate to supply-side federalism? Narrowing the Australian education policy agenda 1987–1996. Paper presented at Australian Association for Research in Education Conference, Singapore.

Lamb, S. (1998). Completing schooling in Australia: trends in the 1990s. *Australian Journal of Education, 42*(1), 5–31.

Lather, P. (1986). Research as praxis. *Harvard Educational Review, 56*(3), 257–277.

Lingard, B. (1998 December). Contextualising and utilising the 'what about the boys' backlash for gender equity goals. Paper presented at the Australian Association for Research in Education Conference, Adelaide.

Lingard, B., Porter, P., Bartlett, L. & Knight, J. (1995). Federal/state mediations in the Australian national education agenda: from AEC to MCEETYA 1987–1993. *Australian Journal of Education, 39*(1), 41–66.

Lohrey, A. (1995). A report on transferability in relation to the key competencies. Sydney: Centre for Workplace Communication and Culture, University of Technology.

Looker, E. (1997). In search of credentials: factors affecting young adults: participation in post-secondary education. *Canadian Journal of Higher Education, 27*(2–3), 1–36.

Looker, E. & Dwyer, P. (1998). Education and negotiated reality: complexities facing rural youth in the 1990s. *Journal of Youth Studies, 1*(1), 5–22.

Luke, C. & Luke, A. (1999). Theorising interracial families and hybrid identity: an Australian perspective. *Educational Theory 49*(2): 223–250.

Luke, T. (1991). Touring hyperreality: critical theory confronts informational society. In P. Wexler (Ed.), *Critical Theory Now* (pp. 1–26). London: Falmer Press.

Luttrell, W. (1996). Becoming somebody in and against school: towards a psychocultural theory of gender and self-making. In B. Levinson, D. Foley & D. Holland (Eds.), *The Cultural Production of the Educated Person: Critical Ethnographies of Schooling and Local Practice* (pp. 93–117). Albany: State University of New York Press.

Mac an Ghaill, M. (1994). *The Making of Men: Masculinities, Sexualities and Schooling*. Buckingham, UK: Open University Press.

MacPherson, P. & Fine, M. (1995). Hungry for us: adolescent girls and adult women negotiating territories of race, gender, class and difference. *Feminism and Psychology, 5*(2), 181–200.

Malone, K. & Hasluck, L. (1998 Autumn). Geographies of exclusion: young people's perceptions and use of public space. *Family Matters, 49*, 20–26.

Margonis, F. (1992). The co-operation of 'at-risk': paradoxes of policy criticism. *Teachers College Record, 94*(2), 343–364.

Martino, R. (1997 December). Boys in schools: addressing the politics of hegemonic masculinities. Paper presented at Australian Association for Research in Education Conference, Brisbane.

McCarthy, C. (1988). Rethinking liberal and radical perspectives on racial inequality in schooling: making the case for nonsynchrony. *Harvard Educational Review, 58*(3), 265–279.

McCarthy, C. & Critchlow, W. (Eds.). (1993). *Race, Identity, and Representation in Education*. New York: Routledge.

McClellans, A., MacDonald, H. & MacDonald, F. (1998). Young people and labour market disadvantage. In Dusseldorp Skills Forum (Ed.), *Australia's Youth: Reality and Risk* (pp. 103–126). Sydney: Dusseldorp Skills Forum.

McInerney, P., Hattam, R., Smyth, J. & Lawson, M. (1999). *Developing Middle Schooling Practices*. Adelaide: Flinders Institute for the Study of Teaching, Flinders University of South Australia.

McLaren, A. (1996). Coercive invitations: how young women in school make sense of mothering and waged labour. *British Journal of Sociology of Education*, 17(3), 279–298.

McLaughlin, T. (1996). *Street Smarts and Critical Theory: Listening to the Vernacular*. Madison: University of Wisconsin Press.

McLeod, J. (1998 December). Friendship, schooling and gender identity work. Paper presented at the Australian Association of Research in Education Conference, Adelaide.

McRobbie, A. (1994). *Postmodernism and Popular Culture*. London: Routledge.

Meadmore, D. & Symes, C. (1996). Of uniform appearance: a symbol of school discipline and governmentality. *Discourse*, 17(2), 209–225.

Mies, M. (1986). *Patriarchy and Accumulation on a World Scale: Women in the International Division of Labour*. London: Zed Books.

Mills, M. (1996). 'Homophobia kills': a disruptive moment in the educational politics of legitimation. *British Journal of Sociology of Education*, 17(3), 315–326.

Ministerial Council on Education, Employment, Training and Youth Affairs. (1997). *Gender Equity: A Framework for Australian Schools*. Canberra: Department of Urban Services, Australian Capital Territory Government.

Ministerial Review of Post-Compulsory Schooling. (1985). *Report: Volume 1*. Melbourne: Ministerial Review of Postcompulsory Schooling.

Moi, T. (1991). Appropriating Bourdieu: feminist theory and Pierre Bourdieu's sociology of culture. *New Literary History*, 22, 1017–1049.

Moore, B. (1993a June–July). The Politics of Victim Construction in Australian Social Justice Policy. Paper presented at the Australian Curriculum Studies Conference, Belconnen, Australian Capital Territory.

Moore, B. (1993b). Anti-racist education: South Australian policy in black perspective. *South Australian Educational Leader*, 4(1), 1–12.

Morton, D. & Zavarzadeh, M. (Eds.). (1991). *Theory/Pedagogy/Politics: Texts for Change*. Urbana & Chicago: University of Illinois Press.

National Board of Employment, Education and Training (1995). *'Where Do They Go?' An Evaluation of Sources of Data Used for the Monitoring of Students' Destinations and Other Educational Outcomes in Australia*. Canberra: Australian Government Printing Service.

National Youth Affairs Research Scheme (1997). *Under-age School Leaving: A Report Examining Approaches to Assisting Young People at Risk of Leaving School before the Legal School Leaving Age*. Hobart: National Clearing House for Youth Studies.

Natriello, G. (1986). School dropouts: patterns and policies, *Teachers College Record* 87(3), 305–306.

New London Group. (1996). A pedagogy of multiliteracies: designing social futures. *Harvard Educational Review*, 66(1), 60–92.

Ng, R. (1995). Teaching against the grain: contradictions and possibilities. In R. Ng, P. Stanton & J. Scare (Eds.), *Anti-Racism, Feminism and Critical Approaches to Education* (pp. 129–152). Westport, CT: Bergin & Garvey.

O'Brien, M. (1984). The commatisation of women: patriarchal fetishism in the sociology of education. *Interchange*, 15(2), 43–60.

Paterson, L. & Raffe, D. (1995). 'Staying-on' in full-time education in Scotland, 1985–1991, *Oxford Review of Education* 21(1), 3–23.

Pearson, N. (1994). A troubling inheritance. *Race and Class*, 35(4), 1–9.

Pring, R. (1989). *The Sorting Machine Revisited: National Education Policy since 1945*. New York: Longman.

Probert, B. (1998 August). Fast Capitalism and New Kinds of Jobs. Paper presented at the Changing Work—Changing Society, VETNETwork Conference, Adelaide.

Proudford, C. & Baker, R. (1995). Schools that make a difference: a sociological perspective on effective schooling. *British Journal of Education*, 16(3), 277–292.

Pusey, M. (1991). *Economic Rationalism in Canberra: A Nation-building State Changes Its Mind*. New York: Cambridge University Press.

Quantz, R. (1992). On critical ethnography (with some postmodern considerations). In M. LeCompte, W. Milroy & J. Preissle (Eds.), *The Handbook of Qualitative Research in Education* (pp. 447–505). San Diego: Academic Press.

Raffe, D. & Willms, J. (1989). Schooling the discouraged worker: local labour market effects on educational participation. *Sociology*, 23(4), 559–581.

Ramsay, E., Trantor, D., Charlton, S. & Sumner, R. (1998). *Higher Education: Access and Equity for Low SES School Leavers*. Canberra: Australian Government Publishing Service.

Reay, D. (1998). Rethinking social class: qualitative perspectives on class and gender. *Sociology*, 32(2), 259–275.

Reid, A. (Ed.). (1998). *Going Public: Education Policy and Public Education in Australia*. Deakin West, Australian Capital Territory: Australian Curriculum Studies Association.

Robertson, R. (1995). Glocalization: time-space and homogeneity-heterogeneity. In M. Featherstone, S. Lash & R. Robertson (Eds.), *Global Modernities* (pp. 23–44). London: Sage.

Robinson, C. & Ball, K. (1998). Young people's participation in and outcomes from vocational education. In Dusseldorp Skills Forum (Ed.), *Australia's Youth: Reality and Risk* (pp. 67–83). Sydney: Dusseldorp Skills Forum.

Roman, L. (1996). Spectacle in the dark: youth as transgression, display, and repression. *Educational Theory*, 46(1), 1–22.

Rudd, P. (1997). From socialisation to post-modernity: a review of theoretical perspectives on the school-to-work transition. *Journal of Education and Work, 10*(3), 257–279.

Rudd, P. & Evans, K. (1998). Structure and agency in youth transitions: student experiences of vocational further education. *Journal of Youth Studies, 1*(1), 39–62.

Sacks, K. (1989). Toward a unified theory of class, race, and gender. *American Ethnologist, 16*, 534–550.

Sarup, M. (1982). *Education, State and Crisis—A Marxist Perspective*. London: Routledge & Kegan Paul.

Seddon, T. (1995 July). Educational Leadership and Teachers' Work. Paper presented at the Educational Leadership Conference, Flinders University of South Australia, Adelaide.

Shacklock, G. (1997). A three phase interview strategy. Unpublished paper for the Students Completing Schooling Project, Flinders Institute for the Study of Teaching, Flinders University of South Australia, Adelaide.

Shacklock G. & Smyth, J. (1997). Conceptualising and capturing voices in drop-out research: methodological issues. Unpublished paper for the Students Completing Schooling Project, Flinders Institute for the Study of Teaching, Flinders University of South Australia, Adelaide.

Shor, I. (1980). *Critical Teaching and Everyday Life*. Chicago: University of Chicago Press.

Shor, I. (1990). Liberation education: an interview with Ira Shor. *Language Arts, 67*(4), 342–352.

Shor, I. (1996). *When Students Have Power: Negotiating Authority in a Critical Pedagogy*. Chicago: Chicago University Press.

Shor, I. & Freire, P. (1987). *A Pedagogy for Liberation: Dialogues on Transforming Education*. South Hadley, MA: Bergin & Garvey.

Sibley, D. (1995). *Geographies of Exclusion: Society and Difference in the West*. London & New York: Routledge.

Simon, R. & Dippo, D. (1987). What schools can do: designing programs for work education that challenge the wisdom of experience. *Journal of Education, 169*(3), 101–116.

Simon, R., Dippo, D. & Schenke, A. (1991). *Learning Work: A Critical Pedagogy of Work Education*. Amherst, MA: Bergin & Garvey.

Skeggs, B. (1997). *Formations of Class and Gender: Becoming Respectable*. London: Sage.

Smith, D. (1999). *Writing the Social: Critique, Theory, and Investigations*. Toronto: University of Toronto Press.

Smyth, J. (1998a December). Dialectical theory building: juxtaposing theory with student voices in the non-completion of schooling. Paper presented at the Australian Association for Research in Education Conference, Adelaide.

Smyth, J. (1998b). Some global economic forces affecting school supervision. In G. Firth & E. Pajak (Eds.), *Handbook of School Supervision* (pp. 1173–1183). New York: Macmillan.

Smyth, J. (1999a). Researching the cultural politics of teachers' learning in J. Loughran (ed.), *Researching Teaching: Methodologies and Practices for Understanding Pedagogy*, London and New York, Falmer Press, pp. 67–82.

Smyth, J. (1999b December). Voiced research: bringing in the epistemologically marginalised. Paper presented at the Australian Association for Research in Education Conference, Melbourne.

Smyth, J. (2003). Making young lives with/against the school credential. *Journal of Education and Work 16*(2), 2003, pp. 128–146.

Smyth, J. & Dow, A. (1998). What's wrong with outcomes? Spotter planes, action plans, and steerage of the educational workplace. *British Journal of Sociology of Education, 19*(3), 291–303.

Smyth, J., Dow, A., Hattam, R., Reid, A. & Shacklock, G. (2000). *Teachers' Work in a Globalizing Economy*. London: Falmer Press.

Smyth, J. & Hattam, R. (2001). Voiced research as a sociology for understanding 'dropping out' of school. *British Journal of Sociology of Education 22* (3), pp. 401–415.

Smyth, J. & Hattam, R. (2002). Early school leaving and the cultural geography of high schools. *British Educational Research Journal 28* (3), 2002, pp. 375–397.

Smyth, J., Hattam, R., Cannon, J., Edwards, J., Wilson, N. & Wurst, S. (2000). *Listen to Me, I'm Leaving: Early School Leaving in South Australian Secondary Schools*. Adelaide: Flinders Institute for the Study of Teaching, Department of Employment, Education and Training, and South Australian Senior Secondary Assessment Board.

Smyth, J., McInerney, P., Hattam, R. & Lawson, M. (1999). *Placing Girls at the Centre of Curriculum: Teachers' Learning and School Reform at Gepps Cross Girls High School*. Adelaide: Flinders Institute for the Study of Teaching, Flinders University of South Australia.

Smyth, J., Shacklock, G. & Hattam, R. (1999). Doing critical cultural studies: an antidote to being done to. *Discourse, 20*(1), 73–87.

Snow, D. & Anderson, L. (1987). Identity work among the homeless: the verbal construction and avowal of personal identities. *American Journal of Sociology, 92*(6), 1336–1371.

Social Development Group (1979). *Developing the Classroom Group*. Research Report. Adelaide: Education Department of South Australia.

Spierings, J. (1995). *Young Australians in the Working Nation. A Review of Youth Employment Policies for the 1990's*. Adelaide: Social Justice Research Foundation, University of Adelaide.

Spoehr, J. (1999). A labour market in crisis? In J. Spoehr (Ed.), *Beyond the Contract State: Ideas for Social and Economic Renewal in South Australia* (pp. 92–106). Adelaide: Wakefield Press.

Stake, R. (1978). The case study method in social inquiry. *Educational Researcher, 7*(2), 5–8.

Stanton-Salazar, R. (1997). A social capital framework for understanding the socialization of racial minority children and youths. *Harvard Educational Review, 67*(1), 1–40.

Suarez-Orozco, M. (1987). 'Becoming somebody': Central American immigrants in U.S. inner-city schools. *Anthropology and Education Quarterly, 18*(4), 287–299.

Tait, G. (1993). Youth, personhood and 'practices of self': some new directions for youth research. *Australian & New Zealand Journal of Sociology, 29*(1), 40–54.

Taylor, C. (1989). *Sources of the Self: The Making of the Modern Identity*. Cambridge, MA: Harvard University Press.

Taylor, S., Rizvi, F., Lingard, B. & Henry, M. (1997). *Educational Policy and the Politics of Change*. London: Routledge.

Teese, R. (1998). Curriculum hierarchy, private schooling and the segmentation of Australian secondary schooling, 1947–1985. *British Journal of Sociology of Education, 19*(3), 401–417.

Teese, R. (2000). *Academic Success and Social Power: Examinations and Inequality*. Carlton South: Melbourne University Press.

Teese, R., Davies, M., Charlton, M. & Polesel, J. (1995). *Who Wins at School? Boys and Girls in Australian Secondary Education*. Canberra: Department of Education, Training and Youth Affairs.

Teese, R., Davies, M., Charlton, M. & Polesel, J. (1997). Who wins at school: which boys, which girls? In J. Kenway (Ed.), *Will Boys Be Boys? Boys' Education in the Context of Gender Reform* (pp. 8–12). Deakin West, Australian Capital Territory: Australian Curriculum Studies Association.

Teese, R., McLean, G. & Polesel, J. (1993). *Equity Outcomes: A Report to the Schools Council's Task Force on a Broadbanded Equity Program for Schools* (Projects of National Significance). Canberra: National Board of Employment, Education and Training.

Walby, S. (1992). Post-post-modernism? Theorising social complexity. In M. Barrett & A. Phillips (Eds.), *Destabilizing Theory: Contemporary Feminist Debates* (pp. 31–53). Cambridge, UK: Polity Press.

Walkerdine, V. (1989). Femininity as performance. *Oxford Review of Education, 15*(3), 267–279.

Walkerdine, V. (1990). *Schoolgirl Fictions*. London: Verso.

Weedon, C. (1999). *Feminism, Theory and the Politics of Difference*. Oxford: Blackwell.

Weis, L. (1988). High school girls in a de-industrializing economy. In L. Weis (Ed.), *Class, Race and Gender in American Education* (pp. 183–208). Albany: State University of New York Press.

Weis, L. (1990). *Working Class without Work: High School Students in a De-industrializing Society*. New York: Routledge.

Weis, L. (1995). Qualitative research in sociology of education. In W. Pink & G. Norblit (Eds.), *Continuity and Contradiction: The Futures of the Sociology of Education* (pp. 157–173). Cresskill, NJ: Hampton Press.

Weis, L., Marusza, J. & Fine, M. (1998). Out of the cupboard: kids, domestic violence, and schools. *British Journal of Sociology of Education, 19*(1), 53–74.

West, C. (1992). A matter of life and death. *October* (61), 20–28.

Wexler, P. (1992). *Becoming Somebody: Towards a Social Psychology of the School.* London: Falmer Press.

White, R. (1996). Schooling and youth alienation. *Education Links, 52,* 23–27.

White, R. & Wyn, J. (1998). Youth agency and social context. *Journal of Sociology, 34*(3), 314–327.

Whitebrook, M. (2001). *Identity, Narrative and Politics.* London & New York: Routledge.

Williams, R. (1976). *Keywords: A Vocabulary of Culture and Society.* Oxford: Oxford University Press.

Williams, T., Long, M., Carpenter, P. & Hayden, M. (1993). *Year 12 in the 1980s.* Canberra: Australian Government Printing Service.

Willis, P. (1977). *Learning to Labour: How Working Class Kids Get Working Class Jobs.* Westmead, UK: Gower.

Willis, P. (1986). Unemployment: the final inequality. *British Journal of Sociology of Education, 7*(2), 155–169.

Woods, P. (1994). Critical students: Breakthroughs in learning. *International Studies in Sociology of Education, 4*(2), 123–146.

Wyn, J. & Dwyer, P. (1999). New directions in research on youth in transition. *Journal of Youth Studies,* 2(1), 5–21.

Wyn, J. & Dwyer, P. (2000). New patterns of youth transition in education. *International Social Science Journal, 164,* 147–159.

Wyn, J. & Lamb, S. (1996). Early school leaving in Australia: issues for education and training policy. *Journal of Education Policy, 11*(2), 259–268.

Wyn, J. & White, R. (1997). *Rethinking Youth.* Sydney: Allen & Unwin.

Yates, L. & Leder, G. (1996). *Student Pathways: A Review of National Databases on Gender Equity.* Canberra: Department of Employment, Education, Training and Youth Affairs.

AUTHOR INDEX

SUBJECT INDEX

glocalization, 40, 48
going for a job, 48, 56, 66
good teaching, 180
government education policy, 135
gradient of inequality, 102
greedy institutions, 169

hanging in at school, 12, 21, 81
harassment, 115, 117, 122–124, 126, 129, 164, 167, 180, 193
Henderson Royal Commission into Poverty in Australia, 101
heuristic, 28
hierarchical observation, 149
hierarchical relationships, 195
hierarchical structuring, 57–58
hierarchy of subjects, 60
high school xi, 18, 58–59, 61, 92, 100, 139, 172, 180
homelessness, 129
homogenizing, 15
homophobia, 27, 122, 193

identity construction as a political project, 191
identity formation, 33, 58, 75, 97, 191
ideological diversion, 9
illegal substances, 74, 81, 164, 170, 176
ill-health, 129
imagination, 9
impediments, 28, 33, 136, 148
inadequate policy explanations, 136
inappropriate pedagogy, 180
inclusion/exclusion, 161, 162
inclusive values, 185
increasingy diversity, 17, 185
independence, 166
indifference towards students, 175
individual/society relation, 68–69
individualist rationality, 148, 168, 185
individualistic ethos, 47, 148, 185, 188
individualization of responsibility, 150, 168
individualization, 144
inequalities of capital among young people, 192
inequitable reproduction of society, 102
inflexibility and inability to accommodate, 146, 158, 165
information technology literacy, 74
innocence, 14, 156

institutional identities, 131–132
institutional leadership, 195
institutional structures, 129
institutionalized refusal, 11
institutionalized teacher-student relationship, 62
institutionally sanctioned discipline policy, 187
intensification of workload, 149, 150, 151
interactive trouble, 33, 131–133 169, 191–193
inter-disciplinary curriculum, 61
interferences to school completion, 12, 28, 32, 73, 117, 127, 156, 172, 191
international competitiveness, 39, 57, 136
international division of labor, 41
internationalization, 41
interrogation of generative themes, 28
interrupting the habitual, 12, 14,
interviews, 25, 27
irregular or contingent jobs, 42

justice, 77

knowledge economy, 39

labor identities, 122
labor market, 43, 66, 194
laminating contradictions, 18
learning by passive absorption, 56
leavers, 23
left floundering, 168
liberal education, 19
linear or propulsion pathway, 33, 38, 135–136, 152
linear progression from school to work, 38, 152
listening, 166–167, 176
logic of competition, 108
lost opportunities, 165
low socioeconomic status, 55, 164, 187

managing time, 150
manipulative power relations, 165
marginalization, 78, 88, 129
masculinities, 74, 114–117, 128, 193
masking asymmetric power relations, 144
meaningful transition, 17
media culture, 33, 74–76
media-saturated culture, 74

Adolescent
Cultures,
School &
Society

Joseph L. DeVitis & Linda Irwin-DeVitis
GENERAL EDITORS

As schools struggle to redefine and restructure themselves, they need to be cognizant of the new realities of adolescents. Thus, this series of monographs and textbooks is committed to depicting the variety of adolescent cultures that exist in today's post-industrial societies. It is intended to be a primarily qualitative research, practice, and policy series devoted to contextual interpretation and analysis that encompasses a broad range of interdisciplinary critique. In addition, this series will seek to provide a pragmatic, pro-active response to the current backlash of conservatism that continues to dominate political discourse, practice, and policy. This series seeks to address issues of curriculum theory and practice; multicultural education; aggression and violence; the media and arts; school dropouts; homeless and runaway youth; alienated youth; at-risk adolescent populations; family structures and parental involvement; and race, ethnicity, class, and gender studies.

Send proposals and manuscripts to the general editors at:

Joseph L. DeVitis & Linda Irwin-DeVitis
College of Education and Human Development
University of Louisville
Louisville, KY 40292-0001

To order other books in this series, please contact our Customer Service Department at:

(800) 770-LANG (within the U.S.)
(212) 647-7706 (outside the U.S.)
(212) 647-7707 FAX

or browse online by series at:

WWW.PETERLANGUSA.COM